The Business of America is Lobbying

The Delegated Welfare State: Medicare, Markets,
and the Governance of Social Policy
Kimberly J. Morgan and Andrea Louise Campbell

Rule and Ruin: The Downfall of Moderation and the Destruction
of the Republican Party, from Eisenhower to the Tea Party
Geoffrey Kabaservice

Engines of Change: Party Factions in American Politics, 1868–2010
Daniel DiSalvo

Follow the Money: How Foundation Dollars Change Public School Politics
Sarah Reckhow

The Allure of Order: High Hopes, Dashed Expectations,
and the Troubled Quest to Remake American Schooling
Jal Mehta

Rich People's Movements: Grassroots Campaigns to Untax the One Percent
Isaac William Martin

The Outrage Industry: Political Opinion Media and the New Incivility
Jeffrey M. Berry and Sarah Sobieraj

Artists of the Possible: Governing Networks and American Policy since 1945
Matt Grossman

Building the Federal Schoolhouse: Localism and
the American Education State
Douglas S. Reed

The First Civil Right: Race and the Rise of the Carceral State
Naomi Murakawa

How Policy Shapes Politics: Rights, Courts, Litigation,
and the Struggle over Injury Compensation
Jeb Barnes and Thomas F. Burke

Ideas with Consequences: The Federalist Society
and the Conservative Counterrevolution
Amanda Hollis-Brusky

The Business of America is Lobbying

How Corporations Became Politicized and Politics Became More Corporate

LEE DRUTMAN

OXFORD
UNIVERSITY PRESS

OXFORD
UNIVERSITY PRESS

Oxford University Press is a department of the University of Oxford.
It furthers the University's objective of excellence in research, scholarship,
and education by publishing worldwide.

Oxford   New York
Auckland   Cape Town   Dar es Salaam   Hong Kong   Karachi
Kuala Lumpur   Madrid   Melbourne   Mexico City   Nairobi
New Delhi   Shanghai   Taipei   Toronto

With offices in
Argentina   Austria   Brazil   Chile   Czech Republic   France   Greece
Guatemala   Hungary   Italy   Japan   Poland   Portugal   Singapore
South Korea   Switzerland   Thailand   Turkey   Ukraine   Vietnam

Oxford is a registered trade mark of Oxford University Press
in the UK and certain other countries.

Published in the United States of America by
Oxford University Press
198 Madison Avenue, New York, NY 10016

Library of Congress Cataloging-in-Publication Data
Drutman, Lee, 1961–
The business of America is lobbying : how corporations became politicized
and politics became more corporate / Lee Drutman.
p.   cm.
ISBN 978–0–19–021551–4 (hardcover)
1. Business and politics—United States. 2. Corporations—Political activity—
United States. 3. Lobbying—United States. I. Title.
JK467.D78 2015
324.40973—dc23
2014028845

1   3   5   7   9   8   6   4   2

Printed in the United States of America on acid-free paper

To Annalise and Elsa

CONTENTS

ACKNOWLEDGMENTS

Writing a book is, to state the obvious, a journey of a thousand steps. I have written this book in phases and stages over the course of almost seven years. Along the way I've benefitted from the wisdom and generosity of many, many wonderful people. To tell the story of how this became a published manuscript is a chance to thank those who made it possible.

This book began as my Ph.D. dissertation at the University of California, Berkeley. I owe incredible gratitude to my dissertation committee at Berkeley, all of whom consistently challenged me to do my very best while giving me the confidence that I could do so. Henry E. Brady, the chair of my committee, taught me to love big data. He was always full of ideas and inspirations, and gave me the confidence to think big. Paul Pierson taught me to think of politics as a dynamic process and helped me to appreciate that the questions most worth answering are almost always the hardest to answer. David Vogel was always generous with his incredible knowledge of business and politics, and his remarkable ability to identify key points. Neil Fligstein helped me to think hard about the role of organizations. In Berkeley, I also learned so much from conversations and friendships with faculty members David Karol, Todd La-Porte, Robert Reich, Gordon Silverstein, and Robert Van Houweling; and with fellow graduate students Devin Caughey, Miguel de Figueiredo, Joshua Green, Matthew Grossmann, Peter Hanson, Iris Hui, Andrew Kelly, Sarah Reckhow, Alex Theodoridis, and Matthew Wright.

In Fall 2007, I moved to Washington, DC, to conduct interviews with lobbyists. I found a home at the University of California's Washington, DC, center, where I was fortunate to connect with Bruce E. Cain, whose encouragement and support have been crucial over the years, and who has since become a co-author. In Fall 2008, I began a 10-month research fellowship at the Brookings Institution, which generously provided me office space and a very stimulating environment in which to do my dissertation writing. There I enjoyed many conversations with my intelligent and very kind colleagues: Sarah Binder, E. J. Dionne Jr., William Galston, Thomas Mann, Pietro Nivola, Jonathan Rauch, R. Kent Weaver, Darrell West, Benjamin Wildavsky, and Benjamin Wittes.

In Fall 2009, I began a 10-month APSA congressional fellowship working in the office of Senator Robert Menendez (D-NJ). I thank Senator Menendez, Danny O'Brien, Karissa Willhite, and Michael Passante for giving me the opportunity to actively participate in the legislative process around the Dodd-Frank Wall Street Reform and Consumer Protection Act, and to be lobbied on almost a daily basis. My understanding of lobbying and the political process was enhanced remarkably by this firsthand experience.

After filing my dissertation in 2010, I let it sit on my website while I moved onto other projects, unsure of my next step. A year later, I was extremely fortunate to connect with Steven M. Teles, editor of Oxford University Press's *Studies in Postwar American Development* series. Steve told me he'd like my dissertation as a book for his series: how soon could I have it ready? I thank Steve for both his patience and his impatience—but especially for his impatience. He gave me a date to present at his graduate seminar at Johns Hopkins University, which meant I had to have something ready. He and his students also provided me wonderful and useful feedback. I thank Steve, and David McBride at Oxford University Press, for their generous support for this project.

I owe a tremendous debt to The Sunlight Foundation, which allowed me to devote several months of salaried time to the writing of this book, and I especially thank Tom Lee and Ellen Miller for making this possible. But even more than time, Sunlight provided me an incredible learning environment. I gained incredible knowledge about data visualization from my brilliant and all-around fabulous colleagues Amy Cesal, Benjamin Chartoff, and Alexander Furnas. I must especially thank Alexander Furnas. This book is much better due to his endless patience in letting me bounce ideas off of him, and his remarkable savvy in telling me which ideas made sense, which ideas didn't make sense, and which ideas I hadn't thought of yet. At Sunlight, I also benefitied from many substantive conversations with my colleagues Kathy Kiely, Bob Lannon, Tom Lee, Eric Mill, Ellen Miller, Lisa Rosenberg, Daniel Schuman, Gabriela Schneider, and John Wonderlich.

Two anonymous reviewers provided incredibly helpful comments. I am also incredibly grateful to Timothy M. LaPira and Maggie McKinley for reading a near-final version of the manuscript and providing me exhaustive and incredibly helpful comments and edits that made this book even better.

In addition to those I've named already, this book has benefitted from conversations with and feedback from many others along the way, including Frank Baumgartner, Ryan Blitstein, Heather Gerken, Adam Gitlin, Jacob Hacker,

Andrew Hall, Richard Hall, Jacob Harold, David Hart, Christopher Hayes, Daniel J. Hopkins, Jonathan Jacoby, Heather Klemick, Lisa Lerer, Jonathan McKernan, Dana Mulhauser, Clay Risen, Thomas Saunders, Katie Selenski, Kay Lehman Schlozman, John Sides, Jim Tankersley, Tom Toles, James Thurber, Elbert Ventura, and Sidney Verba.

And, of course, this book would not have been possible had not 60 professional lobbyists taken the time to talk to me. I thank all of them.

Finally, I thank my mother, Ava Drutman, and my late father, Lowell Drutman, for encouraging me every step of the way, and I thank my brothers, Scott Drutman and Mark Drutman, for doing their best to keep me humble. I owe both the greatest debt and greatest inspiration to my wife, Annalise K. Nelson (who, in an early and audacious act of benevolence, copyedited my entire dissertation when we had only been dating for a few months). Though it sounds like a cliché to say that her love and support made this book possible, I simply can't imagine having written it without her as a constant companion. Our wonderful daughter, Elsa, arrived a few weeks before I sent this manuscript out for review. I thank her for constantly reminding me of the importance of sticking out your tongue for no reason. This book is dedicated to Annalise and Elsa. I love you both so much.

NOTES

This book relies on seven sources. The first three are unique to this book. The remaining four are public sources.

Unique sources

1. Original interviews

Between October 2007 and March 2008, I conducted semi-structured interviews with 60 lobbyists in person in Washington, DC, and on the telephone. I located participants through a mix of targeted and snowball sampling. I first picked a random sample of companies and trade associations in four industries (pharmaceuticals, high-tech, financial services, and retail), and then began calling Washington offices, requesting hour-long interviews. Some lobbyists seemed eager to talk; others brushed me off or didn't return repeated phone calls. In the end, response rates unfortunately varied across industries.

Ultimately, among in-house company lobbyists, I was able to talk to 11 pharmaceutical lobbyists, nine high-tech lobbyists, seven retail lobbyists, and four financial service lobbyists. Among trade associations, I was able to talk to representatives for one pharmaceutical trade association, five high-tech associations, four retail trade associations, and three financial services associations. For-hire lobbyists were the least eager to talk to me, and very few were willing to talk specifically on behalf of companies they represent. I ultimately interviewed 11 for-hire lobbyists. Finally, I also spoke with six additional lobbyists who either represented companies or trade associations outside of my target industries or had prior experience representing companies or trade associations in the four industries on which I had focused. The lobbyists I spoke with represented a range of ages, experience, background, and stature. Some were relatively big names in the world of lobbying while others were just starting out.

The interviews all followed a basic script with variations for the type of lobbyist. I allowed the interviews to be semi-structured because I didn't know the unknown unknowns (to borrow Donald Rumsfeld's famous epistemological category). This was partially because many lobbyists had unique perspectives and histories that I was interested in exploring in more detail. Especially with lobbyists who had been around Washington for a long time, I was particularly interested to learn how, in their estimation, Washington lobbying had changed. The interviews also included two surveys. Most interviews were one hour long. In a few cases, I was unable to complete the interview script because professional demands of lobbyists interrupted our time. In other cases, the lobbyists were happy to talk my ear off and we went past the allotted time.

2. The Washington Representatives directory

I was very fortunate to connect early on in my graduate student career with Henry Brady, Kay Schlozman, and Sidney Verba, who were engaging in the Herculean effort of coding the complete *Washington Representatives* lobbying directory for 1981, 1991, 2001, and 2006. Thanks to them, I have had complete access to the corporate and trade association lobbying data for these years. Also under their aegis, I developed a data set that includes the complete 1981–2004 history of *Washington Representatives* lobbying data for any company that was in the S&P 500 between 1981 and 2006. The *Washington Representatives* directory was published by Columbia Books. It "includes all organizations that are active in Washington politics by virtue of either having an office in the D.C. area or hiring D.C. area consultants or counsel to represent them."[1] The limit of the *Washington Representatives* data is that they depend on whom the editors of the historical volumes were able to identify, both through their own surveys and through careful reading of Washington media.

3. APSA Congressional Fellowship

This book also draws on my personal experience as an APSA Congressional Fellow. From December 2009 through July 2010, I worked as a banking and housing policy staffer for a Democratic senator. This timeline took me through the entire development and passage of the Dodd-Frank Wall Street and Consumer Protection Act and brought me into contact with many corporate lobbyists. My insights on how lobbying works are informed by those experiences.

Public Sources

4. Lobbying Disclosure Act (LDA) reports

The passage of the 1995 Lobbying Disclosure Act meant that all organizations that spend money on federal lobbying must file periodic reports detailing their activities, including their expenditures. These data are available in electronic form going back to 1998. The data have been cleaned by the Center for Responsive Politics. These cleaned data are made public by the Sunlight Foundation.

5. Federal Election Commission (FEC) reports

Data on campaign finance expenditures come from mandatory campaign finance reports filed with the Federal Election Commission. The data has been cleaned by the Center for Responsive Politics. These cleaned data are made public by the Sunlight Foundation.

6. Policy Agendas Project

Data on congressional hearings and bills come from the Policy Agendas Project, a database developed by Bryan Jones and Frank Baumgartner to measure policy activity across different issue areas. I modified a crosswalk between Policy Agendas categories and industry categories developed by Timothy LaPira and Beth Leech.

7. Compustat

Data on company sales, R&D, and profits come from Compustat, a comprehensive database on corporate financial information.

1

The Pervasive Position of Business

"I am in this race to tell the corporate lobbyists that their days of setting the agenda in Washington are over. I have done more than any other candidate in this race to take on lobbyists — and won. They have not funded my campaign, they will not run my White House, and they will not drown out the voices of the American people when I am president." — *Barack Obama, speech in Des Moines, Iowa, November 10, 2007*

This is a book about business lobbying in American national politics. It is a book about how and why for-profit corporations invest billions of dollars each year to influence political outcomes, and why that investment has been growing steadily for decades. It is a book about what lobbying involves and how it operates, and about how the billions of dollars that corporations spend on lobbying alter the priorities and problem-solving capacities of the American government.

Questions about the relationship of capitalism and democracy are as old as, well, both capitalism and democracy. What is new is that, in recent years, large corporations have achieved a pervasive position that is unprecedented in American political history. The most active companies now have upwards of 100 lobbyists representing them who are active on a similar number of different bills in a given session of Congress. They serve as de facto adjunct staff for congressional offices, drafting bills, providing testimony, and generally helping to move legislation forward. They provide policy expertise, helping stretched-too-thin staffers to get up to speed on a wide range of subjects and assisting administrative agencies in writing complex rules. They provide generous funding for think tanks and fill the intellectual environment of Washington with panel discussions and op-eds and subway advertisements. They build large coalitions, mobilize grassroots constituencies, and discredit opponents. They host fundraising events and donate to charities. They hire former congressional staffers and former members of Congress and former agency bureaucrats and former agency heads by the dozens to make sure they have a connection to every person who matters, as well as an insider's understanding on how the process works and how to work the process. They heed the old Washington adage, "if you are not at the table, you are probably on the menu," by showing up at every table.

This book will argue that corporate lobbying has reached its modern pervasive position largely because corporate lobbying has its own internal momentum. In a word, lobbying is "sticky." Hiring lobbyists and creating a government affairs department sets in motion a series of processes that, over time, collectively push companies towards more lobbying. Corporate managers begin to pay more attention to politics. In so doing, they see more reasons why they should be politically active. They develop a comfort and a confidence in being politically engaged. And once a company pays some fixed start-up costs, the marginal cost of additional political activity declines. They find new issues. They get drawn into coalitions and networks and fights. They see value in political engagement they did not see before. In short, lobbying begets lobbying. Once companies encamp on the Potomac, they rarely depart.

Lobbyists are the key drivers of the processes described in the previous paragraph. Lobbyists are responsible for gathering political information and advising on lobbying strategy. Because political developments are often ambiguous and uncertain, and because influence is far more of an art than a science, lobbyists have informational advantages over corporate managers. They can make political engagement seem particularly necessary to companies by overstating threats and opportunities. After all, the more aggressively and expansively companies lobby, the more wealthy and important lobbyists become. Over time, lobbyists teach corporate managers about the value of political engagement, making the case for continued and often expanding lobbying expenditures.

The growth of lobbying has both a quantitative and a qualitative dimension. More lobbying does not just mean more lobbyists spending more time in Washington on behalf of more companies. It also means a more aggressive, comprehensive, and proactive approach to lobbying. As companies lobby more, they have a greater capacity to tackle big issues, and they have more lobbyists encouraging corporate managers to think of public policy as a strategic advantage. Individual corporations once tended to stay out of politics, and corporate executives largely viewed politics as something to be avoided. In modern Washington, corporations are increasingly looking to government as a partner. Corporate lobbying has also become increasingly particularistic, with individual corporations more and more looking out for their own narrow interests, egged on by lobbyists who stand to benefit most from an everyone-for-themselves approach to lobbying (after all, more competition almost always means more lobbying).

Almost 40 years ago, Charles Lindblom famously described the "privileged position of American business."[1] He argued that because government relied on businesses to allocate and mobilize the economic resources essential to the public welfare of the nation, and because business had superior organizational resources, large private corporations enjoyed a political power that undermined democratic responsiveness to any other interest in society. Consider the fact that in 1977, when Lindblom published *Politics and Markets*, American businesses were just getting their political footing after reeling from a remarkable expansion of government regulation of the economy and a general rise in anti-business sentiment.

That era of sparse and mostly defensive business lobbying now seems like a distant memory. Corporations have now fit their way into almost every process of American democratic policymaking. Business has achieved a *pervasive* position. I say *pervasive* rather than *privileged* because this pervasive position guarantees neither influence nor privilege (the range of issues and possible conflicts is far too broad to make such a simple assertion). However, the mere ubiquity of business has important consequences for how policy gets made in Washington.

Major political change has become more difficult. When major legislation does pass, it is increasingly an incoherent set of compromises necessary to buy the support of a wide range of particular interests. As the lobbying industry grows, more and more experienced and talented government staffers become lobbyists, drawing policy expertise and political know-how out of the public sector and into the private sector. The increasing complexity and specialization of policy makes this public–private gap in expertise all the more consequential, as inexperienced staffers come to need to rely on experienced lobbyists to make sense of policy. And as companies invest more and more in politics, they increasingly overwhelm the intellectual environment of Washington, funding endless messaging that over time shapes the way decision-makers even think about issues.

Arguably, these developments make the success of any particular individual lobbying effort more unpredictable than ever before, further complicating scholars' ongoing attempts to demonstrate a consistent correlation between lobbying activity and lobbying success on a any given issue (or set of issues). But collectively, these changes foster a policy environment where resources matter even more. The organizations that are most likely to be the winners in the modern policymaking process are those that:

- are able to lobby on multiple issues over multiple years;
- can pay the increasingly high price of entry necessary for effective participation; and

- gain from policy complexity, both because it gives them more opportunities to insert narrow provisions with limited public scrutiny and because they are more capable of supplying expertise to overworked staffers.

More and more, the only organizations that are capable of marshaling the resources to do all these effectively are business organizations,—both individual companies and the associations that represent them.

A New Theory of Corporate Lobbying

Much of economic analysis starts with the assumption that corporations are rational actors who engage in activity if the expected benefits of the activity exceed the expected costs. Such thinking suffuses an existing body of scholarship that collectively explains the variation in corporate political activity (typically, campaign contributions) as primarily a function of company size, industry structure, government contracts, regulatory burden, potential opposition, and legal issues with the government.[2] "Underlying this research," write Wendy Hansen and Neil Mitchell, "is the assumption that corporate efforts to influence politics are *perceived* by managers to produce benefits for the firm, such as friendlier regulatory environment or additional government contracts"[3] (my italics). In other words, if corporate managers think that lobbying will help their company's bottom line, then they will lobby. If not, then they won't lobby.

Such a cost-benefit approach makes perfect and reasonable sense. But the key word is "perceive." Doing a cost-benefit analysis depends on being able to calculate both the costs and the benefits—but how accurately can managers connect particular policy outcomes with benefits to the bottom line? How reliably can they calculate what the actual costs of engagement will wind up being? Both calculations involve significant guesswork and assumptions. Certainly, some issues are easier to calculate than others, but very little in politics is clear or predictable without the time-sensitive benefit of hindsight.

Managers may behave rationally, but as Arthur Stinchombe puts it, "All rationality is based on predictions of one kind or another, not on knowledge."[4] Decisions to engage are based on predictions of what will happen if a company engages politically. These predictions are based on whatever information is available, and on whoever is around to interpret that information. For this reason, Stinchombe argues that "the core structure of organizations, then, is information processing."[5]

Certainly, objective conditions do matter. Sometimes it is glaringly obvious what is at stake. When companies are highly regulated, sell a lot to the government, and/or have legal troubles that involve the government, it makes sense that they would hire a lobbyist (or several). And the existing literature on corporate political activity does a pretty good job of making this clear. Generalized metrics of what a company has at stake in government policy (e.g., Is it heavily regulated? Does it sell a lot to the government?) tend to be good predictors of whether or not a company is politically active.

However, the literature on corporate political activity generally fails to appreciate the subjective, cognitive dimension of rational action—the way in which benefits and costs must be constructed through information and experience. Managers may *perceive* that there are benefits and costs to political engagement, but the relative numbers they attach to those benefits and costs matter. These calculations determine how and how much corporations will invest in politics.

Managers face a big challenge: politics is uncertain and unpredictable. Politics is not a vending machine where outside forces can put in their dollar, press a few buttons, and reach below for a neatly shrink-wrapped policy outcome. Politics is a multidimensional tug of war between many unpredictable forces across many venues, full of wild swings and random events, in which few things are ever truly resolved.[6] Coalitions emerge and shift the scope of conflict. Public attention comes and goes.

Economists are fond of using the logic of the marketplace to explain politics, leading to the kinds of simplified models in which politicians trade votes and other actions in exchange for the campaign contributions necessary to stay in office.[7] The abstraction of politics as marketplace is helpful in one way. It clarifies a fundamental principle: Companies that engage in politics are seeking to get something (a policy outcome or outcomes) for a price (whatever they spend on lobbying and other political activities).

Politics, however, is a very messy marketplace, one in which interests and prices are ever-shifting. If it is a market, it is most like a byzantine bazaar in which one never knows what will be for sale, and in which the merchandise comes and goes unpredictably. Prices are unmarked and ever-changing. One must pay a price just to enter. The goods are frequently obscure and their value is often unknown ahead of time—it is only upon learning what one has actually purchased that one can determine the value of it. One's access to the goods depends on relationships with the merchants, and relationships take time to build. Often goods are sold as part of an auction in which losing bidders have to forfeit their bids. One never knows ahead of time how many bidders there will be, or how much others will be willing to bid—or when a screaming mob may come through the market, ransacking the place and leading everybody to run for cover. Such a market is not for the inexperienced and uninitiated. One needs a guide. Or several.

If companies want to engage effectively in the bazaar of political influence, company managers need to learn how to locate their interests, properly value outcomes, and adequately assess costs. They need to develop the capacity to get what they want. And as they learn and develop this capacity, they are likely to use it more and more often.

In this process, the lobbyists play a key role. They are the professional persuaders hired to advise corporations on what to do politically and when to actually do it. Since lobbyists are interested in maintaining their jobs and increasing their importance to the company, they have incentives to highlight the ways in which political developments could impact their companies, and then to recommend a maximal strategy for responding. They have incentives to find new issues on which they can deliver clear and traceable benefits to companies, so that they can more easily justify their worth—and increase their salary. And they have incentives to show why companies have to be there in Washington *themselves*, and why leaving representation to trade associations is not enough.

This is a classic principal-agent problem, with corporate managers acting as agents and lobbyists acting as principals. Corporate managers hire lobbyists to deliver political benefits. They would prefer to get more benefit for less cost. Lobbyists, seeking to maximize both their job security and their personal income, want companies to spend as much as possible on lobbying. Because politics is highly uncertain and ambiguous, lobbyists benefit from a powerful information asymmetry. Companies depend on lobbyists to interpret politics for them, and advise them on strategy. Politics is incredibly information-rich. Signal dominates noise. Almost all outcomes (including non-outcomes) are multi-causal. There are ample opportunities for credit-claiming, and equally ample opportunities for blame avoidance. With the right salesperson, many things can seem possible. In such an environment, lobbyists have ample space to convince corporations that there is always an opportunity for more lobbying—*if* they've convinced companies that lobbying is generally a valuable activity.

This "if" qualifier presents an important obstacle for lobbyists. The same ambiguities and uncertainties that give lobbyists room to shape the decision environments of corporate managers can also make it hard for lobbyists to convince corporate decision-makers that political engagement makes a positive, bottom-line difference. Historically, most corporate executives viewed government with distrust and sometimes even disdain.[8] Even today, the vast majority of publicly traded corporations (about 90 percent) don't have their own lobbyists, and to the extent that they are represented in Washington, it is only through trade associations. Politics and business are very different worlds. And lobbyists cost money.

Lobbyists often struggle to prove their worth to the bean-counters. To make the case for their continued presence, they must be able to point to deliverables, to policies they've personally changed in ways that can translate into real bottom-line dollars. These might include changes to the tax code, trade deals that allow companies to expand their markets and/or buy cheaper foreign goods, government contracts, or any of the many other federal policy outcomes that impact corporate profits. Lobbyists have powerful incentives to deliver these particular benefits. Lobbyists benefit when they can show corporate managers why lawmakers and rule-writers need to hear directly from *them*. This includes showing managers that companies cannot simply leave lobbying to the trade associations, because individual corporations have unique perspectives that would be lost. This pushes against business unity and towards particularism. If every lobbyist wants to have something they can point to as theirs, this leads to more complex policy.

As companies increase their political capacity, they tend to become more ambitious. Once capacity is in place, corporate managers become more politically comfortable and confident, and they begin to see government as a tool (instead of as an impediment). This theory is briefly summarized in Figure 1.1.

Existing literature offers other possible explanations for the growth of lobbying: a response to "disturbances" in the socioeconomic environment[9]; a response to government attention[10]; a response to threats in particular[11]; pure rent seeking[12]; necessary counter-action to opponents' lobbying efforts.[13] These theories are all primarily explanations for why political interests mobilize. They do not explore the long-term consequences following mobilization.

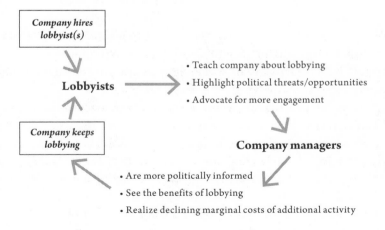

Figure 1.1 The stickiness of lobbying.

This book, by contrast, is far more focused on the self-perpetuating nature of political engagement, and the ways in which, once it gets started, organizational lobbying deepens and expands over time. The causes of political activity may be heterogeneous, as the wide variety of theories explaining mobilization would suggest. But this book argues that once a company starts lobbying, political activity has an institutional stickiness that keeps companies politically engaged, despite ebbs and flows in the political agenda. Once a company hires lobbyists, those lobbyists are very good at making the case why that company needs to not only stay engaged, but become even more engaged.

As companies do more lobbying, they tend to get involved in more and different issues. Additionally, as particular corporations and industries increase their capacity, so do their competitors. Corporations often find themselves enmeshed in coalitions and trade associations, where there is both pressure on them to do their share, as well as incentives for them to devote resources to making sure that they get to shape the policy stances of the coalitions and associations in ways that are favorable to them. Sometimes political battles between two well-resourced industries take on the dynamics of a classic arms race, where more spending only serves to maintain an unresolvable equilibrium. There is often a dynamic relationship between corporations and the political environment. And yet, as we will see, just as often lobbying growth proceeds independently of government attention. Additionally, at least some of the growth of corporate lobbying can be explained by the simple fact that corporations are getting bigger in general.

The Pervasive Position of Business

In 2012, politically active organizations reported $3.31 billion in direct lobbying expenses, down slightly from $3.55 billion in 2010 but up significantly from $1.82 billion just 10 years earlier and, controlling for inflation, almost seven times the estimated $200 million in lobbying expenses in 1983.[14] More than three-quarters of that money has consistently gone towards representing corporate America.

Corporations are highly visible and pervasive political actors in modern Washington. In 2012, 372 companies reported spending at least $1 million on lobbying. The most active, General Electric, reported $21.4 million in lobbying expenditures, followed by Google at $18.2 million. A total of 3,587 individual corporations reported a combined $1.84 billion in lobbying expenditures, roughly 56 percent of *all* the disclosed money spent on lobbying in 2012. Add in another $553 million in spending by trade associations and $175 million in spending by business-wide associations, and that's

$2.57 billion in combined spending—78 *percent* of all the money spent on lobbying in 2012. While these are big numbers, there is good reason to believe that they significantly undercount the true corporate investments in politics, given that so much political influence activity is not covered by lobbying disclosures.[15]

The two empirical observations put forward in here—that the amount of lobbying has been steadily increasing, and that the majority of lobbyists in Washington represent business interests—are two of the most timeless findings in all of political science.[16] Throughout the twentieth century and now into the twenty-first, the number of organizations with representation has increased in every era (though some eras have been more active than others). But regardless of the pace of growth, the data have continued to back up E. E. Schattschneider's quip that "The flaw in the pluralist heaven is that the heavenly chorus sings with a strong upper-class accent."[17] Business interests and the well-off have always had the loudest voices in Washington.[18]

And yet, while American business has always been well represented in Washington, prior to the 1970s, very few companies had their own lobbyists. Trade associations largely handled representation. Even at the trade association level, political engagement was limited and unsophisticated by modern standards. Historically, American businesses tended to view government as something to be avoided, kept at a distance, and only responded to in cases of threat. But since the mid-1970s, American business has increasingly learned how to work with government, and to use government policy in strategic ways. As one lobbyist described the change in corporate lobbying over the last several decades, "It's gone from 'leave us alone' to 'let's work on this together'."[19]

In 1971, a leading corporate lawyer could write credibly that: "As every business executive knows, few elements of American society today have as little influence in government as the American businessman."[20] After all, businesses had been on the losing side of an aggressive growth of government regulation for several years, and had comparatively little presence in Washington by today's standards. But starting in the early 1970s, corporate America began to devote attention and meaningful resources to politics. The current spending levels merely mark the latest moving capstone in a 40-year period of near-continuous expansion of corporate political activity. With almost each passing year, more money is spent to hire more lobbyists to represent more corporate interests. And though there have been periods of slower and faster growth, the 40-year trend has overwhelmingly moved in one direction: *growth.* Corporate lobbying expenditures now dwarf the comparable investments of unions and "diffuse interest" groups (my preferred term for what others more commonly call "public interest groups" or "citizen groups").[21] At various points in American history these groups served as meaningful political counterweights to corporations. But those points are receding further and further into the past.

Corporations now have political operations whose savvy and scope would have seemed unfathomable even a half-century ago, when lobbying could reasonably be described as little more than a straightforward "communication process."[22] This capacity means the ability to pursue a broader range of issues over a longer period of time. Companies with million-dollar budgets have the manpower to be at multiple tables at once. They have the capacity to engage in a kind of "spread betting"[23] approach to lobbying. They can invest in a wide portfolio of policy solutions, knowing that, even though most efforts will be wasted, those that go somewhere will likely more than make up for those that don't. They can send clear messages that they are ready to act aggressively should anybody threaten their favored policies. No single action may be definitive. But as one of the most comprehensive studies of lobbying ever undertaken concludes, "The general pattern is that doing more of anything produces greater success than doing less, regardless of the strategy."[24]

The quantitative story of the growth of corporate lobbying can be told most succinctly in two charts: Figures 1.2 and 1.3. Figure 1.2 covers 1981 to 2004, and reports the average "lobbying presence" among a sample of 1,066 companies that were part of the S&P 500 at some point between 1981 and 2006. My

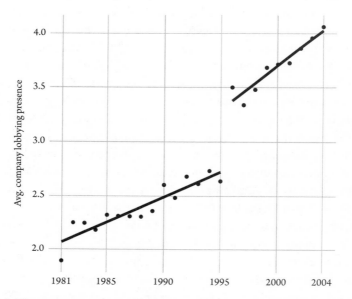

Figure 1.2 The growing corporate "lobbying presence." Source: Author's calculations based on lobbyists listed in the *Washington Representatives* directory for companies in the S&P 500 sample. Annual averages are calculated among companies that were in business that year. "Lobbying presence" measures in-house lobbyists plus outside firms.

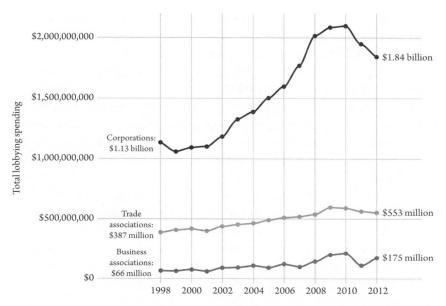

Figure 1.3. The growth of business lobbying spending, 1998–2012. Source: Author's calculations from LDA reports.

measure of "lobbying presence" is the sum total of all individual in-house lobbyists (company employees) and outside (contract) lobbying firms listed as lobbying on behalf of the company in the *Washington Representatives* lobbying directory. These data are described in more detail in Notes on Sources.

The basic story here is that the average lobbying presence of these companies has more than doubled between 1981 and 2004. However, there is an unfortunate uncertainty in this data. In 1996, the number of lobbyists documented by the *Washington Representatives* directory increases by more than one-third across the board. The most likely reason is that Congress passed the Lobbying Disclosure Act in 1995, which helped the editors of the *Washington Representatives* directory identify many more lobbyists in 1996.[25] While this presents an obvious discontinuity, the general trends both before and prior to this discontinuity are both roughly linear, suggesting that the underlying trends are consistent both before and after the passage of this bill. Corporate lobbying does appear to grow slightly more rapidly after 1996 than before.

Figure 1.3 covers 1998 to 2012, taking advantage of the electronic disclosures of lobbying expenditures that began in 1998, which arguably gives us an even better measure of the lobbying intensity than the earlier lobbying presence measure.[26] Figure 1.3 also includes data on trade associations (organizations that represent the interests of a specific industry, e.g., the American

Petroleum Institute [API] or the Pharmaceutical Research and Manufacturers of America [PhRMA] and businesswide associations (organizations that attempt to speak for all businesses, e.g., the U.S. Chamber of Commerce or the Business Roundtable). It also covers *all* lobbying companies, providing the most comprehensive picture possible.

The basic takeaway, again, is one of growth. Between 1998 and 2010, the amount of money all corporations reported spending on their own lobbyists increased by 85 percent, going from $1.13 billion in 1998 to $2.09 billion in 2010 (in constant 2012 dollars).[27] Total corporate spending declined slightly post-2010, down to $1.84 billion.

During same 1998–2010 period, trade associations increased their lobbying spending by 53 percent, from $387 million to $590 million, before declining to $553 million in 2012. Business associations (largely the U.S. Chamber of Commerce) grew from $66 million in 1998 to a high of $214 million in 2010, then down to $175 million in 2012. These post-2010 declines show that business lobbying is not immune from a recession and congressional gridlock (and possibly reduced disclosure). Then again, given the widespread gridlock in Congress and the recession, we might reasonably have expected lobbying to have declined further. Of course, many in Washington believe that lobbying didn't actually decline during this period—just that less and less of it was being counted in public disclosures.[28]

Taken together, figures 1.2 and 1.3 tell a clear story of three decades of continued corporate lobbying growth.

By contrast, countervailing power organizations that might be expected to check the power of business have not kept up. In 1998, organizations representing "diffuse interests" spent a combined $33.7 million on lobbying, and labor unions spent a combined $369 million on lobbying. Between 1998 and 2010, diffuse interest organizations increased their lobbying spending by a mere 23 percent (reaching $41.3 million in 2010), and unions increased their spending by 32 percent (reaching $486 million in 2010). Both dropped their spending in 2011–2012, with diffuse interest groups falling to $29.7 million (less than they spent in 1998, controlling for inflation), and unions falling to $45.6 million.

One way to understand the dominance of business in Washington is to look at the top 100 lobbying organizations, as measured by lobbying expenditures (see Figure 1.4). From 1998–2012, consistently between 90 and 95 of the top 100 spending organizations have been business organizations (individual companies, trade associations, and business-wide associations). In both 2009 and 2010, 96 of the top 100 organizations by spending represented business. In 2012, 95 of the top 100 organizations represented business. Of the top 100 spending organizations in 2012, 71 were individual corporations,

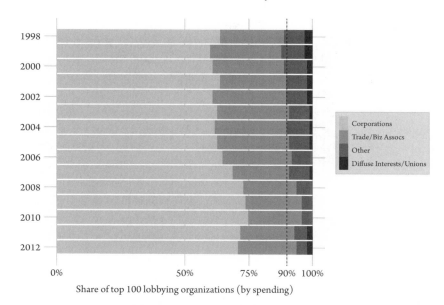

Figure 1.4. Breakdown of the top 100 lobbying organizations (by spending), 1998–2012. Source: Author's calculations from LDA reports.

down slightly from the high-water mark of 75 in 2010. By contrast, diffuse interest groups and unions have never collectively accounted for more than three of the top 100 spending organizations. But they haven't reached that high-water mark since 1998 and 1999. Every year since, they've only been represented either once, twice, or not at all. In 4 of the 15 years (2006, 2008, 2009, and 2010) not a single diffuse interest group or union shows up in the top 100 spending organizations.

Another way to measure the dominance of business is to calculate the annual ratio of lobbying spending by business (corporations, trade associations, and business associations) to diffuse interest and labor union spending over time. In 2012, the ratio was $34 spent by business for every one dollar spent by diffuse interest groups and unions combined. That ratio is up from 22-to-1 in 1998. It was as low as 21-to-1 in 2001, and as high as 35-to-1 in 2008 (see Figure 1.5).

Another way of thinking about the 34-to-1 ratio is that if each dollar bought one calendar day of representation in a year, diffuse interests and unions would have bought only a week-and-a-half of representation (11 days) for every year of representation that business bought. Or, if each dollar bought one minute of time in a typical eight-hour workday, diffuse interests would have bought just 14 minutes of time for every full eight-hour (480-minute) workday business interests purchased.

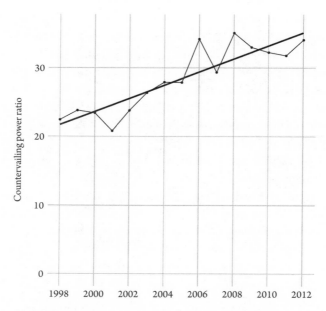

Figure 1.5. The "countervailing power" ratio (combined business lobbying expenditures divided by combined diffuse interest group and labor union lobbying expenditures) Source: Author's calculations from LDA reports.

Had we looked only at diffuse interest groups, we would see that the 2012 ratio was $86 spent by business for every $1 spent by diffuse interest groups—nearly double the 47-to-1 ratio in 1998. That's because, controlling for inflation, diffuse interest spending on lobbying in 2012 was actually down 11 percent from 1998. Had we looked only at unions, we would see that in 2012, businesses spent $56 for every $1 spent by labor unions, up from a 43-to-1 ratio in 1998. Controlling for inflation, union lobbying spending is up 24 percent since 1998. Overall business spending is up 62 percent over the same period. While there are some ups and downs in these numbers, the big picture is clear. An incredibly unequal system of representation is becoming even more unequal.

Of course, these numbers don't take into account the many political activities that are not counted in the disclosed lobbying expenditures, such as grassroots lobbying, talking to the press, and coalition-building, among many others. But it's unlikely to think that these other activities (if measured) would change the ratio much. Unions and diffuse interests might spend more on some things (e.g., grassroots mobilization), businesses might spend more on other things (e.g., funding research).

Businesses account for more than three-quarters of total lobbying expenditures, while diffuse interest groups barely account for one percent. Yet, if one were to sample from the political science literature on interest groups, one could be forgiven for thinking that the imbalance went the other way. Political scientists over the years have devoted far more attention to the political activities of citizen groups and membership groups than they have to the political activities of large corporations. In a 2012 *Annual Review of Political Science* review essay on interest group scholarship from 1996 to 2011, only 11 of the 119 works cited (9 percent) dealt primarily with corporate political activity.[29] Both the seventh and eight editions of *Interest Group Politics* (2006, 2012), a popular edited volume highlighting currents in interest group research, contain only a single essay (out of 16 and 17, respectively) focused primarily on business political involvement (in the 8th edition, I authored that single essay). As Graham K. Wilson noted in 2006: "There are about a hundred political scientists studying parties and elections for every one studying business and politics."[30] Or as David Hart remarked in the 2004 *Annual Review of Political Science,* "If the business of Washington is business, the business of American politics scholarship is anything but. Individual companies are represented in American politics in large numbers. They are doing something, and we ought to learn what and why."[31] Nor is this a new criticism. Back in 1959, Robert Dahl exhorted: "For all the talk and all the public curiosity about the relations between business and politics, there is a remarkable dearth of studies on the subject."[32]

It seems that for as long as business has been dominant in Washington, political scientists have devoted only scant attention to it. This book is an attempt to counter this situation. If we want to understand why then-Senator Obama's 2007 promise to wrest control of Washington from corporate lobbyists (as quoted at the beginning of the chapter) was up against impossible odds, we need to understand business lobbying. If we want to understand lobbying generally, we need to understand business lobbying.

What is Lobbying and Why Focus on It?

I define lobbying quite broadly to mean any activity oriented towards shaping public policy outcomes, and I make the reasonable assumption that all corporate political activity is oriented towards shaping public policy outcomes. For this reason, I will use the terms "lobbying" and "corporate political activity" interchangeably throughout this book.

This goes beyond more familiar definitions of lobbying. The Lobbying Disclosure Act, for example, defines lobbying narrowly as "Lobbying contacts and efforts in support of such contacts, including preparation and planning activities, research and other background work that is intended, at the time it is performed, for use in contacts, and coordination with the lobbying activities of others."[33] Lobbying contacts are in turn defined as "any oral or written communication to a covered executive branch official or a covered legislative branch official." Perhaps the most widely cited definition of lobbying in political science literature comes from Lester Milbrath, who defined lobbying as "the stimulation and transmission of a communication, by someone other than a citizen acting on his own behalf, directed to a governmental decision-maker with the hope of influencing his decision."[34]

Unfortunately, these definitions, focusing as they do on direct communications with Congress, tend to leave out a fair amount of activity. As the American League of Lobbyists argued in 2012: "In today's lobbying environment, grassroots and public relations firms are an integral part of many advocacy efforts. Very large sums of money are spent on the services of those providing these services, as well as those engaged to prepare testimony, studies or op-eds...Determining how to craft a proposal that accomplishes that goal is a complex task that must be dealt with as these proposals are transformed into legislative language."[35] In 2013, The American League of Lobbyists voted to change its name to the Association of Government Relations Professionals, reflecting the inadequacies of "lobbying" in defining what influence professionals actually do.[36]

This book focuses only marginally on campaign contributions. There are two reasons for this. The first and primary reason is that corporations devote far more resources to lobbying than they do to campaign finance. For example, in a study of Enron's political e-mails that I conducted with Daniel J. Hopkins, we observed that: "Election-related e-mails make up only 1 percent of Enron's political e-mails—and even within that 1 percent, there is scant evidence that Enron's staffers considered themselves to be buying the support of candidates."[37] We found Enron far more engaged in the substance of the policy process than in the funding of it. More broadly, from 1998 to 2012, corporations spent on average 12.7 times as much on lobbying as they did on PAC contributions (Figure 1.6). This ratio has been highly consistent for a decade and a half, though it tends to be lower in election years, reflecting the increased giving. The second reason is that there is already a substantial literature on the role of campaign contributions in shaping political outcomes, but it is a literature that has largely exhausted itself at an impasse of inconclusive findings and methodological limitations.[38]

This is not to say that campaign contributions are irrelevant, or even unimportant. Almost all large corporations have PACs. But lobbying is simply where most of the action takes place. Campaign contributions may buy access.[39] However, access is only the first step, and there are many other ways to gain access that don't involve campaign contributions.

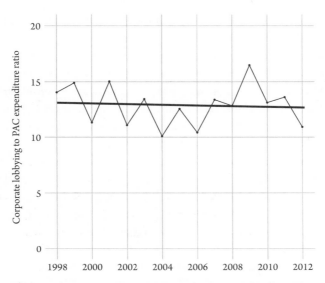

Figure 1.6 Ratio of corporate spending on lobbying to corporate spending on PACs, among individual corporations. Source: Author's calculations from LDA and FEC reports.

Plan of the Book

This book takes a multi-method approach, relying on a tight interplay between rich qualitative detail gained from 60 original lobbyist interviews and large-scale trends gleaned from collecting data from 24 years of *Washington Representatives* directories. Using the two approaches in tandem will reveal a more detailed picture of how corporate lobbying operates and how and why it has grown than we would gain by using either method in isolation. The data sources are described in more detail in the Note on Sources.

The remaining chapters of the book are as follows:

In Chapter 2, I explain how the growth of corporate lobbying changes the policymaking environment. More lobbying makes political change harder, which means both that the beneficiaries of the status quo can more easily continue to enjoy their advantages, and that those seeking to change the status quo require more resources to make anything happen. Both of these changes advantage business interests, who are both most likely to benefit from the status quo, and most capable of allocating the large-scale resources necessary for change. More lobbying also makes legislation more complex (in order to accommodate all the lobbying interests). This creates more opportunities for low-salience lobbying, which corporations are best positioned to take advantage of. As lobbying becomes more competitive and pervasive, companies invest more and more in shaping the "intellectual environment" of Washington. They fund more think tanks, more organizations, more panel discussions and research reports and op-eds and white papers. In the war of ideas, they increasingly fight to make sure that their perspectives and frames and facts are immediately available and familiar. A growing lobbying economy, meanwhile, pulls talent out of the public sector and into the private sector. As K Street becomes a more lucrative place to work, Congress becomes more a farm league for K Street. This contributes to declining government capacity, which means that government policymakers must increasingly rely on lobbyists to help them to develop, pass, and implement policy. In an ever more complex policy environment, the need for expertise becomes greater, but the gap between public sector and private sector expertise is wider. Again, organizations that can supply the expertise are at an advantage. These organizations tend to almost always represent business.

In Chapter 3, I examine the history of corporate lobbying. Prior to the 1970s, very few corporations had Washington offices. To the extent that corporations lobbied, they did so through trade associations. Studies from the 1950s and 1960s describe corporate lobbying as largely threadbare, reactive, and not particularly influential. Then again, public policy was largely pro-industry at the time, so there was less need to lobby. In the mid-to-late 1960s, public opinion and public policy turned against industry, and a new regulatory climate imposed new costs on business. Feeling threatened, business leaders turned to politics and individual corporations devoted substantial attention to politics for the first time—a kind of political awakening. By 1981, businesses had beaten back the existential threats that had mobilized them. But they didn't retreat from politics. They now had government affairs divisions, and that meant lobbyists to help corporate leaders understand the importance of political engagement. Throughout the 1980s, corporations improved their political savvy, as managers slowly but surely became more comfortable with the idea of active political engagement. By the 1990s, corporations began to expand their political presence. Whereas they had once seen government as something to be avoided, corporate leaders increasingly came to see public policy as a way to improve their profits. Rather than merely trying to defend the status quo, lobbyists helped corporations to find more particularistic means of gaining advantages over their competitors, and to think of more aggressive ways to proactively enact new policies while solidifying previous gains. As lobbying became more competitive and more crowded, companies become more comprehensive and innovative in their lobbying strategies, increasingly approaching the pervasive position that they now inhabit.

Chapter 4 describes the contours of modern corporate political engagement and the impressive diversity of both tactics and reasons for being active.

Understanding tactical diversity is important because it shows what increasing amounts of money go towards, and the ways in which political activity can appear infinitely expandable. Because there is an ever-growing range of strategies and tactics that an enterprising government affairs department could possibly recommend, there is the possibility for an ever-expanding level of corporate political expenditures. We will see that with both tactics and reasons, the more companies spend, the more tactics and reasons they list as being important in interviews. Looking closely at both tactics and reasons for being active allows us to see how corporate lobbying can expand from a straightforward approach (narrowly focused on working with congressional allies) to a something more expansive—engaging in all branches, leading coalitions, having an active PR shop, and many other tactics.

Chapter 5 explores the role of trade associations as a way of understanding the tensions between cooperation and competition within industry. In part, associations provide coherence to industry lobbying efforts, helping companies to jointly prioritize issues and strategies, and successfully divide-up-and-conquer. Associations also help move issues forward in ways in which individual companies simply cannot, both because they lack the individual capacity and because key government decision-makers are more likely to take notice when the entire industry says something. But associations can also be a battleground within the industry. Companies compete to shape the industry position. Often this means that associations take on a "least-common-denominator" position, leaving companies to lobby on their own to advocate the specific details that they most want. Trade associations also help foment intra-industry divisions by reminding companies why it is important to participate in setting the agenda of the association, and by sometimes carving out narrow advocacy niches. They do these things to retain and gain membership dues. The changing relationship of companies and associations is both a consequence and cause of the continued growth of corporate lobbying. As companies develop more capacity, they can participate in trade associations more aggressively to try to shape industry positions. But as some companies in an industry do this, so other companies must respond, also participating more. Intra-industry *cooperation* continues to exist, but it is increasingly tinged by intra-industry *competition*.

With a detailed picture of corporate lobbying activities in place, I then turn to the internal dynamics of corporate government affairs to develop a theory of why corporate lobbying is sticky with expansionist tendencies. Chapter 6 examines lobbying from the perspective of corporate managers. It looks at how establishing a government affairs department changes the cost-benefit calculus of political activity. Absent a political operation, corporate managers have a hard time locating their interests, and a hard time making accurate cost-benefit predictions about political engagement. Without internal advocates, without experience, without capacity, without ongoing issues in which they are already invested, political engagement can seem at best an uncertain gamble. But when a company sets up a government affairs department, lobbying has a way of sustaining itself. Managers gain more information about politics, which helps them to see what is at stake, and how they might participate. With more information, and more experience, managers can better develop more realistic policy goals. And as they build capacity, they can feel more confident in their ability to achieve those goals. Political activity has high fixed start-up costs. But once companies invest, there are decreasing marginal costs to additional political activity. All of this pushes companies towards more political activity.

Chapter 7 focuses on the lobbyists as the key actors. Companies hire lobbyists to tell them what is going on in Washington and what they should do about it. The uncertainties and ambiguities of politics give lobbyists room to operate and room to spin. Lobbyists choose details and narratives to persuade managers why the maximalist approach to politics makes the most sense, taking advantage of the informational asymmetries inherent in their position. Over time, lobbyists teach corporate managers why politics is important, helping to shape the cognitive biases and information-processing mechanisms of key corporate decision-makers. They make sure that corporate managers understand the long-term value of engagement, even as they struggle with the culture of quarterly earnings reports. To demonstrate the value of politics, lobbyists seek out bottom-line issues, especially those narrow benefits for which they can claim credit. They make sure that corporate managers understand why the company has unique interests in Washington, and why those interests cannot simply be left to trade associations. Lobbyists benefit from a competitive universe of corporate lobbying. All of this contributes to both the stickiness and the growth of corporate lobbying. Lobbyists are powerful internal advocates for continued lobbying, and once government affairs takes hold within a company it rarely lets go. Once companies start lobbying, they tend to keep lobbying. And the more companies lobby, the more they orient towards proactive and particularistic policy outcomes.

Chapter 8 tests alternative explanations for the growth of lobbying. I analyze three possible explanations: Government is getting "bigger"; government is devoting more attention to issues of concern to the lobbying growth industries; and companies are getting bigger. Government has gotten bigger, and the growing size of government may exert a diffuse pull on corporate lobbying expenditures. Government has also shifted its attention. However, in some of the key growth industries, changes in government attention (as measured by congressional hearings and bill introductions) do very little to explain the growth patterns. Rather, industry-level lobbying seems to have an internal logic of growth. Regardless of the ebbs and flows of industry-specific government attention, the growth patterns across several industries are similar: steady but slow increases throughout the 1980s, and faster increases starting in the early 1990s. Companies have also gotten bigger over the last several decades, and changes in company size can explain a small amount of the increases in lobbying activity. Collectively, these theories leave a significant amount of the variability in corporate lobbying activity unexplained. None of these explanations can offer a theory of why corporate lobbying has expanded and grown as it has.

Chapter 9 provides empirical support for my theory that lobbying is sticky. No matter how I cut the numbers, the evidence is clear: once companies start lobbying, they tend to keep lobbying. By far the best predictor of how much a company will spend on lobbying this year comes from looking at how much it spent on lobbying the year before. The year before that also works well as a predictor, as does the year before that. While bigger companies do lobby more, company lobbying activity is primarily explained by persistence factors. Big changes in presence are rare. Lobbying is indeed very sticky.

In Chapter 10, I conclude by warning about the dangers of continued growth. I argue that the growth of corporate lobbying is ultimately bad for business, because it undermines the problem-solving capacity of the political system necessary for a productive market economy. I also lay out possible reforms, arguing that the best way to counteract the growth of corporate lobbying is to increase the policy capacity of the government and make the political fights fairer, channeling politics to solve political problems.

I conclude this chapter by returning to Obama's aspirational and entirely unfulfilled campaign promise to put an end to the influence of corporate lobbyists in Washington. Many politicians promise to end the influence of corporate lobbyists. So far, none have succeeded. Despite Obama's promises (as well as the promises of many others now in office), corporations continue to devote impressive resources to being the loudest voices in the nation's capital. This book will help us to understand how business has achieved its current pervasive position. It will provide a comprehensive picture of what corporate lobbyists do and why they do it. For those interested in political reform (and not mere campaign promises), this knowledge is the first step. Without this detailed and balanced picture of how corporate lobbying really works, it will be very difficult to formulate effective reforms.

2

Why the Growth of Corporate Lobbying Matters

"Now, less legislation is being passed, but it's more complicated, and the average bill is bigger, more expensive, with more strings attached. The process is more like making sausage than it used to be." – Corporate lobbyist

To look at the polls is to find a public broadly convinced that corporations are buying our democracy—that their lobbyists need only to dangle crisp dollar bills and politicians will fall over themselves to grab them, happily offering up whatever the lobbyists want.[1] The popular stereotype is that Washington is a stinking swamp of corruption, where smooth-talking, cigar-chomping lobbyists with gold watch chains hanging out of their oversized suit vests need only to say "boo" and their loyal devotees on Capitol Hill will fall over themselves to draft the latest multi-million-dollar giveaway. It is easy to come to such conclusions from reading and watching the news. The stories that make headlines are the ones of the lobbyist lavishing a nineteenth-century Louis Philippe commode, among other gifts, upon a congressman in exchange for government contracts.[2] Or of the congressman being discovered with $90,000 worth of cold, hard cash in his freezer, taken in exchange for promoting high-tech businesses abroad[3]—tales of exasperating influence-peddling that offend our civic and moral sensibilities.

Popular books compile suggestive anecdotes of lobbying activities alongside hard-to-justify pro-industry policies, painting a depressing picture of the state of American democracy.[4] However, from a methodological standpoint, these books are guilty of selecting their cases on the outcome variable, choosing only examples where corporations got what they wanted. A corporation may get a win here and there, but do companies consistently get all, or even most of what they ask for? And could the wins have other perfectly legitimate explanations besides politicians being cowed into corporate subservience? These books are not written to explore such questions.

Political scientists, by contrast, tend to tally wins and losses (either in the form of votes or policy victories) and test whether wins correlate with resources invested (either campaign contributions or lobbying). They are more careful to get variation in the independent variables that they think might lead to influence. The general consensus seems to be that neither campaign contributions nor lobbying expenditures systematically increase the likelihood of victory. Contrary to public opinion, politics is not a vending machine.

However, both perspectives face the same fundamental challenge. Measuring political power is a serious methodological challenge because defining political power is a semantic vortex. Is power getting somebody to do something they might not otherwise do?[5] Is power coercion?[6] Is power capacity? Is power cooperation?[7] As Frank Baumgartner and Beth Leech conclude: "Scholars have avoided some basic questions of political power, or have studied those questions in such circumscribed ways that their carefully designed studies can often not be generalized beyond the case on which the evidence is based."[8]

If we were to study political power, which issues should we look at? Only those on the agenda? What about those off the political agenda? How far up the causal chain do we go to measure power? How do we account for the status quo bias of U.S. politics in measuring influence? Should we treat large-scale expenditures of resources as a sign of power, or a sign that the desired outcome will require a major investment because it faces long odds? Over what time period do we measure power? Moreover, if we are to study the power of business, which businesses should we study? Rarely does "business" lobby as a single unified entity. More and more, corporate lobbying involves fights between industries and even between companies. What if some companies get some of what they want, some of the time?

The basic point is that power is difficult to measure because it is such a difficult concept to circumscribe into a manageable analytical frame. We could ask the familiar question: "does corporate lobbying alter policy outcomes?" But that is like asking whether food makes people fat. Some food, in conjunction with other food, in conjunction with various lifestyle choices, in conjunction with various biological and metabolic factors, will likely make some people fat. Other food, as part of a different diet, with a different lifestyle and different metabolism, will not.

Likewise, some types of lobbying, under certain conditions, are more likely to lead to desired policy outcomes than others: Generally, interests are most likely to get what they want on narrow issues of a highly technical nature, with no public scrutiny and with no obvious partisan battle lines.[9] Lobbying is most effective when lobbyists are trusted allies who have long-standing relationships with key decision-makers, and when information and argumentation on one side of an issue overwhelm information and argumentation on the other side of an issue.[10] These conditions, however, do not always guarantee success, nor does the lack of them guarantee failure.

But if we know that certain conditions are more likely to help business interests get what they want than other conditions, the better question to ask might be: how widespread are these conditions (and are they increasing or decreasing)? We might expect corporate lobbyists to have more influence when they are working on more narrow, particularistic issues with limited public scrutiny, with less opposition generally, with more well-connected former government staffers representing them, with more research and analysis backing them up, and in an environment where congressional staffers are more dependent on corporate lobbyists for expertise. Therefore, rather than tallying up wins and losses, we might gain more leverage on influence questions by looking at the ways in which various aspects of policymaking environment have changed, and whether the conditions listed here are becoming more common.

This chapter makes the case that the growth of corporate lobbying has altered the policymaking environment in eight ways that are largely interconnected. Figure 2.1 lays out these eight ways. This chapter will explore these eight changes in detail, with a special focus on how they are likely to benefit corporate interests in comparison to other interests. Mostly, these changes benefit corporate interests because they increase the importance of money, which has always been the most fungible political resource. While other interests may enjoy more legitimacy, corporations have substantially more money, as Chapter 1 made very clear. While none of these changes guarantee corporate victory on any particular issue, generally they play to the advantages that corporations have in being able to allocate substantial resources to politics.

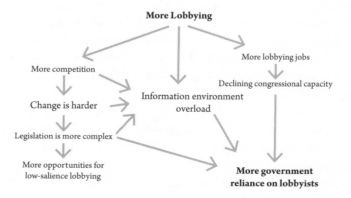

Figure 2.1 How the growth of lobbying changes the policymaking environment

Certainly, the growth of lobbying activity is not limited to corporations. Indeed, almost every sector of the interest group community has increased its presence in Washington over the last several decades.[11] But as I showed in Chapter 1, corporations are increasing their investments in politics more rapidly than the diffuse interests and labor unions that might exert countervailing pressures. More generally, since corporate lobbying consistently accounts for roughly three-quarters of lobbying activity in Washington, the growth of lobbying really is the story of the growth of corporate lobbying. And, as we saw in Chapter 1, of the top 100 most active lobbying organizations, consistently between 90 and 95 now represent business.

More Competition

The first and most basic observation is that while lobbying activity has increased over the years, there are not more days in the year. There are not more senators and representatives. And, most importantly, congressional staffs remained at the same size for more than three decades while the demands on offices have increased dramatically.[12] There are now more lobbyists competing for a finite amount of attention, working harder and harder to attract that attention and demonstrate why their perspectives and priorities are more important than anybody else's perspectives and priorities.

Here's how several veteran lobbyists I interviewed described the change:

- "The biggest change is there are more people doing it. The hallways are more crowded, the hearing rooms are more crowded, everything is more crowded."
- "The noise level has gotten ridiculous. The biggest problem is to be heard."
- "It's gotten more brutal, more cut-throat. . . All in all, it becomes harder to penetrate Capitol Hill because there's so much white noise."
- "The big difference between 1983 [when the lobbyist started] and today, I'd say, is because the healthcare sector is so much more competitive you do sometimes see companies going right directly at each other. You do see more of that now than then."

As we will see in more detail in Chapter 4, corporate lobbying can be quite expansive in scope. Lobbying strategies have become increasingly aggressive, reaching out far beyond the traditional approach of working with congressional allies and communicating positions to Congress.[13] Modern lobbying strategies increasingly have a kind of everywhere-and-everything-at-once approach that includes large-scale coalition building, grassroots activity, a comprehensive media plan, and a broad shaping of the "intellectual environment"—a subject that I will return to in more detail. To be effective, organized interests need to do more. But each expansion or advance in lobbying strategy doesn't remain an advantage for long. To stay ahead, organized interests must always be doing *even more.*

Change Is now Harder

One consequence of this increasingly competitive lobbying environment is that it makes policy change more difficult. Two-and-a-half decades ago, Robert Salisbury observed that a more crowded lobbying landscape had reduced the power of individual lobbying interests.[14] Things have only gotten more congested and more competitive since.

Defenders of the status quo benefit from structural features of the American system of government, with its multiple veto points and, hence, multiple opportunities to stall and delay.[15] Frank Baumgartner and colleagues' *Lobbying and Policy Change* found that being on the side of the status quo was by far the best predictor of lobbying success.[16] After all, defenders of the status quo merely have to keep an issue off the agenda, a task made easier by the scarcity of attention and the doubt inherent in any change. Baumgartner and colleagues also posit an "information-induced equilibrium"—essentially the idea that existing political actors tend to get attached to existing frames and understandings, and absent a major change in the players or in events, there is little possibility of dislodging those frames and understandings. The "unintended consequences" argument always works well to cast doubt on any policy change. As a Senate staffer, I frequently heard some variation of the argument: "The system isn't perfect, but changing it could have *unintended consequences* that might make things *even worse.*" Such arguments harness the risk-avoidance inherent in human cognition and can be quite effective.[17]

Any current state of public policy represents the accumulated victories of many established organized interests, and those organized interests are generally well-mobilized and well-positioned to defend their hard-earned victories. Once a particular interest wins a benefit from the government, that particular interest gets very attached to those benefits. That attachment, and the political engagement that it brings, makes it very hard for the government to ever remove that benefit. Like barnacles attaching to a rock, government programs and subsidies and tax credits almost never go away.[18] Attentive publics watch these programs closely to make sure that members of Congress face stiff costs for challenging them.[19] Many of these benefits fall under the rubric of what James Q. Wilson calls "client politics"—where concentrated interests benefit and a diffuse public absorbs the cost, but because concentrated interests are more likely to mobilize than diffuse interests, they usually win. And because these benefits are hard to take away once created, all it takes is one victory, and that victory is likely to be permanent.[20] Virginia Gray and David Lowery find that in state legislatures, more organized interests correlate to lower rates of bill enactments and even of bill introductions. They offer the following explanation for the negative relationship between bill introductions and interest group density: "When there are many interest organizations, the potential of such introductions to offend someone increases. As a result, introductions may be considered more carefully in dense systems."[21] In other words, the more status quo defenders there are, the less likely legislators are to introduce challenges to the status quo.

The tax code presents a good example of this dynamic. In 2005, a presidential panel noted that, following the Tax Reform Act of 1986, "there has been nearly constant tinkering—more than 100 different acts of Congress have made nearly 15,000 changes to the tax code."[22] But any time someone in Congress starts talking about comprehensive reform, it falls apart because reform challenges the existing benefits of some group of companies and industries. Those companies and industries begin to scream and holler, predicting sure economic doom if their tax preferences are dropped, and sure electoral doom for anyone who would drop those tax preferences. And comprehensive tax reform is promptly tabled. Congress was talking about comprehensive tax reform in 2007 when I began conducting my interviews. The bill at the time—introduced by House Ways and Means Committee Chairman Charles Rangel (D-NY)—was dubbed "The Mother of All Tax Bills."[23] It set off a lobbying frenzy and did not become law. In 2014, as I complete the final draft of this book, another Ways and Means Committee Chairman, Dave Camp (R-MI), has another comprehensive tax reform bill. However, after an even more abbreviated lobbying frenzy, this bill was quickly pronounced dead. It would have altered the tax code in ways that certain industries, most prominently Wall Street, did not like. These industries complained, and congressional leaders promised it would go nowhere.

While the status quo bias is far from a new feature of American politics, the increasing lobbying presence of corporate America and the commensurate thickening of the interest group environment makes the already uphill battle of political change that much harder. Moreover, in a crowded and competitive lobbying environment, with almost every status quo position well-defended and thus well-rooted, it typically requires both considerable resources as well as some luck to challenge a status quo position. This provides another advantage to the well-off: if the status quo is hard to change, those with considerable money and patience will be in a much better position to advocate for proactive changes.

To be sure, many observers of American politics are more likely to blame the current political gridlock on the high degree of partisan polarization that has now descended upon Washington. I would not deny that high levels of partisan polarization have contributed to record lows in congressional legislative productivity. But even were partisan polarization to somehow lessen, the analysis here suggests that the high levels of corporate lobbying would severely constrain the political agenda, cutting off many possible changes to the current status quo. There is also an lobbyist-induced gridlock that makes large-scale policy change difficult regardless of levels of partisanship and polarization.

Legislation Is More Complex

Although a more competitive lobbying environment generally inhibits legislative productivity, it does not entirely choke it. After all, in 2010 Congress passed two landmark pieces of legislation, the Patient Protection and Affordable Care Act (ACA) and the Dodd-Frank Wall Street Reform and Consumer Protection Act. The first became law because a new president made it a top priority and spent considerable political capital on it; the second became law because a major financial crisis (a.k.a., an exogenous shock) demanded a response.

But both bills turned out to be incredibly lengthy, and were almost certainly more complex than they needed to be. Dodd-Frank clocked in at 383,013 words, ACA at 327,911. (For comparison's sake, the Oxford World's Classics edition of *War and Peace* is 561,093 words.)

How did both bills get to be so long? The simplest explanation is that to ensure passage, congressional leaders needed buy-in from many disparate interests and parties. Many lobbyists worked with many different congressional offices to make sure that many different lobbying clients got something in the bill. Though many provisions were narrow and tangential, they each had their rationale, put forward by a lobbyist, and championed by a receptive member of Congress. On Dodd-Frank, at least 900 unique organizations lobbied on the bill. Of these, 509 (56.5 percent) were individual corporations. Another 201 were trade associations.[24] On the Affordable Care Act, 1,483 unique organizations lobbied on the bill. Again, individual businesses were most common— 514 of them lobbied on the bill. Additionally 242 institutions (mostly hospitals) weighed in, 224 trade associations, and 162 professional associations (mostly representing different medical specialists).[25] Each, presumably, had its own particular concerns about the legislation.

Large bills are more and more common. In the 92nd Congress (1971–1972), Congress passed 607 public bills, spanning a total of 2,330 pages, about 3.8

pages per bill. In the 111th Congress (2009–2010), Congress passed just 383 bills, but those bills spanned 7,617 pages, an average of 19.9 pages per bill, an all-time record for average length. The 7,617 pages were just a few short of the previous 110th Congress's record-setting 7,689 pages of legislation, spread across 460 public bills.[26] As one lobbyist noted, "Now, less legislation is being passed, but it's more complicated, and the average bill is bigger, more expensive, with more strings attached, The process is more like making sausage than it used to be."

Complexity tends to grow even more after a bill becomes a law, when agencies write and then figure out how to implement the rules. Consider Dodd-Frank's proposed "Volcker Rule"—an attempt to prevent banks from engaging in "proprietary trading" (basically, gambling with clients' money). The Volcker Rule began as a three-page proposal. It grew to 10 pages in the Dodd-Frank bill. More than a year later, the proposed rule had grown to an unwieldy 298 pages, and regulators faced more than 1,300 question letters on 400 topics. As the *New York Times* reported: "Even the helpful summary prepared by Sullivan & Cromwell, a law firm that represents big banks. . . runs a dense 41 pages."[27] When the rule was finally released in December 2013, it had ballooned to 953 pages. Then-Fed vice-chairwoman Janet Yellen noted, "the absence of a lot of bright-line distinctions."[28] Reports warned of squabbling among financial regulatory agencies over how to implement the new rule,[29] and financial journalists began immediately identifying loopholes.[30]

And while the Volcker Rule stands out because of its contentiousness and resulting difficulty, it was only one of 398 rule-making requirements in Dodd-Frank. Notably, three years since the passage of Dodd-Frank, barely a third (155) of the proposed rules had actually been completed. Few of the directions given by Congress in the original legislation turned out to be straightforward, especially once industry lobbyists had weighed in on them.

To be sure, there are legitimate reasons why policymaking has become more complex. Rapid technological change, increasing globalization, increasing economic segmentation and differentiation—all have contributed to increased policy complexity. Certainly, there is a case to be made for the precision of more complicated laws. As one lobbyist noted, "Legislation itself is by a logarithmic jump far more elegant. It's not as blunt an instrument as it once was when I first came here 30 years ago."

Because the status quo is difficult to change, new tweaks are almost awkwardly grafted onto existing systems, creating additional complexity. Steven Teles has usefully called this condition "kludgeocracy." Public policy, he argues, is increasingly full of "rickety, complicated and self-defeating complexity." And, as Teles argues, this complexity further entrenches the role of business in the political process: "The complexity that makes so much of American public policy vexing and wasteful for ordinary citizens and governments is also what makes it so easy for organized interests to profit from the state's largesse. The power of such interests varies in direct proportion to the visibility of the issue in question . . . corporations are most likely to get their way when political issues are out of the public gaze. Policy complexity is valuable for those seeking to extract rents from government because it makes it hard to see just who is benefitting and how."[31]

More Opportunities for Low-salience Lobbying

Numerous scholars have noted the relationship between salience and business power. As Pepper Culpepper puts it succinctly, "Business power goes down as political salience goes up."[32] But as political salience goes down, business power goes up. Mark Smith reaches similar conclusions in his study of business power: an engaged public can be a formidable match for big business when the two disagree. Smith also notes that this kind of conflict tends to be limited to highly salient issues.[33] When things are too complicated for most people to understand, they generally don't bother to understand them. This leaves a narrow group of interested parties (mostly businesses) and bureaucrats to make policy insulated by the barriers of expertise and the resulting lack of public attention.[34]

There are two ways in which complexity creates more opportunities for low-salience lobbying. One is Teles' point: that the complexity masks the winners and losers. It takes time and expertise for an interested observer to dig in and expose the ways in which various price supports or tax deductions or other complex, low-salience benefits might unfairly pad the profits of particular companies. There are few individuals with that time and expertise—and those who do have the time and expertise are most likely working for the companies and organizations that benefit. Moreover, even if the occasional journalistic or watchdog exposé of a particular loophole causes a stir, most stirs of outrage last only a few days. It takes more than a few days of outrage to change policy.

The other way that complexity contributes to low-salience lobbying is that when the legislative process involves bigger and more complex bills, it is easier to slip small provisions into a massive legislative log-roll. The bigger the bill, the harder for observers to find an offending provision (after all, if the bill is now longer and more confusing to parse, each provision is less likely to be scrutinized). Additionally, once one company or industry gets its pet concerns in the bill, another company or industry can come along and demand that, *out of fairness*, that company or industry's pet concerns also deserve a place in the bill. Pretty soon, everybody who is paying attention has something.

As one lobbyist explained, "What matters is getting stuff put in the bill, a line here, a line there. . . What you are looking to do is put a line in a law, get something tweaked. You're looking to change this line in subsection B. You just need one person to make that change." Another put it more diplomatically: "As things get bigger, and more complex, there are more steps, and more opportunities to have a say."

Tax policy is a good example of low-salience influence. As the authors of the 2005 presidential advisory panel report on tax reform noted about the 15,000 changes to the tax code: "Each one of these changes had a sponsor, and each had a rationale to defend it. Each one was passed by Congress and signed into law. Some of us saw this firsthand, having served in the U.S. Congress for a combined 71 years, including 36 years on the tax-writing committees. Others saw the changes from different perspectives – teaching, interpreting, and even administering the tax code."[35] Almost all of these were small provisions in larger bills. Few received anything close to public scrutiny. As the report acknowledged, this approach has had negative consequences: "In retrospect, it is clear that frequent changes to the tax code, no matter how well-intentioned, ultimately undermine the integrity of the code in real and significant ways."[36] The tax code is now almost 4 million words long.[37]

More Lobbying Jobs

Another consequence of increased lobbying is a growing lobbying sector, with more lobbying jobs. More jobs mean more opportunities for congressional staffers eager to increase their salaries, and more competition among lobbying firms for the most connected congressional staff, pushing salaries up further. In 2012, the median for-hire K Street lobbyist generated $179,667 in reported lobbying revenue, slightly more than the annual salary for a member of Congress ($174,000). Those who reported previous government experience on their lobbying disclosure forms, however, earned significantly more. These lobbyists generated a median revenue of $300,000 in 2012—substantially more than the $112,500 that those lobbyists without government experience generated.[38] Increasing numbers of congressional staffers also go into a vast and growing uncataloged world of "shadow lobbying" (e.g., "strategic advising," "issues management," "public relations") that doesn't show up in lobbying disclosure forms.[39]

The lure of a lobbying/strategic advising job in the ever-expanding office corridors of Washington, DC, exerts a pull on the arc of Washington careers. As one lobbyist said, "Compared to ten years ago. . . you had folks who stayed in government longer. Now you have a situation where anybody can go to

Capitol Hill for two years, three years, come out, and make a decent living. That's one thing you're seeing, compared to ten years ago. People have less experience."

In interviews, several lobbyists who had formerly worked on the Hill made clear the lure of taking a lobbying job after doing their time in Congress.

- "It's tough to live off the government paycheck. You make so little money. One of the big things that's wrong with the system is that somebody finally learns their job and then they have to move on, so you have a bunch of young folks who turn to lobbyists to figure out their jobs."
- "As you get older working on the Hill you realize, one, that you need more money, that you'd like to have more money to support your family, and secondly, it's time to move on. Capitol Hill can be very draining, very rewarding but very draining."
- "I had recently gotten married, had a child, and the ceiling at that point was $116,000, so if I wanted to go out and make any real money and support my family, I'd have to move on."
- "As a lobbyist, you generally don't have to work as hard, but you get more credit. You get rewarded. It's a little bit of an ego thing. You can start your own firm, put your name on it."

As a Congressional Management Foundation report explains it, "Staff typically work exceedingly long, unpredictable hours that leave little time for outside activities; receive lower pay than both private sector and federal executive branch staff; work in cramped quarters with no privacy; exercise minimal control over their work schedules; and have virtually no job security."[40] Additionally, staffers get very little recognition for the work that they do. As Robert Salisbury and Ken Shepsle note, the job requires "if not entire anonymity, at least a willingness to subsist on glory reflected from the principal."[41] But when things go wrong, staff are usually first to be blamed.[42] While working in government has always had its difficulties, what is different now is that the private sector offers more and more lucrative jobs for people with government experience, and the pay gap between public and private policy work continues to grow.

Hiring a well-connected lobbyist does not guarantee victory. However, Baumgartner and colleagues do find that the side with more lobbyists who previously served in government prevailed 63 percent of the time, making this one of the few factors that is reasonably predictive of victory.[43] And in a competitive lobbying marketplace, where business interests have the most to offer lobbyists financially, most of the premier Washington lobbyists will spend most of their time representing business interests. The most experienced Hill staffers do not come cheap when they become lobbyists. Corporate clients can afford to pay their rates. Diffuse interest groups rarely can. This further contributes to the imbalance in representation. That many of best policy minds and most connected people in Washington are far more likely to be working on behalf of private clients than public constituents shapes what issues will get worked on by the most "serious" people, and which arguments and perspectives will be most thoughtfully developed and vigorously advocated for (and which will not). This has obvious consequences for democratic representation and public policy outputs.

Lobbyists are not all the same. Some are extremely well-connected and experienced. Some have a high degree of policy knowledge. Some are skilled tacticians. Some are excellent coalition builders. To be able to hire the best lobbyists on all of these dimensions provides a significant advantage. As more companies and interests lobby, there is more competition for the best lobbyists with knowledge of particular issues, or with access to particular key members. In interviews, some lobbyists described a new phenomenon where companies retained the services of a particular lobbying firm just so that their competitors could not.

In the words of Representative Jim Cooper (D-TN), "Capitol Hill is a farm league for K Street."[44] Congress is the place where you cut your teeth, get some experience, and build some contacts. K Street is the place where you make things happen. Some of this, no doubt, is a consequence of the often-difficult working environment in Congress, and this is where there are some genuine reform possibilities, which I will discuss more in the final chapter. But much of this situation is due to the growing corporate demand for policy expertise and political connections.

Declining Congressional Capacity

The corollary of the pull of K Street is that government is left with less experienced staff. Working in Congress is now more than ever a job for enthusiastic 20- and 30-somethings. According to a 2009 Congressional Management Foundation survey, 27 percent of House legislative directors are under 30 years old, and 87 percent are under 40 years old. More than half (55 percent) have only a bachelor's degree, and only one in six (16 percent) have a law degree. Typically, they have two to three legislative aides working under them, and 80 percent of those aides will have less than three years' experience in Congress.[45] In the House, individual legislative assistants typically cover at least a dozen different issues, far more than they can develop anything resembling expertise on. In the Senate, staffers tend to be a little older, a little more educated, and have a slightly more narrow portfolio, but as I observed working in the Senate, most Senate legislative staff are also stretched too thin and tend to be younger and less experienced than most lobbyists.[46]

While the pull of K Street riches surely has some effect on the tenure of government staff, it is not the only reason government capacity has declined. Another reason is that congressional office staff sizes have remained static since 1979, while constituent demands and policy complexity have dramatically increased. Congressional staffers increasingly find themselves stretched incredibly thin, especially in their ability to deal with substantive policy questions. In 2010, Daniel Schuman found that "there are fewer House staff and fewer legislative support agency personnel now than at any time in the recent past, with data going back to 1979."[47] In 1979, 75 percent of Senate staff were based in DC; in 2005, only 61 percent of staff were. More significantly, the number of Senate committee staff fell from 1,410 in 1979 to 957 in 2005.[48] The House has witnessed similar declines.[49] In 1995, Congress cut off funding for the Office of Technology Assessment, killing the 23-year-old agency that had become a trusted and valuable source for neutral policy expertise.[50]

As Lorelei Kelly explains it, "Many contemporary and urgent questions before our legislators require nuance, genuine deliberation and expert judgment. Congress, however, is missing adequate means for this purpose and depends on outdated and in some cases antiquated systems of information referral, sorting, communicating, and convening."[51] Congressional offices can't keep up. They don't have the resources. Kelly also argues that Congress has lost its "institutional wisdom." High turnover means that staffers lack issue context. Lobbyists are often more likely than staffers to know how members of Congress voted and what they said about a particular issue in the past.[52]

The basic point is simple: few congressional offices have the institutional capacity to develop meaningful policy expertise. While many staffers are bright and energetic, they are forced to cover too many different topics and don't have the background and experience to develop deep knowledge of their subjects. While lobbyists do add value as providers of perspective and information, there is reason to be concerned when staffers depend too much on them.

These observations also extend to the executive branch and government agencies, though not quite as strongly. Executive branch and administrative agencies tend to hire staffers with more targeted expertise, and they generally provide better working conditions and more stable careers. However, even here, agencies almost always pay less than the private sector. Agencies also continually struggle with limited resources (Congress must approve their budgets). Given the complexities of the issues that they must decide and the onslaught of argument and pressure they face from industry, these limited resources often mean more reliance on industry.

Intellectual Environment Overload

One of the key consequences of the increase in corporate lobbying, and especially the increasing competition, is that companies and industries are investing more and more into shaping the "intellectual environment" of Washington. By this, I mean the endless array of articles and op-eds, white papers and speeches, think tank reports and panel discussions, academic studies, Metro ads, and other topics of the "Washington conversation." As Bryan Jones and Frank Baumgartner note, "Oversupply rather than undersupply seems to be the problem. Policymakers generally report that they are bombarded with information of varying quality."[53] Similarly, Richard Hall notes: "Policy-relevant information is abundant, perhaps embarrassingly rich on Capitol Hill."[54] Effective lobbyists always have folders full of justifications—detailed research backing up their legislative ask, specific estimates of jobs that would be lost or created (depending on how the senator voted), and well-honed and well-supported arguments about fairness, economic growth, and American competitiveness.

To understand why this matters, it helps to draw on Hebert Simon's insights into human decision-making. Simon's first basic insight was that people have a limited capacity for attention: "the capacity of the human mind for formulating and solving complex problems is very small compared with the size of the problems whose solution is required for objectively rational behavior in the real world—or even for a reasonable approximation to such objective rationality."[55] Policymaking involves decision-making on some very complex subjects, often far beyond the cognitive capacity of even the most expert individuals, let alone the relatively inexperienced and stretched-too-thin congressional staffers, and the members of Congress who similarly lack anything close to the necessary amounts of time for anything close to policy expertise.

How do decision-makers then cope when faced with a new problem? Simon argues that decision-makers must first enter into a "recognition process." In short, they ask whether the problem is a familiar problem, or at least resembles a familiar problem. If so, there may be a familiar solution that can be applied. Such reactions are often criticized as "knee-jerk responses" in that they happen quickly and automatically.

If a solution does not automatically spring to mind, then a decision-maker will have to search out a solution. But cognitive capacity is limited, and our brains are lazy. Decision-makers don't want to do more work than they have to. This means that they are most likely to seek out information sources that are readily available and/or come to mind quickly. They are most likely to seek out the advice of people they know well and who have shown themselves willing and capable of help in the past.

Typically, humans can keep about at most seven different concepts ("chunks") in active memory.[56] While there may be a wide range of facts and trade-offs to consider in any policy decision, only those that break through the bottleneck of short-term attention can be considered. However, as Simon notes: "A chunk is not an innate measure of storage capacity. A chunk is any stimulus that has become familiar, hence recognizable, through experience. Hence, the capacity of short-term memory is itself determined by learning, and can grow to vast size as individual acts of recognition access larger and richer stores of information in long-term memory."[57]

Building on Simon's insights, Jones and Baumgartner built a theory of policymaking as information processing: "We see information as providing a profound dynamic element to the political process, and we see the pursuit of democratic politics as essential to the processing of information in public policymaking."[58] Jones and Baumgartner, like Simon, argue that attention is the key dynamic in information processing because individuals have a limited amount of it. To make a choice involves first figuring out what problems are worthy of attention in the first place; deciding what aspects of the problem are worth attending to; then figuring out which solutions are worthy of attention; and finally picking a solution. Each stage involves winnowing and filtering.

These insights tell us that it matters very much what information is familiar and what information is top-of-mind. If decision-makers decide based on what they can recognize and/or find quickly, then public policy will depend on what knowledge decision-makers recognize and/or can find quickly. Each individual policy paper, memo, invited panel, or op-ed may by itself be meaningless and forgettable. But if staffers and decision-makers are asked to respond to them, they must engage with them, even if just momentarily. They may listen to the same arguments over and over again. Over time, these arguments begin to sound familiar and, through constant repetition, they achieve a top-of-mind status. They can also come to gradually shape the "causal stories" that underlie policymaking.[59]

Corporations have increasingly figured this out. They are investing considerable sums in saturating the "intellectual environment," overloading the minds of policymakers and their staff so that when the time comes to make a decision, certain arguments and frames will come to mind quicker than others, and certain ideas and solutions will have been pre-legitimated by a wide range of trusted experts. While it is impossible to get comprehensive data on this, there is strong anecdotal evidence for this broad claim. In interviews, lobbyists commonly stressed the importance of working with think tanks:

- "One thing that we do is that there are groups like The New Democrat Network, Main St. Republicans, Third Way, AEI, Brookings. We do retain a relationship with all of those groups. When they are doing something that is of interest to us, they will call us and ask for people in the company to come to participate, and sometimes we contact them on some issue that we want to have more thoroughly examined."

- "We do a lot with different think tanks around town. I like to keep up with new thinking, and I attend a lot of dinners and lecture series, and we commission a lot of research. Some things have been turned into books. We do encourage the knowledge generation business. For example, we've been interested in how poverty is measured. How people get into various federal programs determines how many customers we have coming in through that route. So we fund the Urban Institute."

- "We might go to RAND to put out a study or turn to think tanks in Washington that view health care as primary issue. We came back with Heritage and PPI [Progressive Policy Institute], a think tank on the right and center left, and we ended up partnering with them. We said, let's sit down and look at health information technology."

- "Think tanks have been drivers behind coalitions. A lot of companies are involved. Most don't want to be mentioned on record."

One tech company lobbyist said that, "we think of [lobbying] as thought leadership. In the area of internet infrastructure, we want to be the premier thought leader." Another tech company I visited had named its conference room "The Center for IT Thought Leadership." R. Kent Weaver and Andrew Rich found that between 1970 and 1996, the number of Washington think tanks tripled, from 100 to 306. As they note, "because most public officials care about policy as well as political outcomes, they have an almost insatiable demand for information about policy problems, how current policies work (or do not work), and potential alternatives."[60] Detailed policy analysis and thought leadership costs money—and corporations are willing to pay for it.[61]

Consider the case of the Bipartisan Policy Center, which claims that it "drives principled solutions through rigorous analysis, reasoned negotiation and respectful dialogue." The Center was founded in 2007 by retired Senate heavyweights Howard Baker, Tom Daschle, Bob Dole, and George Mitchell, Republican and Democratic leaders. Over the course of just a few months in 2013, the Center was publicly criticized for taking: (1) money from Walmart to promote an industry-backed plan to handle workplace conditions in Bangladeshi garment factories; (2) oil and gas industry money to write a report promoting more drilling; and (3) Citigroup and American Banking Association money to create a "Financial Regulatory Reform Initiative" to steer the implementation of Dodd-Frank in a way that would be favorable to industry. At the time of the third revelation, John Coffee, a Columbia Law professor on the task force, resigned, saying, "The Task Force has been bipartisan in terms of political parties. But it was not bipartisan in terms of the critical division in Washington: The financial services party and the reform party."[62]

Or consider the Center for American Progress (CAP), a leading Democratic think tank. CAP maintains something called the "American Progress Business Alliance" that (according to a fact sheet) "has proven to be a successful way to keep CAP and its experts connected with and cognizant of business perspectives on issues of highest priority in our work." For a $100,000 annual contribution, alliance members get invited to participate in the Global Progress Summit and a private meeting with the American Progress Executive Committee.[63] The alliance counts among its supporters Comcast, Walmart, General Motors, Pacific Gas and Electric, General Electric, Boeing, Lockheed, the University of Phoenix, and many other leading corporations. As journalist Ken Silverstein, who shed light on the undisclosed program, notes: "Nowadays, many Washington think tanks effectively serve as unregistered lobbyists for corporate donors, and companies strategically contribute to them just as they hire a PR or lobby shop or make campaign donations."[64]

Or consider the case of Google. According to a *Washington Post* analysis, in 2013, the company gave money to "nearly 140 business trade groups, advocacy organizations and think tanks." Reporters Tom Hamburger and Matea Gold noted that, "Google 'fellows'—young lawyers, writers and thinkers paid by the company—populate elite think tanks such as the Cato Institute, the Competitive Enterprise Institute and the New America Foundation. To critics, Google's investments have effectively shifted the national discussion away from Internet policy questions that could affect the company's business practices. Groups that might ordinarily challenge the policies and practices of a major corporation are holding their fire, those critics say."[65] The article describes how after receiving money from Google, the Heritage Foundation came out against an antitrust investigation into Google and joined Google in opposing the Stop Online Piracy Act (SOPA).

Several excellent books have documented the ways in which pro-market conservative donors, along with corporations, invested large sums of money to develop and spread the intellectual justifications for limited government and low taxes by supporting think tanks (most famously the Heritage Foundation, the American Enterprise Institute, and the Cato Institute). These think tanks helped provide a cognitive and policy framework for a generation of Reagan Republicans. Andrew Rich argues that "while millions of dollars have supported the proliferation of hundreds of think tanks since the 1970s" competing ideological think tanks whose reports only show up in the late stages of policy deliberation have "in many respects neutralized the power of expertise in American policymaking."[66] When everybody has a study to draw on, it becomes harder to mediate competing claims of expertise. Yet, even if think tank reports have lost their ability to command respect and authority in the way that they once did (in an earlier era when think tanks were less partisan, and neutral expertise was more valued), this does not mean they are irrelevant.

One reason all this information matters is that lobbyists and policymakers need to have some confidence that they are enacting policies that will work. Esterling, for example, makes the distinction between two kinds of arguments, "normative" and "instrumental." While "normative" arguments merely tell Congress what it *should* do, "instrumental" arguments help to lay out the causal logic behind a policy. Esterling argues that absent "instrumental" arguments, Congress is unlikely to support a policy. Accredited researchers and policy experts, be they in think tanks, academia, or elsewhere, can lend legitimacy to policies by providing the "instrumental" arguments. Advocates who lobby without such legitimizing rationales are at a serious disadvantage. Policy ideas need to go through a legitimizing stage to be taken seriously.[67] Think tanks and other research institutions can provide that legitimacy. For example, the restaurant industry funded a group called the Employment Policies Institute to produce research demonstrating negative consequences for increasing the minimum wage. As one lobbyist told the *New York Times:* "Once you have the study, you can point it to it to prove your case—even if you paid to get it written."[68]

Cass Sunstein wrote that he never saw anybody "cave in" to interest group pressure during his four years as head of the White House Office of Information and Regulatory Affairs (OIRA), where he was in charge of evaluating cost-benefit analysis for all major regulatory rulemakings. "But," he wrote, "if people in the private sector presented arguments, with evidence, about the importance of going in a particular direction, those arguments could matter." Such outside analysis "could, and did, narrow and clarify the stakes, often bringing people together regardless of what they had heard or what they thought they were most concerned about."[69] Sunstein also recounted that "those with an incentive to oppose the rules will tend to overstate the costs and perhaps even claim that if the rules are finalized, the sky will fall." He saw this happen "at least once a month." And yet, he wrote, "if the industry overstates costs, regulators may not have enough information to make a correction"[70] This is an important point. Often, the intellectual environment is overwhelming on one side of the issue, but is sparse on the other side of the issue. When this happens, it can be very difficult for decision-makers not to be swayed, especially given the limited government policy capacity we discussed earlier.

Again, each report, each white paper, each panel discussion, each op-ed does not need to convince in and of itself. It merely needs to add to an echo chamber, to repeat itself, to say the same thing over and over again. Hear something enough times, and it starts to achieve familiarity. After a while familiarity has a ring of truth. Read the same thing again and again, written by somebody with a Ph.D., and you might actually come to believe it. Or at least think of it when it comes time to make a decision. Because you keep hearing it over and over. Because it is familiar.

More Government Reliance on Lobbyists

Let's add up three key stylized facts that we've accumulated up to this point: complexity is increasing; "intellectual environment" overload is increasing; and congressional capacity is decreasing. All of this means that, in order to make policy, congressional offices need more outside help. As Kevin Esterling notes, "it is difficult for Congress to know about the current research-based state of knowledge for the full array of policies before it."[71] He finds that demonstrated technical expertise improves access.[72] Corporate lobbyists are the most ready source of that technical expertise. In one recent survey, two-thirds of staffers described lobbyists as "necessary to the process" as either "collaborators" or "educators." Staffers also frequently referred to lobbyists as "partners."[73] Occasional pieces of investigative reporting reveal what most lobbyists will proudly acknowledge—that they are deeply involved in the developing and drafting of legislative policy.[74] My analysis of Enron's political e-mails with Daniel J. Hopkins found Enron's government affairs team spent much of its time making energy policy arguments on their merits. As we argued, Enron's greatest resource was "its monopoly on policy-relevant information about electricity, natural gas, and communications markets, information that policy makers could not easily obtain elsewhere."[75]

Often, lobbyists do more than just share expertise. They also help congressional offices to draft legislation, develop the talking points and explanations for why the legislation makes sense, write speeches and letters in support of it, seek out co-sponsors and supporters both within and outside of government, and generally see a bill through from start to finish. Richard Hall and Alan Deardorff have formalized congressional reliance on lobbyists into their theory of "lobbying as legislative subsidy." As they note, "[I]t's an unhappy fact that members of Congress do not have the time to vigorously represent all of their constituents on all issues that concern them." The problem is "that subsidies help legislators to work harder primarily on behalf of the interests that can afford the high costs, not only of organizing and making campaign contributions, but of paying professional lobbyists and financing the organizations that support them."[76]

In interviews, lobbyists noted that expertise and analysis had become increasingly important in their work. In the past, perhaps, it was enough merely to know the right people and make the right phone calls at the right time. Of course, access remains an important part of the lobbying business.[77] But a foot in the door is only the first step. Success requires policy expertise alongside that foot in the door. Here are two quotes from experienced lobbyists that help to clarify this point:

- "What I'm finding is people take the data and take the analysis much more seriously today, and I think that's growth in sophistication in terms of both members and staff, and the healthcare industry in general in terms of gathering the right data."
- "[Over 18 years] It has morphed from being very relationship oriented, who do you know on the Hill, to much more policy oriented – how can you convince people that your case is the best case? The biggest thing is that the issues have become more complex and the level of sophistication of members and staff on policy issues has just grown quite a bit."

To be sure, lobbyists have every interest in representing their jobs as largely substantive. But this author's personal experiences working in the Senate found that the majority of corporate lobbyists do know an incredible amount about their particular policy area, and are indeed very helpful as researchers and analysts. Moreover, in an information-rich environment, staffers frequently turn to the lobbyists who have showed up with friendly promises to assist them. Lobbyist Nick Allard argues one of the most important ways in which lobbyists help congressional staffers is "by sifting information and noise, putting information into a coherent framework, and by challenging or checking facts on impossibly short time deadlines."[78]

Policy expertise is even more important in the green eyeshade work of federal rule-making, where political appeals are less likely to resonate because the public pays much less attention and doesn't have the same levers to pressure career government employees as they do members of Congress. The bureaucrats writing the rules tend to be most interested in finding a workable solution, especially one that will minimize headaches and complaints for the agency.

As a result, businesses tend to have a particular advantage in agency rule-making. Businesses tend to have the know-how and resources to provide the detailed analyses that the rule-writers want.[79] This matters, because as Amy McKay and Susan Webb Yackee find, when lobbying is "imbalanced" (as it often is), agency rule-making tends to be responsive to the side that participates most. As they note: "lobbying requires considerable time and money to monitor agencies, research policies, and convince the bureaucrats that a group's position is the right one."[80] Nolan McCarty argues that, "as policy becomes more complex, regulatory outcomes are increasingly biased toward those preferred by the firm." McCarty's reasoning is straightforward: "bureaucrats find it very difficult to establish autonomous sources of information and expertise about the consequences of different policies." As a result, they must rely on industry-provided lobbyists.[81] James Kwak notes that in many cases, industries exert a kind of "cultural capture" on regulated agencies through "group identification, status, and relationship networks." In short, regulators spend time with people in the industry, look up to them, and wind up thinking like them as a result.[82]

The economic consequences of lobbying growth

While this chapter has largely focused on the political consequences of corporate lobbying growth, there are also economic consequences of this changed political environment. One important consequence is that a harder-to-dislodge status quo tends to protect incumbent market players, thus limiting the capacity of the government to support policies would encourage innovation. Jacob Hacker and Paul Pierson argue that "policy drift" (i.e., when policymakers choose not to update policies "due to pressure from intense minority interests or political actors exploiting veto points in the political process") benefits the wealthy disproportionately, since the wealthy are most likely to benefit from maintaining the status quo.[83]

Lobbying might also be a diversion of resources for corporations. If profitability depends more on the rules and regulations and the subsidies and tax loopholes than it does on the quality of goods and services, will corporate managers focus more on politics and less on innovation? Jonathan Rauch makes a compelling case for this in *Government's End*. He worries that too much internal focus on corporate lobbying will lead to a "parasite economy" where, "The negative sums of transfer-seeking, then, are the sums that would have been produced but are not: the inventions not developed, the crops not planted, the equipment not bought, the employees not hired, and, in all other forms, the investments forgone."[84]

Take General Electric, which filed a 57,000-page tax return in 2010 that enabled it to pay nothing in federal taxes.[85] As Alex Tabarrok astutely commented: "Consider the resources that GE spends to lowers its tax bill, not just the many millions spent on clever accounting and accountants and the many millions spent on lobbying but also the many inefficient ways that GE structures its businesses just to avoid paying taxes and the many millions it invests in socially wasteful projects just in order to produce privately valuable tax credits."[86] Moreover, if tax rates are a product of lobbying, this creates another set of economic concerns. Tabarrok goes on to bemoan "the allocational inefficiencies of taxing some firms at different rates than others." And argues that it generates, "a corporate tax system which wastes a lot of resources and raises relatively little revenue."[87]

General Electric has an estimated 1,000 employees dedicated preparing its tax returns.[88] The IRS estimates that American individuals and businesses spend 6.1 billion hours and $163 billion preparing their taxes each year (or about 20 hours and $543 per person).[89] What productivity is lost in the endless complexity of regulations, many of which have become complex in order to accommodate the special pleadings of thousands of corporate lobbyists over the years? These questions go beyond the scope of this book but are still worth raising.

A note on the balance of power

All of this is not to deny that diffuse interest groups are still important voices in the political process. Jeffrey Berry, for example, found "citizen groups" testifying in hearings and being cited in the media at rates far higher than the raw lobbying expenditures might suggest.[90] Likewise, Baumgartner and colleagues found that citizen groups were named as a "major player" more often than any other kind of interest group.[91] Certainly, many diffuse interest groups enjoy legitimacy far beyond their lobbying spending. But in a highly competitive lobbying environment, it is not merely enough to be legitimate, or to testify or be quoted in the press. One needs to also have the resources to move legislation. This often involves working with corporate interests. Baumgartner et al. note that corporations try to pair with "citizen groups." After all, the citizen groups can provide the legitimacy, while the corporate groups can provide the resources. But while corporate groups can create their own "citizen groups" (and often do), it is much harder for "citizen groups" to create their own corporate sponsors. Hence, they have less agenda control.

Consider the battle over the Stop Online Piracy Act (SOPA). Netroots activists cheered the impressive mobilization to stop the bill from moving forward: as many as 3 million e-mails and 3.9 million tweets hit Congress on or around January 18, 2012, all in opposition to a bill that many feared would create unnecessarily harsh rules and penalties for sharing copyrighted content on the Internet and give prosecutors dangerous powers to to crack down on service providers who might be abetting intellectual property violators. Many diffuse interest groups advocating an open Internet had been opposing the bill for a while. Up until January 18, 2012, it appeared that the legislation, drafted at the behest of and in consultation with Hollywood, would move forward. But then Facebook, Google, and Wikipedia, giants of content on the Internet, used their home pages in a coordinated way to raise awareness of the issue. As it turned out, it was actually a reasonably balanced lobbying fight in Washington: computer and Internet companies hired 246 lobbyists to oppose SOPA, as compared to the 241 lobbyists the TV, music and movie industry hired to pass SOPA. Both numbers were far higher than the counts of lobbyists working on behalf of open Internet groups, even as these groups became the public face of a battle between two corporate giants.[92]

This particular battle helps to illustrate a few key points from this discussion. First, it was (and as of this writing, continues to be) a very competitive political battle, and the status quo has been difficult to change. Second, the legislation deals with some very complex issues about how the Internet actually works, and hearings surrounding the bill revealed remarkable confessions of congressional ignorance, including one member of Congress openly admitting ignorance of basic Internet concepts like DNS servers—essential knowledge for someone legislating on the issue. As one anti-SOPA advocate wrote in trenchantly titled and widely shared blog post during the SOPA battle, "Dear Congress, It's No Longer OK to Not Know How the Internet Works."[93] Third, both sides had plenty of former government officials lobbying for them. For example, former Connecticut senator Chris Dodd (D-CT) was heading the Motion Picture Association of America in January 2012; shortly after the January 18 participatory explosion, Google hired former representative Susan Molinari (R-NY) to head its Washington lobbying shop.[94] Finally, as of this writing more than two years since January 2012, the issue has not gone away. Though the legislation was effectively killed for the 112th Congress, similar provisions to those in SOPA found themselves into drafts of the Trans-Pacific Partnership, a proposed free trade agreement.[95] Like many issues, there are deep pockets on both sides, and it is difficult to predict how this issue will be resolved, or whether the status quo will ever change. But a safe prediction is that many lobbyists will earn sizeable revenues from its continuation.

Conclusion

The pervasive nature of modern corporate lobbying investments changes the policymaking environment in several ways. More lobbying makes political change harder, which means both that the beneficiaries of the status quo can more easily continue to enjoy their advantages, and that those seeking to change the status quo require more resources to make anything happen. Both of these changes are advantages for business interests, who are both most likely to benefit from the status quo, and most capable of allocating the large-scale resources necessary for change. More lobbying also makes legislation more complex (in order to accommodate all the lobbying interests). This creates more opportunities for low-salience lobbying, which corporations are best positioned to take advantage of.

As lobbying becomes more competitive and pervasive, companies invest more and more in shaping the "intellectual environment" of Washington. They fund more think tanks, more organizations, more panel discussions and research reports and op-eds and white papers. In the war of ideas, they increasingly fight to make sure that their perspectives and frames and facts are immediately available and familiar.

A growing lobbying economy, meanwhile, pulls talent out of the public sector and into the private sector. As K Street becomes more lucrative, Congress becomes more a farm league for K Street. This contributes to declining government capacity, which means that government policymakers must increasingly rely on lobbyists to help them to develop, pass, and implement policy. In an ever-more-complex policy environment, the need for expertise becomes greater, but the gap between public sector and private sector expertise is wider. Again, organizations that can supply the expertise are at an advantage. These organizations tend to be corporations and trade and business associations.

None of this guarantees influence for any particular company. If anything, all the competition makes the relationship between political activity and policy outcomes more uncertain and unpredictable than ever before. The price of entry is higher, and there are more necessary but not sufficient conditions for influence. That more lobbying leads to more uncertainty is not a new argument. Heinz and colleagues make similar observations: the more resources organizations put into influence, the more "these efforts at control exacerbate problems of coordination and information exchange and may ultimately contribute to greater levels of uncertainty in policy systems generally."[96]

While the relationship between inputs and outputs may be far from predictable, the conditions under which lobbying now takes place are more favorable than ever to the corporations who can afford to build multi-million-dollar lobbying operations that allow them to invest their resources everywhere and anywhere. In a competitive policy environment, the price of entry is high. In a policymaking process marked by increasing complexity and big bills, it is easier to insert a provision here and there with limited scrutiny, and to become the go-to source for policy expertise for stretched-too-thin congressional staffers and even agency rule-makers. Collectively, these change give businesses a more central role in the policymaking process, since businesses are best-positioned to take advantage given their ability to marshal significant financial resources to politics.

Perhaps the biggest beneficiaries of this environment, however, are the lobbyists themselves. More lobbying makes everything more uncertain. This means that lobbying campaigns typically require more work and more patience, and hence bigger investments. Lobbyists enjoy both the financial rewards of increased revenues as well as the psychic rewards of being central players in the policy process. For these reasons, lobbyists have incentives to continue to make lobbying more competitive, and therefore more labor intensive. We will return to these incentives in more detail later in this book.

The Growth of Corporate Lobbying

"Government relations plans and goals got built into and integrated into the general business of organizations. A lot of companies became more sophisticated about how they viewed government relations. And what happened was that companies had a lot of things they wanted government relations departments to do." – *Corporate lobbyist*

In 1991, a proposed NASA space station, over-budget and behind schedule, faced "sudden death."[1] The Boeing Corporation, which as lead contractor stood to benefit significantly from the construction of the space station, faced a significant loss of business. So the company's lobbyists decided to launch a major campaign to save the space station. They put together a very large coalition. They brought in math and science teachers. They brought in other governments—Canada, Japan, several European nations. By 1992, both the House and Senate had voted to keep funding the space station, overcoming arguments that it was an "orbiting tin can" that was forcing the country to "take out a $120 billion, 30-year mortgage on our nation's future" at a time when Congress was very concerned about the growing national debt.[2] For Boeing, it had been a major legislative undertaking, much bigger than anything it had done before. "Early on we would not have taken on things this big," said a former Boeing lobbyist in an interview. "We would have just argued that the space station program not be closed." In 1981, Boeing had nine lobbyists, all in-house. By 1991, it had grown to 15 in-house lobbyists, plus three outside firms.

In 1995, Boeing started thinking even bigger. China was on the verge of not buying U.S. aircraft anymore, and the Executive Council at Boeing decided it wanted to lead an effort to normalize trade relations with China. Again, the company put together a large coalition. Five years later, Clinton successfully pushed Congress to officially grant Permanent Normal Trade Relations (PNTR) to China. In 2008, Boeing jets made up about 60 percent of China's air fleet.[3] The campaign to normalize trade relations was more ambitious than the campaign to save the space station. Saving the space station, after all, was just trying to preserve the status quo. Here, with PNTR, Boeing affected a substantial and proactive change in U.S. trade policy. "This is not something we would have tried even in the late 1980s," said the company's former lobbyist. "We wouldn't have thought we had the ability."

Back in the early 1980s, the lobbyist said, Boeing's lobbying efforts were 75 percent defense (preserving the status quo). Twenty years later, they had become 75 percent offense (trying to change the status quo). "We set the stage so we didn't have to defend," said the lobbyist. "We had already fought that battle. You'd start seeing things coming many years out and you'd be prepared." By 1995, Boeing had grown to 19 in-house lobbyists, plus six firms. And by 1998, after Boeing had acquired Rockwell International and merged with McDonnell-Douglas, Boeing had 26 in-house lobbyists, and had also hired 28 outside lobbying firms, bringing its total "lobbying presence" to 54.

Boeing's history offers one example of what happens when a company expands its Washington presence. It develops the ability to think big. It begins to move from defense to offense, from being reactive to being proactive. Boeing remains one of the most politically active firms in Washington. In 2012, Boeing spent $15.6 million on lobbying, with 26 in-house lobbyists, plus 15 outside firms. A total of 115 lobbyists registered to represent Boeing. The company's top issues were defense, trade, appropriations, and homeland security.

Though Boeing has always been one of the most politically active companies, the trajectory of its political activity conforms to the larger historical pattern. Once a company gets drawn into politics, its managers learn to value politics more. The company begins treating public policy as an opportunity instead of merely a threat. Quotes from different lobbyists all tell the same basic story:

- "I think twenty years ago, you had a Washington office to keep the government out of your business, and I think people have evolved to understand now that there are opportunities, partnerships with government. Private-public partnerships are good. We don't want to be sort of business-versus-government. That doesn't work. We try to get out in front of issues."
- "Sometime after 2000, I think there was a real realization that the industry needed to be more accessible, more open, and more willing to talk to government and not look at them as a combatant."
- "The managerial level of people doing government relations moved higher into the institutional chain. They developed a better ability to anticipate, and did a better job of making sure they drove the issues that came up."

- "Twenty-five years ago, our companies were run by engineers and it was 'just keep the government out of our business, we want to do what we want to,' and gradually that's changed to 'how can we make the government our partners?' It's gone from 'leave us alone' to 'let's work on this together.'"

In broad outline, the progression of corporate political activity occurred in three stages that roughly conform to three decades:

- The 1970s: the political awakening of corporate lobbying
- The 1980s: the political entrenchment of corporate lobbying
- The 1990s (and beyond): the political expansion of corporate lobbying

This chapter traces these different stages, situating them in a broader political-economic context. But before we discuss these stages, it is helpful first to understand what came before.

The Backstory (pre-1970)

Corporate lobbying is not a new invention. Business interests have been trying to shape American politics for as long as businesses have had something at stake in American government (in other words, always). Accounts of lobbying from the nineteenth century and earlier describe a world where whiskey and food and women and good old-fashioned cash predominated. Early in the nineteenth century, the Bank of the United States paid Senator Daniel Webster, a sitting member of Congress, to represent its interests.[4] A story from the mid-1850s tells of efforts by Samuel Colt to extend the patent on his pistol by seven years. Colt's tactics involved putting together parties where young ladies were first sold on the critical importance of a patent extension (they were given Parisian gloves) and then instructed to use their charms to convince members of Congress to extend the patents. Colt's lobbyist at the time adopted the following couplet as his approach to lobbying: "To reach the heart or get the vote / the surest way is down the throat." Samuel Ward, the "King of the Lobby" during Reconstruction, was known primarily for his stores of wine, liquor, and cigars.[5]

The Progressive Era was in many ways a response to the influence of corporate power. In general, progressive reformers saw their role as breaking up the large corporate institutions that had dominated Gilded Age through antitrust enforcements, taking a market-oriented approach to corporate regulation. The most direct strike at corporate political influence was the 1907 Tillman Act, which banned direct corporate contributions to candidates.

Another significant change was that during the first two decades of the twentieth century, "organized interests—unprecedented in number, variety, and professionalism—became active in federal politics"[6] A broadening network of civic groups emerged to hold Congress more accountable. Old-fashioned "down the throat" influence became harder to execute.

By the 1920s, the pendulum had swung back in favor of business. President Coolidge proudly stated that the business of America was business and proclaimed that, "the man who builds a factory builds a temple." The Department of Commerce began encouraging industries to organize into trade associations in the hopes of rationalizing and strengthening the economy, a movement that is most associated with Commerce Secretary and later President Herbert Hoover. Hoover advocated "cooperative competition" as a form of self-regulation in the spirit of scientific administration.

This thinking also guided the 1933 National Industrial Recovery Act, which abandoned the Progressive Era focus on market competition. Instead, the Roosevelt administration worried about too much competition—"ruinous competition," as some called it. New Deal policymakers argued that stability was more important. Therefore, they should encourage companies to organize together as industries so as to avoid undercharging and/or overproducing. Marc Eisner has called this era the "associational regime." As Eisner explains, "The advocacy of markets and the decentralization of economic power was replaced by the active support of economic associations negotiating over the amounts to be produced and the prices to be charged."[7]

During the 1950s and into the early 1960s, both government policy and the public mood were largely pro-business.[8] In 1964, for example, historian Richard Hofstadter wrote, "The existence and workings of the corporation are largely accepted and in the main they are assumed to be fundamentally benign."[9] In 1965, 88 percent of Americans agreed that, "large companies are essential for the nation's growth and expansion."[10] The often-quoted encapsulation of the spirit of the times came from Eisenhower's Secretary of Defense Charles Wilson. When asked before a Senate Committee whether his former position as president of General Motors would create a conflict of interest, he responded by saying he could not imagine such a conflict, "because for years I thought what was good for the country was good for General Motors and vice versa."

The lack of any pressing government threat to business autonomy also meant that there was little reason for companies to spend much money on politics. Graham K. Wilson has written of the era that, "business was relatively immune from public criticism, and did not need to concern itself with any of the most detailed of issues."[11]

Nor were individual businesses in need of significant government assistance. The 1950s and 1960s were a time of steady economic growth. With the rest of the industrialized world still recovering from World War II, U.S. manufacturers had unprecedented dominance of global markets, and plenty of wealth to go around. In many industries, companies could essentially manage demand on their own and intra-industry competition was limited.[12]

During this era, corporations invested small amounts in Washington lobbying. Two landmark studies published in 1963 (Lester Milbrath's *The Washington Lobbyists*, and Raymond A. Bauer, Ithiel de Sola Pool, and Lewis A. Dexter's *American Business and Public Policy*) describe corporate lobbying in the 1950s and 1960s as a sporadic, tinpot, and largely reactive activity. Few companies saw the need to have their own representation in Washington. In 1961, only 130 corporations had registered lobbyists in Washington, and only 50 had Washington addresses.[13] Instead, most corporate managers were content largely to leave politics to the trade associations. The associations, meanwhile, took a sleepy approach to politics, and the lobbyists that they placed in Washington primarily were there just to report back to headquarters. Rather than pressure members of Congress, the more common relationship was that of congressional offices enlisting the lobbyists to help rally support for members' legislative priorities. Here's what Bauer, Pool, and Dexter concluded after an extensive look at business lobbying on trade policy:

- "Lobbies were on the whole poorly financed, ill-managed, out of contact with Congress, and at best only marginally effective in supporting tendencies and measures which had already had behind them considerable Congressional impetus from other sources . . . When we look at the typical lobby, we find its opportunities to maneuver are sharply limited, its staff mediocre, and its typical problem not the influencing of Congressional votes but finding the clients and contributors to enable it to survive at all."[14]

They found little evidence of persuasion or meaningful pressure. Instead, they famously described corporate lobbyists as "service bureaus" for members of Congress who already shared their perspectives. Most of their time was spent simply "channeling communications." Of 166 large firms Bauer, Pool, and Dexter surveyed, only 37 had undertaken any communications at all with Congress.

Milbrath's surveys similarly painted lobbying as little more than a communications process: "The weight of the evidence that this study brings to bear suggests that there is relatively little influence or power in lobbying per se . . . Most careful observers of governmental decision-making have concluded that the over-all impact of lobbying is relatively minor. This point was made by both lobbyist and congressional correspondents and agrees with the observation of other writers on the subject."[15] Like Bauer, Pool, and Dexter, Milbrath found lobbyists wielding little direct influence.

At the same time, critics of this relatively pro-business era observed the cozy ways in which regulated agencies, congressional committees, and affected industries all worked together to keep policy stable and pro-industry. These scholars wrote of "iron triangles" and "agency capture" and worried that these behind-the-scenes dealings were working against the public interest.[16] Such arrangements followed logically from the associational regime put in place in the 1920s and 1930s, when government policy was oriented towards stabilizing business and even bordered on encouraging cartelization. Elite theorists also described the close personal relationships between the leaders of government and the captains of industry, arguing that the dense social networks of shared loyalties also worked against the public interest.[17]

How could these scholars come to such different conclusions? The simple answer is that different scholars were examining different "faces of power." In a seminal article, Peter Bachrach and Morton Baratz argued that there were two "faces" of power.[18] The first face of power is observed in public conflict. To study it, one can simply look at the actual political battles that are fought publicly and determine who wins and who loses. It assumes that the winners win because they have power. Its advantage is that it is highly empirical. But its critics have noted that it is limited to issues where there is observable public political conflict. What of all the issues that are left off the agenda? What of all the deals cut in back rooms? What about the implied threats that constrain the realm of the possible? The second face of power, by contrast, attempts to construct the space of possible policies and then asks why some issues are on the agenda, while others never get discussed. It argues that true power is the power to shape the agenda, and the power to keep certain issues from ever being debated at all. The empirical challenge is that it is both difficult to construct the space of all possible issues and difficult to observe power that is exercised by the absence of activity.

The critics of "agency capture" and "iron triangles" were largely making second face of power arguments. They frequently described relationships that took place in the background, where power arises from shared understandings and shared incentives and a desire to keep the scope of conflict narrow and limited. Everybody benefited from maintaining a pro-industry policy and so nobody had any political reason to challenge it. By contrast, both Bauer, Dexter, and Pool, and Milbrath focused more on the first face of power. They were looking for cases where business lobbyists actively changed minds and positions, where there was overt political conflict. But these cases were rare. They were cases where either there was a lack of consensus in the business community (e.g., the trade policy that Bauer, Dexter, and Pool studied) or where the scope of conflict had already widened beyond the iron triangle—exactly the circumstances where business was bound to be at a disadvantage. While Bauer, Pool, and Dexter dismissed lobbyists as merely "service bureaus" for congressional offices, this was largely because congressional offices did not need convincing to support industry, particularly local industry. They were already eager and ready to do so. There was no need to convince.

To the extent that business did lobby prior to the mid-1970s, it was primarily through trade associations. For example, of Milbrath's 114 survey participants, 43 came from "small trade" groups and another 9 came from "large trade" groups. His survey covered 52 trade association representatives, as compared to just 17 corporation representatives. Of the 52 association representatives, Milbrath most commonly (14 times) interviewed the association executive. He found that these individuals were not particularly disposed to spend much effort on lobbying, preferring instead to focus on business issues: "Most trade association executives dislike lobbying, though they realize that it is important. Many are grateful that it occupies only part of their time; the major portion of their time is devoted to the administration of the association's affairs."[19] Though it's hard to be certain how many trade associations were active in Washington at the time, it's worth noting that 54.3 percent of associations (943 of 1,737) listed in the *Washington Representatives Directory* in either 1981, 1991, 2001, or 2006, and for which founding dates are available, list their founding dates as earlier than 1970.[20]

Of the 17 corporations Milbrath interviewed, the majority (eight) were represented by lawyers. Milbrath writes of the lawyers: "Lawyer-consultants come to mind when organizations have problems relating to government . . . Most lawyers consider themselves lawyers first and lobbyists second. Lobbying positions come to them in the course of their general legal practice. Some do not care for lobbying and do it only because an old and favored client has a problem that requires legislative assistance . . . Other lawyers enjoy lobbying and seek to expand that aspect of their practice. Even these, however, do mainly legal work."[21] In other words, to the extent that companies had hired representatives in 1958 (when Milbrath conducted his survey), it was largely because they had legal troubles in Washington.

Three of the 17 corporations in Milbrath's study had "Washington Representatives," yet Milbrath was quick to dismiss the power of these "Washington Representatives," casting them as stretched-too-thin generalists whose primary tool of influence was making pleasantries: "These lobbyists are Washington envoys for organizations that have headquarters in another city. As members of a small staff or perhaps as the sole person on the staff, the Washington representatives tend to become 'jacks-of-all-trades.' . . . They cannot carry on comprehensive lobbying campaigns. Generally they restrict their role primarily to that of watchdog for the interests of their clients."[22]

A 1962 study, *The Business Representative in Washington*, found that the majority of company representatives were in Washington first and foremost to market and sell their companies' products to the government.[23] By contrast, "The legislative role of the representative appears to be substantially smaller than might be supposed."[24] The authors described the Washington representatives more as "diplomats" than "ambassadors," suggesting that their ability was constrained by their own lack of authority. Looking back on the period from the vantage point of 1979, Phyllis McGrath noted in a *Conference Board* report that, "The Washington office used to be the place where you shipped your soon-to-retire executive."[25] Others writing retrospectively also describe businesses as out-of-touch with politics during this era. As a 1984 book, *Business Strategy for the Political Arena*, notes, "In the past, business has by and large abstained from a continuing commitment toward developing political strategies." As a result, "the visiting business executive to Washington was like the proverbial bull in a china shop."[26]

Business leaders' political indifference had two important consequences. The first, and most important, is that it created space for the political reform movement that emerged in the 1960s. When Congress passed a series of new regulations starting in the mid-1960s, corporations barely fought back. Had corporations then built up the lobbying presence they have now established, it seems almost inconceivable that much of the social regulation that passed during that period would have become law.

The second consequence was that most business leaders were left alone to nurture what David Vogel has called an "underlying suspicion and mistrust of government."[27] This anti-government philosophy had deep roots in American business. "What is so striking about American business ideology," wrote Vogel, "is the remarkable consistency of business attitudes toward government over the last one hundred and twenty-five years. A sense of suspicion towards the state has managed to survive the most impressive political triumphs."[28]

The anti-government sentiment ran quite deep in the business community. John Kenneth Galbraith, writing in 1958, observed that, "the widespread suspicion and even hostility of businessmen to government, even when, as in the case of the Eisenhower Administration, it was presumptively sympathetic to business, is one of the greatest constants in our political life."[29] A 1953 study of the political opinions expressed in major business journal found four extreme anti-government, pro-market propositions occurring over and over again: (1) "The state is intrinsically evil"; (2) "Freedom is defined as freedom *from* governmental intervention in economic affairs"; (3) "There is an exclusive identification of *free enterprise* . . . with freedom, morality, and economic opportunity"; and (4) "All good things flow from free, unfettered operations of the free enterprise society."[30] Similarly, *The American Business Creed*,[31] a survey of business materials from 1948 and 1949, concluded that, "Business comments on government are rarely complimentary; that the government should have only limited powers and be restrained in their use is a fundamental and ever-recurring proposition in the business creed."[32] E. E. Schattschneider, writing in 1960, claimed that big business had two political priorities: (1) "to be left alone" and (2) "to preserve the solidarity of the business community."[33]

Of course, it should be noted that some business leaders during this period did take on the mantle of "corporate statesmanship," and those who did so tended to accept government intervention in the economy. For example, IBM CEO Thomas J. Watson, writing in 1963, argued that, "much as we may dislike it, I think we've got to realize that in our kind of society there are times when government has to step in and help people with some of their more difficult problems ... Programs which assist Americans by reducing the hazards of a free market system without damaging the system itself are necessary, I believe to its survival."[34] Mark Mizruchi documented a similar progressive corporate statesmanship during this period, largely organized through the Committee for Economic Development and the Council on Foreign Relations—organizations that were devoted to a public-spirited, research-based problem solving that included a prominent role for government.[35] Meanwhile, business organizations that nurtured free market fundamentalism, like the U.S. Chamber of Commerce, were largely marginalized in Washington.[36] Some of this relatively progressive corporate statesmanship was no doubt a luxury of the times. Business was profitable, and looked to be so for the foreseeable future.

The 1970s: The Political Awakening of Corporate Lobbying

Circumstances began to change in the mid-1960s. Most broadly, the 1960s happened, and brought with it a cultural shift that challenged the authority of the staid corporate culture of the previous era. More specifically, a new consumer movement, led by Ralph Nader, began calling attention to unsafe products, environmental pollution, and other alleged excesses of corporate America, and began demanding political solutions in the form of new laws and regulatory agencies. A number of entrepreneurial senators took up the crusade, often working closely with Nader.[37] Between 1965 and 1977, the president signed 44 major regulatory laws dealing with all manner of health, safety, and environmental issues, heaping billions upon billions of dollars in compliance costs on businesses, whose managers had grown accustomed to a high level of autonomy and deference. Between 1970 and 1975, the annual number of pages in the *Federal Register* tripled from 20,000 to 60,000, as did the budget for federal regulatory agencies, going from $1.5 to $4.3 billion.[38]

To a modern observer, perhaps the most surprising part of the story is that corporations did little to nothing to stop it all from happening. David Vogel notes that, "business didn't even want to try to fight against something with a consumer handle on it."[39] When Ralph Nader began his crusade against the automobile industry that ultimately resulted in the creation of the National Highway Traffic Safety Administration, General Motors did not have a single lobbyist in Washington. Rather than make a public argument against regulation, or hire a bunch of lobbyists to make their case in Washington, the company tried to discredit Nader personally. It sent private detectives to spy on him, made threatening phone calls, and sent young women (probably prostitutes) to entrap him while he shopped for groceries at the Safeway supermarket. The publicity surrounding the case only served to further raise Nader's political stock and may have even helped to speed the passage of the legislation that created the National Highway Traffic Safety Administration. Ultimately, GM wound up paying $425,000 to settle a harassment lawsuit, money that Nader used to fund more watchdog organizations.[40]

Even as late as 1970, one congressional representative described General Motors' political operations as entirely inept: "It's just that management has this disdain for relations in Washington."[41] In my interviews, one veteran lobbyist recalled that in the early 1970s, companies "had a simple understanding of a few big issues. They were marginally involved and had a low level of sophistication." For years, corporate leaders had either maintained productive personal working relationships with government or they had ignored politics entirely. But the idea of investing significant resources into a Washington lobbying office was not something many businesses had contemplated at the time.

In addition to the new regulation, corporate leaders also faced sluggish economic conditions in the 1970s. In the golden era following World War II, few U.S. companies faced any serious competition from abroad. After all, most of its economic rivals had been decimated by World War II, and it would take decades for them to return to their pre-war capacity. By the late 1960s, European and Asian companies were once again competitive. At home, rising labor costs and high inflation further cut into corporate profits.

Then, at a time when businesses felt least able to absorb it, a new army of federal bureaucrats began telling corporate managers what they could and couldn't do. Public opinion that had largely been pro-business turned anti-business. Young people no longer trusted capitalism, or even the profit motive. They no longer saw corporations in a positive light. As David Yoffie has written, "Government became more of a threat to business . . . imposing greater constraints on private initiative. New regulations squeezed corporate profitability and sharply limited the autonomy of firms and their executives."[42] By the early 1970s, the business leaders were approaching a moment of panic: " "The issue is survival!" they cried. "Survival of capitalism, survival of free enterprise, survival of America."[43]

In 1971, future Supreme Court Justice Lewis F. Powell Jr. (then still an attorney in private practice) wrote a "Confidential Memorandum" entitled "Attack on American Enterprise System" for the Chamber of Commerce.[44] In it, Powell documented the political ineptitude of business, and called for a new approach.

> "As every business executive knows, few elements of American society today have as little influence in government as the American businessman, the corporation, or even the millions of corporate stockholders. If one doubts this, let him undertake the role of "lobbyist" for the business point of view before Congressional committees. The same situation obtains in the legislative halls of most states and major cities. One does not exaggerate to say that, in terms of political influence with respect to the course of legislation and government action, the American business executive is truly the 'forgotten man'."

The solution, Powell argued, was for business leaders to throw themselves into politics.

> "One should not postpone more direct political action, while awaiting the gradual change in public opinion to be effected through education and information. Business must learn the lesson, long ago learned by labor and other self-interest groups. This is the lesson that political power is necessary; that such power must be assiduously (*sic*) cultivated; and that when necessary, it must be used aggressively and with determination – without embarrassment and without the reluctance which has been so characteristic of American business."

The Chamber of Commerce had for years been a marginal player in Washington, focused primarily on anti-communism and free-market fundamentalism. Around this time, it became more mainstream and grew dramatically in size and scope. From 36,000 members in 1967, the Chamber's membership doubled to 80,000 members in 1974, and doubled again to 160,000 by 1980. It also tripled its budget between 1974 and 1980, growing to $55 million. Even more impressively, the National Federal of Independent Businesses grew from 300 companies in 1970 to 600,000 in 1979.[45]

In 1972, a community of leading CEOs formed the Business Roundtable, an organization devoted explicitly to lobbying. Alcoa CEO John Harper, one of the founders, said at the time, "I think we all recognize that the time has come when we must stop talking about it, and get busy and do something about it."[46] In December 1972, Burt F. Raynes, the National Association of

Manufacturers (NAM) chair, said: "We have been in New York since before the turn of the century, because we regarded this city as the center of business and industry. But the thing that affects business most today is government. The inter-relationship of business with business is no longer so important as the inter-relationship of business with government. In the last several years, that has become very apparent to us." In 1974, NAM completed its move to Washington.[47] David Vogel writes that, "By the end of the decade, 'Washington knowledge' had replaced industry familiarity as the most important qualification for trade-association directors."[48]

A large number of individual corporations, which had largely eschewed politics, set up Washington offices for the first time. Between 1971 and 1982, the number of firms with registered lobbyists in Washington grew from 175 to 2,445. Between 1976 and 1980, the number of corporations with political action committees more than quadrupled, from 294 to 1,204. In 1970, public affairs offices were a rarity in corporate America. By 1980, 80 percent of Fortune 500 companies had some kind of "external relations department." In 1978, Fortune 1000 CEOs reported devoting about 40 percent of their time to "public issues"—twice what they had reported only two years earlier.[49]

The 1970s were a contentious time. Business waged battles against price controls, the costs of existing regulations, and the threat of new regulations. Perhaps the most important battle was the several-year struggle over a proposed Consumer Protection Agency, which would have institutionalized government-funded consumer advocates as part of the regulatory process, with the power to compel companies to provide data. Throughout the 1970s, business lobbyists somehow managed to hold passage of the CPA at bay through a few well-chosen congressional allies and their clever procedural tactics, buying time to turn public opinion against it through aggressive grassroots activities and issue advertising warning of a new nanny state. Business argued that the agency would make goods cost more, and painted the consumer movement as a special interest. In the early 1970s, the legislation to create the agency seemed almost certain to become law, passing by wide margins in each chamber in separate Congresses, but for procedural reasons failing to pass both chambers in the same session. In 1978, the legislation suffered a final 227-to-189 defeat in the House. Public Citizen's then-director, Mark Green, complained that while legislators said they were with him on the merits, they feared being labeled by their constituents as supporters of big government. "The business mobilization against the CPA succeeded," Benjamin Waterhouse concluded, "because it mixed sophisticated lobbying tactics with the enthusiasm of vast networks of political and intellectual allies, both of which encouraged prominent business leaders to deploy their own resources and political capital."[50] Business also defeated the Humphrey-Hawkins

Full Employment Act, a Labor-pushed plan to mandate government intervention to promote full employment.

By the late 1970s, tides were clearly turning. In 1974, President Ford's Executive Order 11,821 had been the first to put in place a mandatory system of
cost-benefit analysis for new regulations. President Carter added to that with
Executive Order 12,044, directing all executive agencies to construct "simple
and clear" regulations that "did not impose unnecessary burdens on the economy, on individuals, on public or private organizations, or on State and local
governments."[51] Carter also passed the "Paperwork Reduction Act" in 1980,
which created the Office of Information and Regulatory Affairs, which would
serve as an executive office check on the potential costs of new regulations.

Surveying the landscape for the Business Roundtable in 1979, Phyllis Mc-
Grath reported that: "Now Washington offices are headed by lawyers, experienced public affairs people, and people with first-hand government experience.
And back at corporate headquarters, a full-blown government relations communication program is in effect – to develop awareness, to teach corporate
staff the intricacies of the government process, and bring all facets of management into the government relations effort. The chief executive officer, the government relations executive, the technical experts, staff officers, and even
plant managers, have all been drawn into the development of new
strategies."[52]

Ninety percent of executives polled in 1979 said that over the last three
years, their companies' "concern with and involvement in federal government
relations" had gone up, and for 61 percent, the increase had been "extremely
strong." Nine in ten also felt confident that the increase would continue over
the next three years.[53]

Moreover, companies were, for the first time, starting to understand how to
play the Washington game. They were identifying "allies of business among
the electorate – stockholders, the community, and so forth," reported Mc-
Grath. "Business is also placing a great deal of emphasis on the politicizing of
employees, particularly at the local operating level."[54] Companies were developing formal issues-identification programs and internal government relations newsletters. As McGrath concluded, "The government relations
department is now a more firmly established fact of life on more and more corporate organization charts."[55]

The 1980s: The Political Entrenchment of Corporate Lobbying

When Ronald Reagan was sworn in as the 40th President of the United States
in 1981, American business leaders had, for the first time in six decades, a

president who spoke their language of free enterprise and small government, and who owed his position, at least in part, to active campaigning by companies and trade associations. He placed a moratorium on all new regulations that had been written (but were yet to go into effect), required cost-benefit analysis for all rules over $100 million, dismantled the Council on Wage and Price Stability, created a new Presidential Task Force on Regulatory Relief, and appointed "department heads who shared his animus toward the regulatory project in general and thus achieved weaker enforcement, and lower compliance costs, by sheer dint of their inactivity."[56] For example, between 1981 and 1982, the EPA reduced its case referrals to the Justice Department by 84 percent.[57] There was also a marked shift in antitrust enforcement. New horizontal merger guidelines introduced in 1982 demanded a high threshold of proof that competition would actually be harmed (mere industry concentration was no longer enough). Merger challenges by the Justice Department and the Federal Trade Commission declined notably, and they have stayed low since.[58]

In 1981, The Economic Tax Recovery Act delivered $169 billion in business tax cuts. The supply-siders got their individual across-the-board tax cuts, and manufacturers got their accelerated and simplified depreciation schedule known as "10–5–3": depreciate buildings in 10 years, vehicles in 5 years, and equipment in 3 years. It also sent a signal that lobbying could be more than just about stopping things. Businesses played a key role in shepherding the legislation through Congress. As one contemporary book noted, "With the help of a massive lobbying effort by business, the administration was able to twist enough legislative arms to get the tax cuts through Congress. Corporate tax reduction had been a hot topic in the business community for years, and many of the provisions of the tax bill had originally been proposed in meetings of representatives of the major employer associations in Washington."[59]

In 1982, a Harris Poll of corporate leaders found 90 percent saying that they were better able to get their message out than five years ago, 75 percent saying that they felt business has more clout than it did in the recent past. "They are purring," wrote the Harris Poll. "Business is much more self-confident about its power than it was."[60] The existential threats that had propelled corporations into the political arena had largely subsided. As Mark Mizruchi notes, "By the early 1980s, government and labor were no longer capable of exercising their previous level of constraint on business. Business had won the war."[61]

By the early 1980s, neither big government nor big labor posed the same existential threat to business, and thus neither provided the same rationale for business unity.[62] Meanwhile, new debates over trade policy, hostile takeovers, the federal deficit, and tax policy created splits within the business community. While the 1981 tax bill made everybody in the business community happy, a year later, a sluggish economy plus rising debt made it clear that something had to give. And so "the long-simmering tensions between supply-side and capital accumulation oriented business leaders finally boiled over."[63] At the Chamber of Commerce, "divisions over tax policy nearly ripped the venerable organization apart."[64] While firms that invested heavily in buildings, vehicles, and equipment wanted to maintain the accelerated depreciation, other firms cared more about the high interest rates that debt would bring and the ways in which it would crowd out private borrowing and raise the trade deficit by raising the cost of the dollar. Unlike the previous round of tax legislation, the 1982 tax bill now picked winners and losers. By the time of the 1986 Tax Reform Act, the splits in the business community were more pronounced, and the idea of a unified business position seemed increasingly quaint.[65] As Waterhouse writes: "Although organized business associations saw their collective unity wane, corporate lobbying itself boomed. Indeed, the fracture of the once-unified community of business associations created new opportunities for firm- and industry-specific lobbyists to negotiate for special tax benefits and government appropriations for their clients."[66]

The economy also became more competitive. Some of the competition came from abroad, as European and Asian manufacturers began to out-compete U.S. goods for the first time in decades. As one measure of both the increasing competitiveness of the global economy and the increasing tendency of industry to look to the federal government for help, the number of industries seeking (and receiving) trade protection rose dramatically in the 1980s. Between 1980 and 1989, industries initiated 345 countervailing duty investigations and 438 antidumping investigations with the U.S. International Trade Commission. Relief was granted in slightly more than half of both types of investigations. By comparison, between 1934 and 1974, there had only been 200 countervailing duty investigations, with only 15 resulting in relief.[67]

Meanwhile, a new "shareholder primacy" movement took hold in the stock market, putting corporate managers under increased pressure to generate consistent and strong earnings. A disappointing quarter and a low stock price could leave a company vulnerable to a leveraged buyout.[68] Mizruchi also describes a cultural shift: "the new corporate leader who emerged in the 1980s was a brash, swashbuckling celebrity, far more colorful than his predecessors, yet often viewed as lacking responsibility to anyone but himself, and perhaps his shareholders."[69]

Some of the increasing competition also came as a result of government deregulation, which broke up anti-competitive regimes in transportation, energy, finance, and telecommunications (with the breakup of AT&T). Whereas once these industries had been regulated to maximize stability, critics both left and right argued that industry-specific regulation had led to captured regulators allowing incumbent market players to maintain unacceptably high prices and poor service. Economists and good government types agreed: introduce competition, and let the market itself discipline the excess.[70] While this put an end to the old iron triangles, it did not depoliticize the issues. Companies continued to lobby. But they now fought each other.

Robert Reich argues that the massive business investments in Washington since the 1980s can be seen as market competition by other means. In a highly competitive economy where corporate leaders face intense pressure to deliver profits, corporations have had little choice but to seek political advantages to help them, creating an escalating cycle of political investments.[71]

All of these larger political-economic changes have no doubt contributed to both the growth of business lobbying as well as its balkanization. But there is another important factor behind both this growth and balkanization of corporate lobbying: the lobbyists themselves. While the changing political economy certainly created the conditions for the expanding and fracturing of business lobbying, lobbyists also took advantage of these conditions, amplifying and deepening the competition and instability inherent in the political economic changes. As I will explore in much more detail in the chapters to come, lobbyists have powerful incentives to foster an increasingly narrow outlook by individual corporations, since this typically translates into a need for more lobbying.

While the 1970s provided a "critical juncture" for corporations to begin to attend to politics in a new, expanded way, it was not clear at the beginning of the 1980s that this political capacity would produce the kind of "lock-in" effects that it did (to borrow some terminology from the theory of path dependence).[72] Rather, it took affirmative actions by the lobbyists within the companies to solidify the corporate commitments to full-scale political engagement. After all, from the modern vantage point, lobbying in the 1980s was a relatively limited affair. Government affairs hadn't been well-integrated into corporate decision-making. Lobbying remained more reactive than proactive. Companies simply didn't have the same capacity and know-how that they do today. Here is what several lobbyists had to say looking back on the period:

- "In the 1980s, the Washington office was run by a glad-handing goodwill ambassador, as opposed to a real policy professional. The guy's slogan was: if you're working more than 30 hours a week, you're doing something wrong."
- "When I started (1983), people didn't really understand government affairs. They questioned why you would need a Washington office, what does a Washington office do? I think they saw it as a necessary evil. All of our competitors had Washington offices, so it was more, well we need to have a presence there and just something we had to do. . . . We had various projects

with people within the business of the corporate units, but it wasn't like an understanding that was corporate-wide."

- "Back in the early 1980s, lobbyists didn't always know the process as well."
- "The DC office slogan used to 'be hire one person, and leave 'em there.' It was difficult to show a bottom-line value."
- "The person in Washington was there to put out problems. There was a real lack of communication. They didn't do a good job letting the executives know what the value was, what the accomplishments were. The company was not bringing that person in on bigger picture issues."

A 1995 book entitled *The New Corporate Activism* describes the old corporate attitude towards Washington (which persisted into the early 1980s) as a "Fix-it" mentality: "They had a problem. They hired a lobbyist . . . to bury the problem. It was an approach to influencing government that remained dominant until about a decade ago."[73] Still, by 1984, some observers could claim that, "Business lobbies are learning to attractively package proposals that serve their self-interest and to market their agendas more successfully to the public. It is not sufficient to cry 'Cost!' or to raise the specter of socialism."[74]

Over time, government affairs departments helped to socialize political activity into the culture of large corporations, allowing managers to learn to see politics differently than they had before (which was usually not at all). As one lobbyist I interviewed explained it, "Government relations plans and goals got built into and integrated into the general business of organizations. A lot of companies became more sophisticated about how they viewed government relations. And what happened was that companies had a lot of things they wanted government relations departments to do."

The 1990s (and Beyond): The Political Expansion of Corporate America

By 1993, when the debate over healthcare reform enveloped Washington, corporate lobbying had reached a new level of pervasiveness. As one lobbyist noted, there was something new about the scope and all-encompassing nature of the battle over healthcare: "The healthcare fight was the first time that huge coalitions were formed. Grassroots, grasstops, academics. Things happening on lots of levels. There were broad-based coalitions, with elite constituents." Several pharmaceutical lobbyists described the 1993–1994 healthcare debate as a wake-up political moment for industry, an observation that fits with empirical evidence showing that the number of healthcare companies with a Washington lobbying presence almost doubled between 1992 and 1994.[75]

The Republican takeover of Congress in 1995 also provided a new opportunity for lobbying to expand. Republican leaders, after all, were not shy about wanting to build a lasting alliance with business lobbyists on K Street.[76] "We say to the lobbyists, 'help us,'" then-House Majority Whip Tom DeLay said. "We know what we want to do and we find the people to help us do that. We go to the lobbyists and say, 'Help us get this in the appropriations bill.'"[77] Consider the initial meeting of Tom DeLay's pro-business "Project Relief" in 1995, as described by two *Washington Post* reporters:

> "He now stood before him with a lineup of pals who had eased his rise to the top. They were lobbyists representing some of the most powerful companies in America, assembled in his office on mismatched chairs amid packing boxes, an unplugged copying machine, and constantly ringing telephones. DeLay was delighted to see them. He could not wait to get started on what he considered the driving mission of his political career: the demise of the modern era of government regulation."[78]

DeLay helped to set up the well-known "K Street project," which worked with lobbying shops to ensure that congressional Republican staffers would have jobs waiting for them on K Street when they left Capitol Hill, a well-oiled machine that worked to create a symbiotic power relationship between corporate America and the Republican Party.[79]

Notably, it is after 1995 that we start to see examples of major legislative victories across several industries. The Telecommunications Act of 1996, the Gramm-Leach-Bliley Act of 1999, and the Medicare Modernization Act of 2003 are all examples of companies taking a proactive approach to public policy, actively pushing for advantageous policy changes.

The Medicare Modernization Act offers a particularly telling example of the changing relationship between increased political capacity and public policy. For a long time, pharmaceutical lobbyists told me, the drug industry opposed a Medicare prescription drug benefit, because the industry was convinced that it would mean bulk government purchasing, which would undoubtedly cut into industry profits. Such was the traditional way in which businesses thought about public policy: the less government involvement, the better. But sometime around 2000, industry lobbyists began to hatch an idea: what if you had a Medicare prescription drug benefit, but without bulk government purchasing? That idea became the 2003 Medicare Modernization Act, a boon to the industry that one study estimated at $242 billion over 10 years[80]—almost 2,000 times the $130 million the industry spent lobbying in 2003.

The Medicare Modernization Act also gave pharmaceutical companies continued reasons to lobby the government. Now that Medicare covered prescription drugs, companies had a strong financial interest in making sure the drugs that they produced were reimbursed by Medicare at the highest possible rate. Several pharmaceutical lobbyists I interviewed talked about reimbursement rates as an important issue, and noted that they had increased their Washington presence to lobby the Centers for Medicare & Medicaid Services (CMS) on reimbursement issues.

- "I really have to say, the Medicare drug benefit in 2003 really opened our company's eyes to how much the government can control and be involved in our business, and since that time our staff has grown from 5 to 25."
- "For our industry, it really picked up with the Medicare drug benefit. . . There are now a lot of private insurance companies that follow and have followed what Medicare and Medicaid recommend in terms of that, so knowing that it's also the precedent that it sets for private sectors too, that was when you really saw growth, even for companies that had just this one product."
- "The Medicare drug benefit really increased things. That's when PhRMA [the industry trade group] increased staff, and a lot of companies took on more lobbyists, and that really got everyone's attention. So I think that was the biggest factor."

The Growth of Corporate Lobbying, by the Numbers

Now let us turn to the data in an attempt to quantify the story I've told above. In Chapter 1, I plotted the bird's-eye view of growth between 1981 and 2004 (Figure 1.2). To refresh the basic finding: in 1981, the average company had a lobbying presence of 1.9. By 2004, the average company had a lobbying presence of 4.1—more than double. That number has been steadily increasing throughout the entire period.

But now we can go a little deeper and break down the growth into two separate trends: more companies are lobbying, and the companies that lobby are hiring more lobbyists. The first trend is visualized in Figure 3.1. For most of the 1980s and into the early 1990s, the share of companies in my sample with Washington lobbyists remained roughly the same—hovering in the 52 to 54 percent range. Then, starting in 1996, the share of companies with Washington lobbying started to increase, going from 59 percent in 1996 to 69 percent in 2004. Some of the gap between 1995 and 1996 may be due to the enactment of the 1995 Lobbying Disclosure Act, which, as I've noted, almost certainly

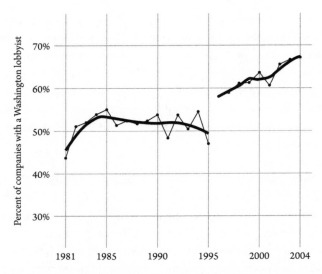

Figure 3.1 The growing percentage of companies with a Washington presence. Source: Author's calculations based on lobbyists listed in the *Washington Representatives* directory for companies in the S&P 500 sample. Annual percentages are calculated among companies that were in business that year.

allowed the editors of the *Washington Representatives* directory to unearth more lobbyists. However, 55 percent of active companies had lobbyists in 1994, so the discontinuity should not be overly troubling. The basic takeaway from Figure 3.1 is that population of companies in Washington remained pretty stable throughout the 1980s and into the early 1990s. But sometime in the mid-1990s, more and more companies started directing their attention to Washington. This change corresponds to the anecdotal evidence from interviews suggesting that the mid-to-late 1990s were a second political awakening for corporate America. The Clinton healthcare plan, followed by the Republican takeover of Congress, followed by the Microsoft antitrust suit—all sent the message to companies that politics matters.

The second trend is that the companies that are active have been steadily increasing their presence (see Figure 3.2). Politically active companies (that is, those with Washington lobbyists) have increased their average presence from 4.3 in 1981 to 6.1 in 2004. (Again, presence is a measure of the number of in-house lobbyists plus outside lobbying firms retained.) The average growth does slow down after 1996, but this is to be expected, since there are more new entrants into the ranks of lobbying. New entrants tend to lobby less. This pulls down the overall average.

Digging deeper into the numbers, we can observe that lobbying growth has been far from uniform throughout the economy. Certain sectors have grown

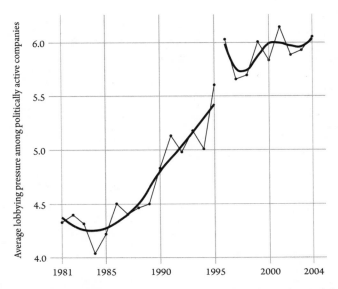

Figure 3.2 The growing lobbying presence of companies with Washington lobbyists.
Source: Author's calculations based on lobbyists listed in the *Washington Representatives* directory for companies in the S&P 500 sample. Annual averages are calculated among companies that were in business that year. "Lobbying presence" measures in-house lobbyists plus outside firms.

much faster than other sectors. A few sectors have grown hardly at all, and a few have even declined. Figure 3.3 visualizes the changes by sector. The sectors are ordered from fastest-growing to slowest-growing to declining. The changes are mapped by the distance between the two dots. The first dot marks the average lobbying presence among active companies in the industry in 1981. The second dot marks the average lobbying presence in 2004. The size of the dots represents the number of companies in my sample that were active that year. For example, there are only two tobacco companies in my sample, but there were 61 financial services companies in 1981 and 77 in 2004, and 32 pharmaceutical companies in 1981 and 31 in 2004. The number of defense aerospace/electronic companies (another prominent industry) declined from 25 to 15.

Within my sample, tobacco was the industry with the sharpest increase in presence. This makes sense, given the way in which government regulation and litigation fundamentally changed the tobacco industry (there were also only two tobacco companies in my sample). Defense contractors and telecom companies also had a very sharp increase, which also makes sense, given the importance of the federal government to these industries. Interestingly, of the 10 industries with the biggest increases, four (telecom, trucking, air transport, and railroads) experienced pro-competitive de-regulation around the start of this time series.

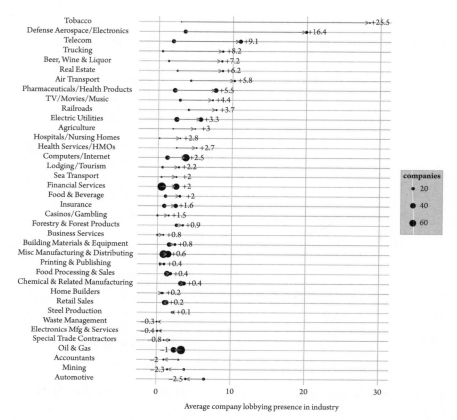

Figure 3.3 Changes in industry lobbying presence, 1981–2004. Source: Author's calculations based on lobbyists listed in the *Washington Representatives* directory for companies in the S&P 500 sample. Annual averages are calculated among companies that were in business that year. "Lobbying presence" measures in-house lobbyists plus outside firms.

While there are plenty of plausible stories to explain why certain industries grew faster than others, it is important to note that the growth trends across the fastest-growing industries all look somewhat similar. Figure 3.4 describes the growth of average company lobbying presence within the top nine industries (nine makes an easy 3 × 3 matrix). Again, the size of the dots reflects the number of companies. Generally, the trends are remarkably consistent across industries: a steadiness through the 1980s, with a pick up of growth in the 1990s. In some cases, the growth continues into the 2000s. In others it stabilizes. Only two industries—real estate, and television/movies/music (entertainment)—exhibit any notable jerkiness in the time trends (real estate's early 1990s peak is almost certainly a response to the savings and loan crisis; the entertainment industry's mid-1990s peak is almost certainly due to debates over digital copyright policy). Otherwise, there is a general consistency in the

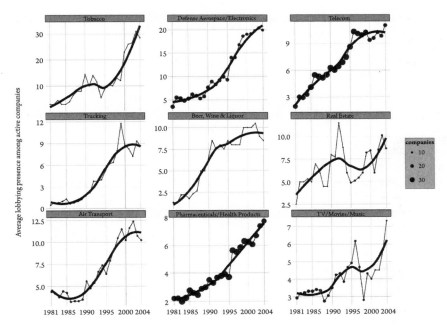

Figure 3.4 Growth patterns for the nine industries that increased their average lobbying presence the most, 1981–2004. Source: Author's calculations based on lobbyists listed in the *Washington Representatives* directory for companies in the S&P 500 sample. Annual averages are calculated among companies that were in business that year. "Lobbying presence" measures in-house lobbyists plus outside firms.

growth trends. Though the nine industries all have different political concerns, they have all grown in roughly the same manner.

We can also learn something about the growth of corporate lobbying by looking more closely at the nine companies in my sample that lobbied the most during the 24-year period this data covers. The companies are arranged in Figure 3.5 in decreasing order of average annual lobbying presence over period.

Two types of trajectories emerge. The first, and most common, is the trajectory of growth. This is the most common pattern, exemplified by five of the nine companies: AT&T, Boeing, Lockheed Martin, Fannie Mae, and Altria. All companies increased their lobbying presence substantially. Given the importance of government to all of these companies, it is not hard to explain why they all would have grown their lobbying during this period. Boeing and Lockheed Martin also both grew through a series of major mergers, which almost certainly boosted their lobbying presence. But what is also notable about these companies is that, at a certain size, the growth does seem to level out. It suggests companies may reach a point of diminishing returns at a certain lobbying presence.

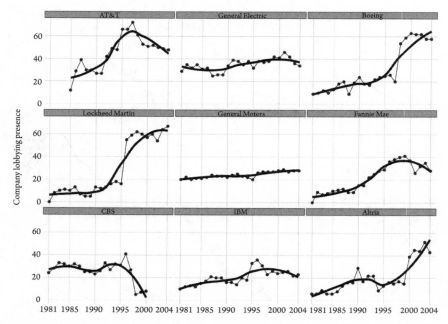

Figure 3.5 Growth patterns for the nine companies with the highest overall lobbying presence, 1981–2004. Source: Author's calculations based on lobbyists listed in the *Washington Representatives* directory for companies in the S&P 500 sample. "Lobbying presence" measures in-house lobbyists plus outside firms.

The second pattern is general stability, as exemplified by the three manufacturing giants in the middle column: General Electric, General Motors, and IBM. All have roughly maintained the same presence that they had in 1981, with a slight increase. Given the ups and downs of policy during this period, the stability is impressive. But then again, these are stalwarts of the economy. At any given moment, there are undoubtedly many policies under consideration that are relevant to them, and many more policies they would like to see under consideration. The Columbia Broadcasting System (CBS) also follows this pattern, at least until it becomes part of the Westinghouse Electric Company, in 1995. Soon after the number of CBS lobbyists declines to zero.

Collectively, these lobbying time trends of the nine most-committed lobbying companies express patterns that combine some steady increases, and some plateaus, and only a few very minor jumps. We will return to these data in more detail in Chapter 9, when I will provide more detailed empirical analysis to support the claim that lobbying is very sticky. But for now, as we move forward, it is helpful to have a few industry-level and company-level examples of what growth looks like.

Conclusion

Prior to the 1970s, very few corporations had Washington offices. To the extent that corporations lobbied, they did so through trade associations. Studies from the 1950s and 1960s describe corporate lobbying as largely threadbare, reactive, and not particularly influential. Then again, public policy was largely pro-industry at the time. There was less need to lobby. In the mid-to-late 1960s, public opinion and public policy turned against industry, and a new regulatory climate imposed new costs on business. Feeling threatened, business leaders turned to politics and individual corporations devoted substantial attention to politics for the first time, a kind of political awakening. Old associations, like the Chamber of Commerce, were revitalized. New associations, like the Business Roundtable, formed. Individual corporations began hiring lobbyists and setting up political action committees, and successfully defeated major legislation that would have created a new consumer protection agency and major labor law reform.

By 1981, businesses had beaten back the existential threats that had mobilized them. But they didn't retreat from politics. They now had government affairs divisions, and that meant lobbyists to help corporate leaders understand the importance of political engagement. The big business vs. government battles of the 1970s over regulation gave way to business vs. business battles in the 1980s, most notably over tax policy. Whereas business had once lobbied as a class, companies and industries began to lobby more for their own narrow interests. Throughout the 1980s, corporations improved their political savvy, as managers slowly but surely became more and more comfortable with the idea of active political engagement. Corporations became entrenched in Washington.

By the 1990s, corporations began to expand their political presence. Whereas they had once seen government as something to be avoided, corporate leaders increasingly came to see public policy as a way to improve their profits. Rather than merely trying to defend the status quo, lobbyists helped corporations to find more particularistic means of gaining advantages over their competitors, and to think of more aggressive ways to proactively enact new policies while solidifying previous gains. As lobbying became more competitive and more crowded, companies become more comprehensive and innovative in their lobbying strategies, increasingly approaching the pervasive position that they now inhabit.

How and Why Corporations Lobby

"As opposed to a simple or a linear model of influence, the lobby-ing profession is in fact a multi-faceted and competitive enterprise, on large issues almost always requiring Rubik's Cube-like, multi-dimensional, and multi-phase advocacy strategies." – *Nick Allard, Patton Boggs*[1]

What does it mean to lobby? When companies lobby, what are they lobbying for? How much do different companies lobby, and how do some companies manage to spend upwards of $10 million a year on lobbying? In this chapter, we will see that there are many reasons why companies lobby. This matters be-cause the more potential reasons there are to lobby, the more reasons there are for corporations to expand their lobbying activity. Lobbying is tactically di-verse, and understanding this diversity helps us to see how lobbying expands, and what lobbying looks like in its most pervasive expression. It also clarifies that lobbying is far more of an art than a science. In this chapter, we will look at what companies lobby for, how lobbying strategies vary across companies, and what it means for companies to be *fully* engaged in lobbying.

Why Do Companies Lobby?

To understand why corporations lobby, I began by asking their lobbyists. In interviews, I asked in-house corporate lobbyists to rate the relevance of seven potential reasons why companies might be politically active. Each reason was rated on a scale of 1 to 7, with seven being the highest. Table 4.1 reports the results.

The most highly rated reason was that companies need to be in Washington "to protect the company against changes in government policy (or other gov-ernment actions) that could be harmful." On average, lobbyists rated this a 6.2 out of 7. Notably, not a single lobbyist I asked rated it below a 4 on a 7-point

Table 4.1 **Company reasons for a Washington office**

Reason	Mean
Need to protect against changes in government policy (or other government actions) that could be harmful.	6.2
Need to improve ability to compete by seeking favorable changes in government policy.	5.7
Need to maintain ongoing relationships with policymakers.	5.7
Need to navigate compliance, licensing, and other regulatory interactions with the federal government on a regular basis.	4.4
Need to respond to critics and counter negative publicity.	4.3
Because other companies in the industry are politically active.	4.2
Government is a direct purchaser of company's products or services.	3.6

Source: Author interviews with in-house company lobbyists. Ratings are on a scale of 1 (lowest) to 7 (highest).

scale, and 27 of the 31 company lobbyists rated it at least a 5. In other words, the most important reason for lobbying is preserving the status quo.

But right behind defense was offense. In my survey, "Need to improve ability to compete by seeking favorable changes in government" averaged 5.7 out of 7. Almost 90 percent of the company lobbyists—27 of 31—rated it at least a 5, and only a single lobbyist ranked it at 1 (the lowest ranking on the scale). "Need to maintain ongoing relationships" also averaged a 5.7 rating in my survey. This indicates that companies have come to see lobbying as a long-term value proposition.

Reasons relating to lobbying competition got more mixed reviews. The "need to respond to critics and counter negative publicity" averaged a rating of 4.3, and "because other companies in the industry are politically active" rated on average 4.2. The reason with the lowest average rating (3.6) is that the "government is a direct purchaser of a company's products or services." However, this reason had a very bimodal distribution—for roughly half the companies it was very important; for the other half it was largely irrelevant.

Figure 4.1 shows the relationship between each company's 2007 lobbying expenditures and the value that company's lobbyist placed on different reasons for being active. The seven reasons are arranged by the correlation between the two variables, from least correlated to most correlated. The flatter the slope, the lower the correlation.

Going from least correlated to most correlated is a way of measuring the universality of the different reasons for being active. Interestingly, there is no

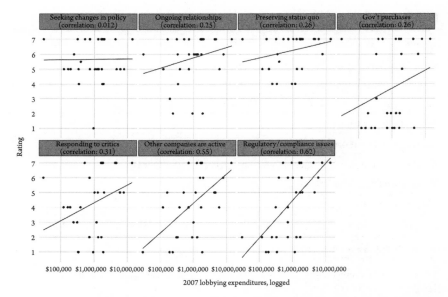

Figure 4.1 The relationship between reasons for lobbying and lobbying expenditures. Source: Author calculations from LDA reports and author interviews with in-house company lobbyists. Interviews covered 53 issues across 31 companies. Reasons are ordered by correlation, from low to high.

statistical relationship between how highly a company's lobbyists value "seeking favorable changes in government policy" and how much the company spends on lobbying. By contrast, both regulatory/compliance issues and the political activity of other companies are highly correlated with the amount that a company spends on lobbying. The companies that spend the most on lobbying tend to be most concerned about regulatory issues, and most motivated by the competiveness of lobbying in their industry. However, from correlations alone it is unclear whether these reasons are causes of or consequences of increased spending. We will return to these questions later in the book.

What do Companies Lobby for?

With these reasons in mind, we can now dig a little deeper and ask more specifically: What are companies lobbying for? What outcomes are they actually trying to achieve? How much attention do they devote to preserving the status quo and how much do they devote changing it? How much time do they spend lobbying for narrow benefits as opposed to industry benefits? How much do they compete with as opposed to cooperate with other companies in the same industry?

Table 4.2 **The four types of issues/examples**

	Collective (Industry)	*Selective (Company)*
Proactive	Medicare Modernization Act of 2003; new industry tax break	Medicare coverage for specific company drug; specific company tax break; new government contract
Reactive	preserving existing industry tax break (under threat); stopping proposed regulation that industry opposes	preserving existing company government contract (under threat)

We can begin by organizing issues into two-by-two matrix: selective vs. collective benefits, and proactive vs. reactive lobbying. Table 4.2 provides a simple overview.

The collective/selective dimension has long been the central dimension in the study of interest groups. The proactive/reactive dimension has enjoyed much less prominence. Both are important. I will discuss them in some detail to show why we care how lobbying breaks down across these various dimensions. Then I will move on to assessing their relative balance.

Collective vs. selective benefits

Ever since Mancur Olson argued that individual actors' rational self-interest undermines their ability to come together for collective political action, interest group scholars have devoted nearly endless energy to demonstrating the ways in which he was wrong or right.[2] Olson's logic was, at heart, pretty straightforward: since everybody wants to free-ride on somebody else's hard work to advocate for collective political benefits, nobody winds up advocating for collective political benefits. For example, many people in a city might want more public parks, but each individual person is busy. They don't want to spend their time attending city council meetings, or even contributing to a group that will do so on their behalf. On the other hand, the single developer, who stands to benefit greatly if he can turn that land into condos, has so much at stake personally that he will attend every city council meeting and lobby the mayor any way he can. For the developer, turning city land into condos is a selective benefit. For the community of park enthusiasts, turning city land into a public park is a collective benefit and a public good. Olson's contribution was an elegant description of why the diffuse park enthusiasts would almost always have a hard time going up against the single developer—or even a small group of developers, whose close personal relationships and high stakes in the outcome would make it easier for them to work together. The basic logic still goes a long way towards explaining why diffuse interest groups have a hard time organizing and maintaining themselves politically, and why corporations lobbying for narrow benefits have a structural advantage that goes beyond even the monetary resources they are able to draw on.

In response to Olson's logic, scholars of corporate political activity have diligently included industry concentration measures (typically the Herfindahl index, which measures how much of economic activity of an industry is concentrated in the top 50 firms, or a variation on this index) as independent variables in regression models explaining corporate political activity. These variables are intended to measure the difficulty companies in an industry might have in overcoming the collective action problem.

Yet in the more than two dozen studies that try to explain the variation in corporate political activity, industry concentration is almost never a statistically significant predictor of corporate political activity, no matter how it is measured.[3] Despite what Olson predicted, industries that are more concentrated do not engage in political activity more than industries that are less concentrated, all else equal. Ken Godwin and colleagues, drawing on interviews, argue that the majority of corporate lobbying is oriented around targeted, distributive benefits where collective action concerns are unlikely to arise.[4] After an exhaustive battery of statistical tests failing to find any consistent relationship between industry concentration and political activity, Wendy Hansen and colleagues reach similar conclusions about the importance of narrow, company-focused lobbying goals.[5]

The relative balance of collective and selective issues matters for two reasons. The first comes directly from Olson's logic. If businesses are lobbying for industry or even business-wide benefits, corporate lobbying runs the risk of being under-provisioned. Companies might not see a reason to have their own lobbyists, given that they have nothing differentially at stake. By contrast, if corporate lobbying is substantially oriented towards selective benefits, companies are more likely to see the direct benefits of their participation, and continue to lobby to gain these benefits. In other words, if corporate lobbying is mostly cooperative, we should expect less of it. If it is mostly competitive, we should expect more of it.

The second reason we should care about the balance of selective and collective benefits is that companies are more likely to get what they want when they lobby for selective benefits. The simple reason for this is that selective benefits tend to involve less public scrutiny because of their narrow and often technical nature. Usually, the public doesn't pay attention, and rarely do diffuse interest groups get involved. Hence, businesses face little opposition.[6]

Proactive vs. reactive lobbying

It is generally acknowledged that it is easier to play defense than offense in American politics. As I argued in Chapter 2, the increasingly competitive lobbying environment has made policy change even more difficult, particularly on major issues. But this hasn't stopped companies from trying to make changes, both big and small. It has just raised the cost.

The balance of proactive and reactive lobbying is important for two reasons. First, it is an indirect measure of power. Being on defense means something is under threat, and the best possible outcome is not losing the status quo. By contrast, being on offense means that maintaining the status quo is the worst outcome. In economic terms, the expected payoff to lobbying is far greater when a company plays offense. Thus, it is better to be actively trying to improve on the status quo. If a company is working to gain ground as opposed to defending ground, this implies a position of power.

Second, proactive lobbying is more likely to require more spending than reactive lobbying, because changing the status quo requires more work than preserving the status quo. Thus, a turn to more proactive lobbying is also a turn towards more aggressive, resource-intensive lobbying. Sometimes preserving the status quo can be as simple as monitoring developments, having as-needed conversations, and maintaining enough of a presence to execute a "peace through strength" strategy that scares off potential challengers. Changing the status quo requires significantly more work.

As I've suggested, increasing amounts of corporate lobbying activity are now devoted to changing the status quo than trying to protect it. However, it is important to note that lobbying activity is by nature limited to issues on which there is actual political activity. Companies may be keeping issues *off* the agenda by their mere presence, exercising what Peter Bachrach and Morton Baratz described as the "second face of power."[7] This is difficult to measure. However, since corporate lobbyists almost universally listed protecting against changes as their top reason for maintaining a Washington office, it seems that we can reasonably assume that they do feel at least somewhat threatened.

The Issues from my Interviews

In interviews, I asked lobbyists to describe the main issues they were currently working on. The company lobbyists I interviewed described a total of 53 issues. I then coded those issues as either industry-specific or company-specific, and either proactive or reactive. Table 4.3 shows the counts in each category.

Table 4.3 **The frequency of the four types of issues among surveyed in-house company lobbyists**

	Industry	*Company*	*Total*
Proactive	19 (36%)	18 (34%)	37 (70%)
Reactive	13 (25%)	3 (6%)	16 (30%)
Total	32 (60%)	21 (40%)	

Source: Author interviews with in-house company lobbyists. Interviews covered 53 issues across 31 companies.

The clearest conclusion is that corporate lobbying activity is largely proactive. More than two thirds of the issues were attempts to change the status quo. These were split roughly equally between industry issues and company issues. Additionally, 40 percent of lobbying issues were on company-level benefits. Both balances were similar across different sizes of companies. There are no noticeable differences in the relationship of company lobbying expenditures and the balance of issues devoted to selective/collective benefits or proactive/reactive lobbying.

There are obvious limits to this sample, since it is based on the issues that company lobbyists volunteered to discuss. It is also based on issues that were actually on the political agenda, and it is unclear how much behind-the-scenes work goes into keeping certain issues off the agenda.

I also asked companies to identify their primary opponent on the issues on which they lobbied. Table 4.4 presents the frequency of different types of opponents. The question was open-ended, and I applied the categories after. A striking observation is that across all 53 issues, not a single diffuse interest

Table 4.4 **Who corporate lobbyists list as their opponents on specific issues**

Primary Opponent	*Pct of Issues*
Member(s) of Congress	26%
Getting Visibility	26%
Other Industry	21%
Government Bureaucrats	13%
No Opponent	11%
Other Business	2%
Diffuse Interest Group or Union	0%

Source: Author interviews with in-house company lobbyists. Interviews covered 53 issues across 31 companies.

group or union was named as the primary opponent.[8] Partially, this may be a reflection of the fact that companies don't like to consider themselves opposed to diffuse interest groups, which may explain why they did not volunteer any of them as opponents. It may also reflect the fact that individual companies and trade associations are not working on the types of highly salient issues where they might go up against public interest groups or unions, and instead leave those battles to business-wide associations like the Chamber of Commerce. But it is consistent with the observation from Chapter 1 that business interests now outspend diffuse interest groups and unions *combined* by a 34-to-1 margin. So perhaps it's no surprise to not see a single one of these groups identified as a primary opponent.

The most common opponent identified is a member of Congress (26%). And for 37% of issues, there is either no opponent (11%) or the main concern is just getting visibility (26%), which is consistent with the 40% of issues that are selective benefits. Industry vs. industry fights describe 20% of the issues, which suggests that a substantial amount of lobbying involves market conflicts spilling over into politics. Only one issue was an explicit company vs. company fight. While I will argue in the Chapter 5 that there is plenty of intra-industry jostling, there is a difference between jostling and outright opposition. It is the difference between a crowd of people shoving to be first on the train to get the best seats as opposed to two people fighting for the very last spot on the train. In the fighting-for-seats condition (i.e., intra-industry jostling), everybody has an interest in the train running (as opposed to being stalled). If the train doesn't move, nobody gets a seat.

Tactical Diversity

Companies have many things they would like to accomplish politically. And their lobbyists have a wide range of tactics and approaches for accomplishing those outcomes. This is not a new observation. As Anthony Nownes puts it, "Lobbying is a complex and heterogeneous phenomenon."[9] Frank Baumgartner and Beth Leech write that, "asking what lobbyists usually do is like asking Pete Sampras whether he usually hits backhands or forehands."[10] But it is an important truth, because two important implications follow. One, it helps us to see the ways in which lobbying can expand from very basic to pervasive. And two, it helps us to see how difficult lobbying can be to evaluate externally, given the wide variety of ways in influence might (or might not) happen.

We can begin with the summary results from my survey. I asked lobbyists to rate the relevance of 21 different tactics and approaches on specific issues on which they were working. Table 4.5 reports the results. Perhaps the most basic

Table 4.5 **Relevance of different tactics**

Tactic	Mean
Contacting congressional staffers directly to present your point of view	6.4
Monitoring developments closely	6.3
Identifying allies in Congress who might serve as "champions" for your cause	6.2
Contacting members of Congress directly to present your point of view	6.1
Consulting with members of Congress and/or their staff to plan legislative strategy	5.5
Entering into coalitions with other organizations	5.5
Consulting with other organizations to plan legislative strategy	5.3
Helping to draft legislation	5.3
Contacting members of the executive branch directly to present your point of view	5.1
Identifying allies in the executive branch who might serve as "champions" for your cause	5.1
Presenting research results or technical information	5.1
Contacting undecided members	5.0
Writing position papers	4.7
Mobilizing constituents to contact their representatives	4.4
Talking to members of the media	4.4
Contacting members who are opposed to your position	4.1
Testifying at hearings	4.1
Attending political fundraisers	4.1
Consulting with members of the executive branch to plan legislative strategy	3.9
Organizing political fundraisers	3.2
Using issue advertising	2.7

Source: Author interviews with in-house company lobbyists. Interviews covered 53 issues across 31 companies. Ratings are on a scale of 1 (lowest) to 7 (highest).

takeaway is resounding support for the tactical diversity of lobbying. Of the 21 issues, only three (planning legislative strategy with the executive branch, organizing political fundraisers, and using issue advertising) fell below the median on a seven-point scale.

This diversity is important because it helps us to understand why it is hard for corporate managers to monitor and evaluate lobbying (a topic to which we will devote more attention later). If lobbying were simple and involved just a few straightforward tactics, corporations could apply it cookbook-style: a cup of campaign contribution here, a tablespoon of grassroots mobilization, a *soupçon* of Hill meetings, and voila: favorable policy outcome! Things do not work this way. Every situation is different, and for each issue, the optimal mix of approaches is almost debatable, even after the issue is resolved.

To better understand the different approaches to lobbying, I conducted a k-means clustering analysis to identify four different clusters of lobbying strategy in the 53 issues. The clusters in effect measure the intensity of the lobbying efforts and help us more easily understand the ways in which lobbying can go from basic to comprehensive. In the parlance of modern marketing, we might think of these as four types of lobbying plans: bronze, silver, gold, and platinum.

Table 4.6 summarizes the clusters briefly. In the "bronze" cluster, the average tactic is rated 3.4 on a scale of 1 to 7. In the "platinum" cluster, the average tactic is rated at 5.8—significantly higher. The "silver" and "gold" clusters fall in between, with both demonstrating high regard for a range of tactics. Figure 4.2 allows us to better see how they differ. As we might expect, the companies engaging in "platinum" lobbying approaches report the highest median lobbying expenditures (see Figure 4.3), though interestingly, the lowest median spending is in one of the silver clusters.

A close look at Figure 4.2 helps us to see how lobbying approaches can vary. The "bronze" lobbying plan involves much of what we might traditionally think of as lobbying (and much of what would be covered under the Lobbying Disclosure Act): a heavy emphasis on contacting government officials, keeping a close eye on what is happening in Congress, thinking about who would be a good ally, and building coalitions and strategizing. Note also what is largely left out of this approach to lobbying: fundraising, trying to sway opponents and undecided members, mobilizing constituents, drafting legislation, and presenting research. These more aggressive tactics, by contrast, are

Table 4.6 **The four lobbying tactic clusters**

Cluster	Mean across all Tactics	Issues	Median Company Spending
Bronze	3.4	11	$940,000
Silver	4.6	12	$530,000
Gold	4.9	10	$1,020,000
Platinum	5.8	20	$1,700,000

Source: Author interviews with in-house company lobbyists. Interviews covered 53 issues across 31 companies; LDA data.

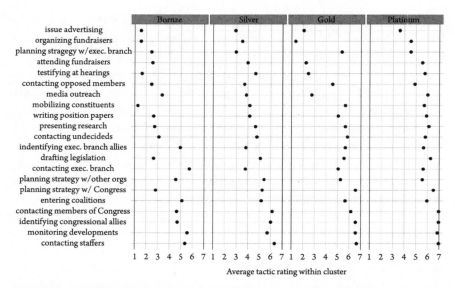

Figure 4.2 The four lobbying tactic clusters. Source: Author interviews with in-house company lobbyists. Interviews covered 53 issues across 31 companies. Ratings are on a scale of 1 (lowest) to 7 (highest). Clusters are determined using *k*-means clustering.

common among those employing the "platinum" strategy—a kind of everywhere, all-the-time, do-all-you-can approach to lobbying. Under this approach, every tactic is important. This is the maximalist, pervasive approach to lobbying. Notably, it is also the most common cluster: lobbying on 20 of the 53 issues fell into the "platinum" cluster.

Though the silver and gold plans' strategies share the most similarities, they differ in a few important ways. The silver plan generally places more emphasis on testifying, reaching out to the media, and being involved in fundraisers, while the gold plan generally places more emphasis on working with the executive branch and mobilizing constituents. Notably, the silver plan is associated with a lower median lobbying expenditure. This is consistent with the gold plan having broader involvement. But given the limited sample sizes, it is dangerous to infer too much. The more notable and significant differences are between the "bronze" and "platinum" approaches, and the differences are substantial.

Of course, it is worth noting that while these clusters place a certain degree of coherence on the results from my surveys, no two issues had the exact same valuation of tactics. Each issue is different, and requires a different strategy.

It is also worth highlighting that all approaches to lobbying have a strong monitoring component. In a separate study, Daniel J. Hopkins and I found that monitoring developments took up a substantial amount of time for Enron's political team.[11] Other surveys also find that a good deal of lobbying activity simply involves staying constantly informed—knowing where different offices stand on various issues and when different bills are likely to move.[12] Most of the time, very little is actually happening in Congress on a given issue, so there are limited opportunities for meaningful influence. Attention is sufficient. But when things do happen, they often happen very quickly, placing a premium on preexisting networks and information. "Windows of opportunity" are rare in politics, and they must be seized on when they do occur.[13] As we will see later, informing clients and bosses about developments in Washington is a key part of what lobbyists do. So it is not surprising that, no matter the strategic approach, collecting information is always a part of it.

The Many Sizes of Corporate Lobbying

From the small sample of companies I interviewed, we've started to appreciate the ways in which corporate political activity can range from minimal to maximal. Now we will turn to the larger population of corporations to see how many companies lobby at different intensities, breaking down companies by the amount they spend on lobbying. This will help to further understand the different range of approaches to lobbying, and help to further see what maximalist approaches to lobbying look like in contrast to minimalist approaches.

While several thousand companies will hire lobbyists in a given year, the vast majority of companies spend under $250,000 a year and engage in a targeted way. Only a few hundred companies each year are major political players (in that they spend substantial sums on lobbying). For analytical purposes, I break companies into four categories,[14] based on their annual lobbying expenditures, adjusted to constant 2012 dollars:

- **Small**: companies with lobbying expenditures of less than $50,000
- **Medium:** companies with lobbying expenditures of between $50,000 and $250,000
- **Large:** companies with lobbying expenditures of between $250,000 and $1,000,000
- **Major:** companies with lobbying expenditures of more than $1,000,000

Figure 4.3 captures the impressive growth in the number of small and medium-sized companies coming to Washington between 1998 and 2009, and then their equally precipitous retreat from 2010–2012. By contrast, the population of largest companies is more stable. Here's the brief rundown of what happened in these various size categories between 1998 and 2012.

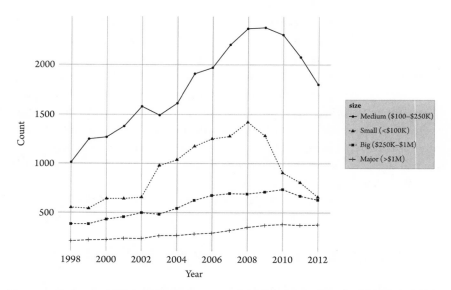

Figure 4.3 Counts of active companies by lobbying expenditure category, 1998–2012. Source: Author calculations from LDA reports.

- The number of "small" companies (those spending less than $50,000, in 2012 dollars) grew from 553 in 1998 to a high of 1,424 in 2008, falling right back down to 660 in 2012.
- "Medium" companies (between $50,000 and $250,000, in 2012 dollars) grew in number from 1,010 in 1998 to 2,375 in 2009, falling back down to 1,804 in 2012.
- "Large" companies (between $250,000 and $1 million) grew in number from 384 in 1998 to a high of 736 in 2010, before slipping back to 630 in 2012
- "Major" companies (those spending more than $1 million) grew in number from 216 in 1998 to 382 in 2010, falling only down to 379 in 2012.

Overall, the number of companies with registered lobbyists grew from 2,163 in 1998 to a high of 4,831 in 2008, but fell to 3,473 by 2012.

While the number of companies with lobbyists does decline starting in 2009, it is important to note that the companies bowing out of lobbying are the companies who did the least lobbying, and thus had the most tenuous connection to politics. They didn't institutionalize lobbying. So it makes sense that these small and medium-sized lobbying companies would drop out when the economy went downhill, Congress fell into gridlock, earmarks largely disappeared, and defense spending declined. But notice: the population of the "big" and "major" lobbying companies stays stable during this period. These are the companies that have committed most thoroughly to political engagement, and they are thus least likely to be deterred by the short-term changes. They are in politics for the long haul. The trends in Figure 4.3 are thus very consistent with my claim that serious investments in lobbying tend to be sticky.

Though small and medium-sized companies make up the majority of the companies with representation, the majority of the spending comes from the "major" companies (Figure 4.4). While 4,496 companies reported spending money on lobbying in 2007, only 297 (6.6 percent) reported spending at least $1 million. The distribution of company-level lobbying expenditures follows a basic power-law distribution. Most companies spend a little. A few companies spend very much. The 297 companies that spent more than $1 million in 2007 accounted for 62.6 percent of all lobbying expenditures made by individual corporations, and the 127 companies that spent more than $2.5 million accounted for almost half (45.7 percent) of all lobbying expenditures. It is these highly engaged companies that we ought to care about most, because they are deeply involved in the political process, whereas the smaller companies are only peripherally involved. They tend to be much more oriented towards small, targeted outcomes, most commonly appropriations and government contracts.

Table 4.7 provides an overview of the 20 companies that spent the most on lobbying in 2007. Not surprisingly, they are all big blue-chip companies, though they cover a range of sectors: Three defense companies, three pharmaceutical

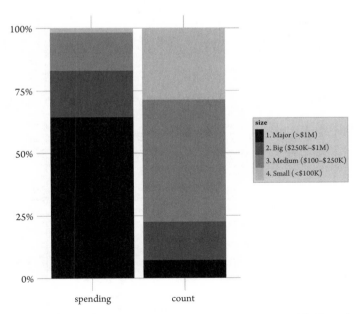

Figure 4.4 The balance of lobbying spending and population by lobbying expenditure category, 2007. Source: 2007 author calculations from LDA reports.

Table 4.7 **Top spending companies, 2007**

Company	Spending (MM)	Outside Lobbying Firms	In-house Lobbyists	Total Registered Lobbyists	Issue Areas Lobbied	Total Agencies Lobbied	Total Bills lobbied	Top issue	Top issue Share (of all lobbying)
General Electric	$20.3	37	32	123	26	28	148	Taxes	17%
Altria Group	$19.1	23	8	81	24	14	121	Tobacco	25%
AT&T Inc	$17.2	47	17	174	18	18	109	Telecommunications	51%
Exxon Mobil	$16.9	16	10	65	26	22	114	Energy & Nuclear Power	16%
Amgen Inc	$16.3	43	18	156	8	17	29	Medicare & Medicaid	36%
Southern Co	$14.7	18	11	67	13	18	31	Energy & Nuclear Power	31%
General Motors	$14.3	26	21	104	22	35	84	Energy & Nuclear Power	15%
Pfizer Inc	$13.8	24	13	108	18	16	63	Health Issues	26%
Verizon Communications	$12.7	58	21	206	22	30	64	Telecommunications	44%
American International Group	$11.4	13	10	52	12	11	26	Taxes	34%

Company								
Northrop Grumman	$11.0	24	10	67	12	20	28	Defense	60%
Boeing Co	$10.8	25	17	87	13	12	53	Defense	38%
Blue Cross/Blue Shield	$10.8	30	56	164	10	12	68	Health Issues	37%
Lockheed Martin	$10.7	53	31	179	19	27	57	Defense	33%
Union Pacific Corp	$9.7	8	5	33	9	7	33	Railroads	30%
IBM Corp	$9.1	7	24	44	21	41	60	Defense	15%
Roche Holdings	$9.0	39	9	184	14	22	49	Health Issues	28%
Chevron Corp	$9.0	10	14	43	16	21	59	Trade	20%
Microsoft Corp	$9.0	27	20	130	22	27	48	Immigration	19%
Comcast Corp	$8.9	25	12	94	10	11	22	Radio & TV Broadcasting	39%

Source: LDA reports.

companies, three energy companies, three telecom companies, plus two tech companies, one tobacco company, one insurance company, one railroad company, one HMO, and one conglomerate.

The reach of what these top 20 companies do is impressive. In addition to having, on average, 18 full-time lobbyists, the average company contracted with 28 different Washington lobbying firms. On average, they have weighed in on 17 different issue areas, before 20 agencies, and on 63 different pieces of legislation. These are major parts of the Washington, DC, community, and all excellent examples of the pervasive position of large corporations.

More on Size and Scope

As I've already argued, companies that spend more on lobbying have more reasons for lobbying and tend to engage in more lobbying tactics. Next, I examine the relationship between lobbying spending and four other measures of lobbying scope: issues, bills, targets, and lobbying presence (Figures 4.5 to

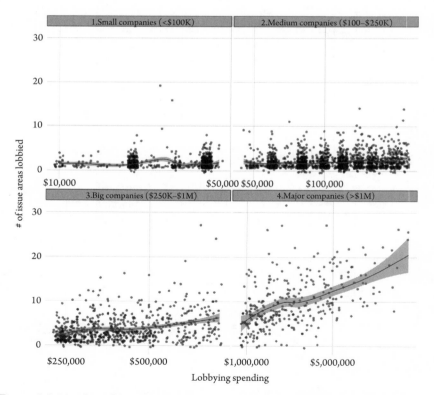

Figure 4.5 Number of issue areas lobbied on and company lobbying expenditures.
Source: 2007 author calculations from LDA reports.

4.9). I will use a series of faceted scatterplots, and continue to stick with 2007 data for consistency's sake. Each dot represents a company. The observations are jittered slightly to enable us to see more observations. The darkness of the dots is a measure of the number of observations at a particular set of coordinates—the darker the dots, the more observations. I also employ a simple Loess smoother to estimate the relationship between lobbying expenditures and the different measures of scope.

The main takeaway is consistent across the figures. As we move through the four types of companies, it's not until we get to the million-dollar companies that we start to see the truly pervasive lobbying efforts. The vast majority of individual companies are engaging in narrow, targeted ways. But as companies cross the million-dollar threshold, we start to see a consistent pattern between expenditures and the pervasiveness of lobbying. At the far end of the spectrum, we can observe an impressively wide scope: companies that really do appear to be everywhere, and involved in everything.

Issue diversity

Lobbying disclosure reports allow filers to identify 80 different issue areas. At the high end, 3M identified 32 different issue areas in its lobbying reports, followed by Hewlett Packard, Koch Industries, and Jacobs Engineering Group at 27, and General Electric and Exxon Mobil at 26. Among the smallest companies, the average number of issue areas is 1.5; among medium companies, 2.0; among large companies, 3.7, and among major companies, 9.7. The Pearson's correlation between total issues and lobbying expenditures is 0.63.

Bills and targets

The next two faceted scatterplots (Figures 4.6 and 4.7) represent total bill mentions and total government targets (each house of Congress and each executive agency counts as a target), two additional dimensions of lobbying scope. The same pattern follows as before, so there is no need for extensive elaboration. Small and medium-sized companies tend to be narrowly focused. As we get into the big and major companies, the scope expands into increasing comprehensiveness. This pattern seems especially pronounced when it comes to the number of bills. The Pearson's correlation between total bills lobbied and company lobbying expenditures is 0.67; the Pearson's correlation between total targets lobbied and company lobbying expenditures is 0.58.

The top five companies lobbying on the most different bills were Principal Financial Group (236), Deere & Co (168), Visa (155), Citigroup (153), and General Electric (136). A total of 11 companies listed at least 100 different

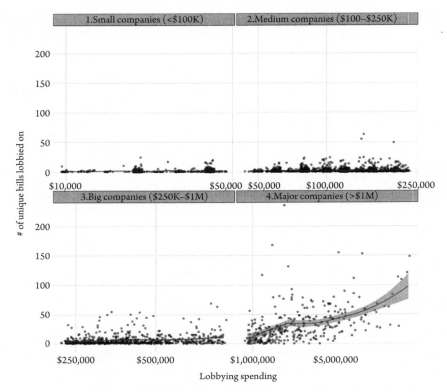

Figure 4.6 Number of unique bills lobbied on and company lobbying expenditures.
Source: 2007 author calculations from LDA reports.

bills, and 65 companies listed at least 50 different bills. On average, small companies lobbied on 1.6 bills, medium companies lobbied on 2.2 bills, big companies on 5.9 bills, and major companies on 31.2 bills.

The top five companies lobbying the most different government targets (each house of Congress and each executive agency counts as a target) were IBM (41), Hewlett-Packard (36), General Motors (35), Citigroup (32), and Reed Elsevier (31). On average, small companies lobbied 3.0 targets, medium companies lobbied 3.8 targets, big companies lobbied 5.7 different targets, and major companies lobbied 11.9 targets. A total of 50 different companies listed at least 20 government targets on their lobbying disclosure forms.

Lobbying presence

Finally, we can look at the "lobbying presence" of companies (Figure 4.8). I use "lobbying presence" throughout this book to mean the total number of in-house lobbyists a company has plus the number of different outside lobbying

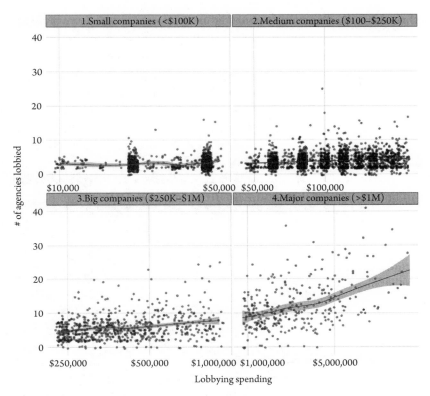

Figure 4.7 Number of government targets lobbied and company lobbying expenditures.
Source: 2007 author calculations from LDA reports.

firms it has retained. Lobbying expenditures and lobbying presence are closely correlated (0.85). Because of this correlation, I use these measures in a roughly interchangeable manner throughout this book.

Blue Cross/Blue Shield had the biggest lobbying presence in 2007, at 86. In addition to having 56 in-house lobbyists, it also retained the services of 30 different Washington lobbying firms. The second-largest lobbying presence was held by defense contractor Lockheed Martin (31 in-house lobbyists + 53 outside firms = 84), while Verizon was next (21 in-house lobbyists + 58 outside firms = 79). Put simply, the more bodies on the ground a company has, the more places it can be at once. In a town where relationships remain important, the ability to be at many tables and in many conversations is an important measure of influence. For small companies, the average lobbying presence is 1.16; for medium companies, it is not much more: 1.42. For big companies, the average is 3.41. But for the major companies, the average presence is 13.9. This is a qualitative difference as well as a quantitative one. Having such a presence allows a company to be in many places at the same time.

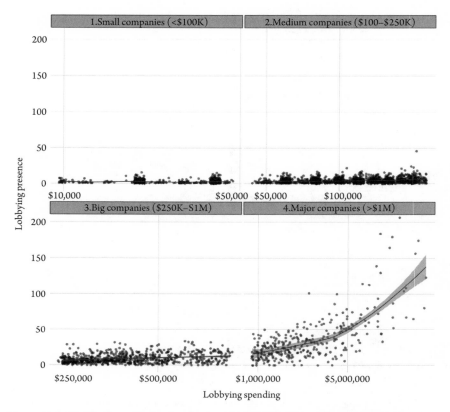

Figure 4.8 "Lobbying presence" and company lobbying expenditures. Source: 2007 author calculations from LDA reports.

What Companies Report Lobbying on

Another way to understand what companies are trying to achieve in Washington is to look at what they disclose lobbying on.[15] This will also allow us to see how companies vary in their priorities depending on how much they lobby. Figure 4.9 looks at the share of lobbying companies in the four size categories devote to the nine issue areas with the most overall lobbying. Again, we will continue to work with 2007 data.

Looking at Figure 4.9 in detail, we can see that companies that do more lobbying tend to devote more of their lobbying budget to taxes. Trade, telecommunications, and particularly, copyright issues are also of more interest to the companies that lobby more. By contrast, the smaller the company, the more of its lobbying budget gets devoted to appropriations and defense issues.

The takeaway here is that big and major companies are more likely to lobby on issues that affect their competitive market position, like taxes, trade, and

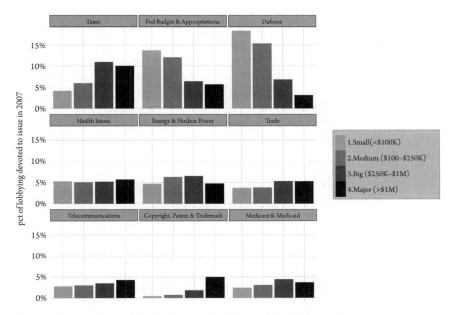

Figure 4.9 How companies' lobbying priorities vary by their lobbying intensity.
Source: Author calculations from LDA reports. Issues are arranged by total lobbying expenditures devoted to the issue.

copyright. Small companies are more likely to be in Washington only to seek very narrow benefits, like government contracts or earmarks. Of course, big and major companies also lobby on defense and appropriations issues. It's just that they have wider portfolios.

Campaign Finance

Finally, there is the issue of campaign finance. As I showed in Chapter 1, companies spend roughly 13 times more on lobbying than they do on their PACs. But campaign finance is an important tactic, and the lobbyists I interviewed shed some light on its uses.

First, some data, as presented in Table 4.8 (again, this is 2007 data).[16] Only 3 percent of the small (under $50,000 in lobbying spending) companies have a PAC, and even those who do have a tiny PAC: on average it is $22,124, and only contributes to 8.5 candidates. By contrast, the "major" companies, those spending over $1 million in lobbying, have large PACs, on average $354,391, contributing to 131.4 candidates—when they have PACs that make contributions. However, it is notable that even among the most active companies, more than one-third do not have a PAC. Among the smallest companies, the ratio of

Table 4.8 **Campaign finance activity of companies, 2007**

	Share Making PAC Contributions in 2007	Average PAC Size among Companies with a PAC	Average # of Candidates Receiving Money from PACs	Ratio of Lobbying Spending to PAC Spending
Small	3.4%	$22,124	8.5	40.9
Medium	8.2%	$37,530	15.0	35.5
Big	31.1%	$82,063	32.3	16.5
Major	63.9%	$354,391	131.4	14.1

Sources: FEC reports, author calculations from LDA reports.

lobbying spending to PAC spending is 40.9 to 1. Among medium companies it is 35.5 to 1. Among big companies it is 16.5 to 1. Even among the major companies (those spending over $1 million on lobbying, the companies that are most politically involved), the ratio of lobbying spending to PAC spending is 14.1. Of course, these numbers are for 2007, which is not an election year, and PAC contributions do tend to be slightly lower in election years. Still, these numbers reiterate a point that I made in Chapter 1. Companies simply devote much more of their resources to lobbying than they do to campaign finance.

None of this, however, is to suggest that campaign contributions are irrelevant. In general, lobbyists I interviewed found making campaign donations was a good way to build and maintain relationships.

- "It's all about having prior relationships, which is why fundraisers are important. It's a lot easier working on an agenda with someone you helped get into office than someone you opposed."
- "I think there's always a need to attend political events, to meet with members and build that relationship, and that's just the way the town works."
- "Political fundraisers are part and parcel of doing business. You want to thank those who have supported you, you want to support them, but there's no quid pro quo. Sometimes you organize fundraisers because you want to show your gratitude, you want to go the extra mile."

Lobbyists also described fundraisers as useful events where they get to see members of Congress and get a sense of what they are thinking about issues of interest. Said one lobbyist: "Usually, you go to the fundraiser and the lobbyists introduce themselves. The member gives comments, opens it up for questions and people say: senator, as you are probably aware, Congress is considering X, Y, and Z and we want you to know how we feel. You throw a little bread in the water—you want to see if they're interested enough to say why don't you come up and we'll talk about it." Another lobbyist described making campaign contributions as "showing respect for the process." This fits with the general consensus in academic political science that campaign money buys access,[17] but little consensus as to whether it does anything more than that.[18]

Lobbyists offered a range of views on the importance of campaign contributions. Some described campaign contributions as very important, and tend to give to almost everybody (no reason not to make friends wherever you can!). Others represented companies with PACs that were more selective about their contributions, limiting their giving only to close friends. For example, one lobbyist expressed extreme enthusiasm for the value of making campaign contributions:

- "It's an 8 [on a 7-point scale]. It's incredibly important. It gives you credibility that you're serious about what Washington is and about the political process. It gets you phone calls from people who would not necessarily ever care about who you are or what you did. When you can hold up a card that says you're with [company omitted], that carries a lot of weight. When people know you have a $2 million PAC, it makes a lot more impact than if they know you have a $100,000 PAC. PACs are important. They're great ways to create relationships, a great way for us to carry the weight we need to get some of things we get done done."

At the other extreme, one lobbyist viewed fundraising as primarily an annoyance:

- "The biggest headache is dealing with volume of calls and e-mails requesting money. If you have a PAC . . . everybody asks. At the end of the day we have screens on who we'll give to and how much we can give and I apply those screens. But on any given day I'll get 25 faxed invitations to Washington-based fundraisers."

Most lobbyists fell somewhere in the middle. The most consistent takeaway point from my interviews was that making campaign contributions and attending fundraisers is simply part of the Washington culture. Lobbyists and companies are constantly asked for money, and most give it to remain in good standing. After all, if companies are going to be asking congressional offices for help, they want to show that they are happy to do their part by contributing. It's an act of goodwill. Lobbyists readily point out that their contributions are so small (only a few thousand dollars in a multi-million-dollar campaign) that they can't possibly have much of an effect. Certainly, this puts a positive spin on things, and runs against more popular perceptions of how money works. But this is how the lobbyists see it. At the very least, the interviews help us to see that companies approach making PAC contributions in a variety of ways, and some see it as more important than others.

Conclusion

There are many reasons why companies lobby, and many ways in which their lobbyists try to influence political outcomes. In general, the more a company spends on lobbying, the more strongly felt reasons its lobbyists have for why that company is active, and the more highly its lobbyists report valuing more tactics. The most important reason companies give for being politically active is to preserve the status quo, closely followed by wanting to change the status quo and wanting to maintain ongoing relationships. Companies that do the most lobbying are much more likely to cite regulatory issues and intra-industry competition as reasons to be active in Washington than companies that do the least lobbying. Companies lobby on a range of company-specific and industry-relevant issues. In my interviews, more than two-thirds of the issues on which companies were actively lobbying were attempts to change the status quo.

Lobbying is very tactically diverse, and this is important for two reasons. One, it helps us to see the ways in which lobbying can expand from very basic to pervasive. And two, it helps us to see how difficult lobbying can be to evaluate externally, given the wide variety of ways influence might (or might not) happen. Using clustering analysis, I showed how the basic approach to lobbying (which I call the "bronze strategy") differs from the comprehensive approach (which I call the "platinum strategy"). The "bronze" strategy involves much of what we might traditionally think of as lobbying: a heavy emphasis on contacting government officials, keeping a close eye on what is happening in Congress, thinking about who would be a good ally, and building coalitions and strategizing. By contrast, the "platinum" strategy is a kind of everywhere, all-the-time, do-all-you-can approach to lobbying: fundraising, trying to sway opponents and undecided members, mobilizing constituents, drafting legislation, and presenting research.

The truly large companies are active across a wide range of issues, bills, and agencies, and have impressively large numbers of lobbyists who register on their behalf. This allows them to take up considerable space in the public policy ecosystem, and puts them in an increasingly pervasive position. At its fullest expression, the modern corporate government relations operation employs upwards of 100 lobbyists, lobbying on upwards of 100 bills and reaching out to two dozen different agencies. It has many different reasons for being active, and is capable of utilizing the full toolkit of modern lobbying tactics. It is an impressive operation, the likes of which have rarely before been seen in American political history.

5

How Corporations Cooperate
and Compete

"We're all competitors. You walk into a congressional office and behind you is your buddy from the other firm, and you're telling him what you think, and the next guy comes in and tells them something different, so you have to come back in and say wait a minute. Some people do try to use government to advantage their business and to disadvantage others." – *Company lobbyist*

As we saw in Chapter 3, prior to the 1970s, very few individual corporations had their own Washington lobbying offices. Instead, trade associations handled almost all industry lobbying. But starting in the 1970s, when companies first hired their own lobbyists en masse, the balance of lobbying began to shift towards companies. Companies now spend substantially more on lobbying than do trade associations, and company-level spending on lobbying is growing faster than association spending. While associations still play an important role, their leadership capacity is diminishing as individual companies narrow their political focus and intra-industry competition grows. This chapter provides an insight into the complicated tensions between competition and cooperation within industries, examining the role of trade associations to better understand how these tensions play out. We will see how companies jostle with other companies in their industry, and how this competition (some of it friendly, some of it not-so-friendly) contributes to more lobbying over time.

While classic theorizing on political activity[1] dichotomizes between selective and collective benefits, the reality is almost always more complicated. On many industry issues, most companies might agree on general high-level issues, but they often have their own particular concerns on the aspects of the policy that might affect them differentially. Since no two companies are exactly the same, there are plenty of opportunities for slight particularism—especially when enterprising lobbyists are eager to make the case for additional corporate political engagement. Ken Godwin and colleagues argue that corporate lobbying can be modeled as a two-stage game. First, companies join together in order to get an issue onto the agenda, aware that it often takes a large coalition to break the threshold of attention. Then, once the issue gets serious consideration, companies break off and advocate for themselves. In Godwin et al.'s survey one chemical company's lobbyist summarized this process: "In the beginning most of us cooperate to get Congress's ear, but in subcommittee it's every man for himself." Another lobbyist in their survey provided a similar perspective on lobbying the bureaucracy: "When EPA is considering a new rule, we [the firms in her industry] stick together. In the end though, I need to have the final rule written for [her firm], not for [her firm's major competitor]."[2]

This model is useful in that it clarifies how agenda-setting is different from policy development. Companies in an industry might all agree that Congress should deal with a particular issue. But when somebody actually starts writing a bill, there are many details to be worked out. Almost always, those details will impact different companies within an industry differently. There is rarely, if ever, true policy consensus within an industry once it comes time to delve into the specifics.

The best way to understand the competing pulls of competition and cooperation within industry is to understand the role of trade associations. Trade associations are forums where organizations ostensibly cooperate, but also often jostle against each other to shift the industry position to better serve them individually. Though more lobbying spending occurs through individual corporate lobbying ($1.84 billion in 2012), trade associations are still significant players in the Washington corporate lobbying ecosystem—they spent $553 billion on lobbying in 2012.

The Importance of Trade Associations

Participation in trade associations is virtually universal among large companies. In one survey of 250 large companies, all reported belonging to a relevant trade association.[3] As one in-house company lobbyist told me, "We belong to them all. They're a very, very useful and important tool in the process, just incredibly important." Another in-house company lobbyist noted that, "trade associations are going to exist no matter what." He noted that not to participate would be to cede leadership to other companies in the industry with slightly different priorities or perspectives. We will revisit this point in more detail shortly.

A typical large company is likely to be a dues-paying member of several trade associations, with the amount of dues generally based on company size.

Microsoft, for example, disclosed in 2012 that it had contributed $12.7 million to 40 different national and state-level trade associations, though the bulk of its dues went to two associations: The Software Alliance ($6.2 million) and the Association for Competitive Technology ($2.4 million). Microsoft also contributed $532,261 to the World Economic Forum, $442,500 to the U.S. Chamber of Commerce, and $370,750 to the Information Tech Industry council.[4]

Xerox, a smaller company, spent $1.1 million in 2011 with 13 associations, most prominently the Business Roundtable ($235,000), the Technology CEO Council ($225,000), and the U.S. Chamber of Commerce ($140,000)

Other companies are more focused. Bristol-Myers Squibb, for example, disclosed contributions to only three trade associations: $1,572,503 to PhRMA, $172,800 to the Biotechnology Industry Organization (BIO), and a tiny payment of $6,815 to the Healthcare Institute of New Jersey.

A unique insight into the translation of trade association dues into lobbying comes from Prudential, which discloses both its total dues to trade associations and the amount of that money that funded lobbying activities. In 2011, Prudential contributed a total of $5.80 million to 18 different trade associations, $1.66 of which (28.6 percent) went to pay for lobbying. By comparison, Prudential spent $8.64 million on its own lobbyists in 2011.[5] Table 5.1 details Prudential's disclosed contributions. Unfortunately, there systematic data on corporate-level contributions to associations are not available, since there are no legal requirements that corporations disclose these contributions.[6]

How Trade Associations Operate

Trade associations serve many functions within an industry, many of which have nothing to do with politics. Associations organize conferences and trade shows, set standards, produce trade publications, and provide a legally sanctioned forum for companies to coordinate and share information. However, since our interest is in political activity, we will focus on the politics.

Trade associations typically have a high-level executive committee or committees that meet occasionally and set the general political priorities of the association for the year. As one lobbyist explained it, "The board of directors or the executive committee within the board of directors sets the initial huge goals and major year priorities, and we work on those issues." Generally, companies pay association membership dues based on their size. Large companies pay more, small companies pay less. Member companies that pay higher dues tend to be better represented on association committees. As one trade association representative explained, "You pay to play. You pay to get on an executive

Table 5.1 **Prudential's contributions to trade associations, 2011**

Association	Lobbying	Total
American Council of Life Insurers	$325,000	$1,625,000
United States Institute for Legal Reform	$750,000	$1,000,000
United States Chamber of Commerce	$287,500	$570,000
Corporate Executive Board	$0	$531,148
Life Insurance and Market Research Assoc.	$0	$420,328
APARK, Inc.	$0	$250,000
Business Roundtable	$106,002	$235,560
Association for Advanced Life Underwriting	$25,490	$226,500
Financial Services Forum	$94,000	$200,000
Securities Industry & Financial Markets Assoc.	$21,000	$140,000
National Structured Settlements Trade Assoc.	$11,700	$130,000
Metro Hartford Alliance	$1,230	$123,000
Association of California Life & Health Insurance Companies	$9,140	$91,400
The Geneva Association	$0	$76,000
Institute of International Finance	$0	$62,500
Life Insurance Council of New York, Inc	$13,800	$60,000
The Insurance Federation of Pennsylvania	$12,000	$60,000
Total	$1,656,862	$5,801,436

Source: Company disclosures

committee." Many associations also have annual events where all paying members get a chance to chime in:

- "Every year we have a CEO summit. All of our CEOs come out for a meeting and talk about the issues that are pending, what we need to focus on, what are the key issues – it's all pretty much decided there."
- "Twice a year, we get together with all our companies and open it up to everyone and let them know our priorities for the next year. We see what we got through, what we didn't get through, and what we think we can get accomplished, and then we have a three-hour planning session."
- "Each year in December, we kind of take a look at the landscape and oftentimes you can tell what's a really hot issue. What are leaders in Congress talking about what they want to do? Look at what's out there that's being debated. And then we also say: what is problematic for our industry, where

can we be impactful and helpful? We have a government affairs committee that sets our agenda that we have calls with. Depending on makeup, once a month or every other month, we say, here's the landscape of issues, and here's where we can play."

Many associations also have more specialized policy committees that set priorities in particular policy areas. For example, one lobbyist said, "Our committees meet two or three times a year, augmented by conference calls. We're getting ready for the tax committee now, because there is tax legislation pending. The committee will provide us technical input and then we'll respond accordingly. But it's not cookie-cutter."

With these general priorities in place, association lobbyists then watch and monitor and try to respond as best they can to events as they develop. Adjustments tend to be made in consultation with Washington offices of companies, and therefore companies who participate the most actively generally also have the most capacity to push and pull agendas and positions. Because trade associations want to stay in business and staying in business means keeping their highest-paying companies happy, associations are most likely to listen to them.

However, since different companies in the industry have different priorities or different takes on shared priorities, this sometimes limits what associations can do. Several lobbyists called this the "least-common-denominator" problem: association lobbying is limited only to issues of general consensus. The fact that this problem commonly exists may offer one explanation as to why, as we will see, the growth of company lobbying is outpacing the growth of trade association lobbying. As individual companies lobby more, associations face limits on the issues where they can effectively lobby without upsetting member companies. Individual companies, by contrast, face no such constraints.

Trade Associations and Cooperation

It is clear, however, that associations are valuable, and companies generally like having strong industry associations. One reason is that trade associations tend to play a coordinating role in industry lobbying efforts. In interviews, company lobbyists frequently described the value of having an association to set priorities and provide a basic framework for where companies in the industry should direct their efforts.

- "They play a role in developing an industry consensus. When you have industry consensus, you're much more effective, so trade associations develop that consensus; they move that issue forward."

- "They help to organize around long-term issues and impact that relate to an industry and are really, really good at the less-than-precise efforts that need to go into winning or losing industry-wide efforts."

Company lobbyists appreciate this coordination. They generally realize that, on industry issues, it is difficult for companies to be effective if they can't present a unified front. As Marie Hojnacki notes, corporate interests especially benefit from coalitions because of their need to "broaden the scope of support for their policy objectives, and to provide a more positive image for their policy interests."[7] Several lobbyists echoed this point:

- "PhRMA has a lot more lobbyists than we do, and I think there are some issues where they can consider all of the company concerns and present those as the industry concerns they look less self-interested than we as a company would . . . there's a lot of value in the relationship building that trade associations provide."
- "Trade associations are an important tool to amplify and leverage our voice. It's not as effective if we have to do it on our own."
- "There is value when we say something is important, but when the whole industry says it, well, it's just more important to go in as the industry as a whole."

Different companies tend to have relationships with different congressional offices, based both on which members represent districts where the companies operate and which lobbyists used to work in which offices. Associations often help companies divide up their contacting so that everybody reaches out to their best allies, thus extending the influence of the entire industry.

- "PhRMA tends to play a coordinating role, and allows companies to come together [to] divide up assignments."
- "They help us see what is out there, what can be done. We may block and tackle and say, you guys meet with this member, we meet with that member; you have a relationship with this guy; we have a relationship with that guy, and we're generally jointly agreed upon that it's really important to keep focused."

This divide-up-and-conquer strategy provides a key insight into the way in which an association can help to overcome the collective action problem. Because different companies have relationships with different members of Congress, they are providing a unique contribution to the collective lobbying effort, which puts more pressure on them to carry out their part. Mancur Olson argued that the social pressure inherent in small groups (where everybody can observe everybody else's contributions) can help overcome the collective action problem.[8] Arguably, in such a divide-up-and-conquer strategy, each contact is essential, so it is more difficult for individual companies to shirk and not do their part. In their interviews, Godwin and colleagues find that industry coalitions pressure large companies in the industry to lobby on issues because their absence would undermine the industry lobbying efforts.[9]

But such contributions to industry lobbying are not entirely altruistic. Because company lobbyists have their own interest in maintaining close relationships with their home state delegation, they would almost certainly prefer to do the lobbying themselves. Moreover, since different companies are likely to have their own particular takes on the issue, there is a benefit to being the one to contact members. So, while the association may organize the broader lobbying effort and general parameters, and even put some pressure on companies to participate, each company wants to make sure its interests are represented. If a train is leaving the station, it's better to be on it.

Often, associations take proactive steps to facilitate the ability of companies to lobby by helping to set up meetings and actively soliciting companies to participate.

- "We have 3–4 member of Congress meetings a week, and we track companies to see who's attending. If we see one company not able to make it for a couple of weeks, we give 'em a call and ask, how's everything going? How are we doing? What are you struggling with on government relations that what can we push for you, what can we do less of? Are there any members of Congress you want to meet?" (trade association lobbyist)
- "They give resources to companies to express views, they give the Hill a place to communicate with the industry, and they give even regulators a place to kind of congregate and talk about and shape the direction a lot of times on industry issues." (company lobbyist)

While several company lobbyists said they appreciated the door-opening capacities that associations tend to provide, one was a bit more cynical: "Trade associations want membership dues, so they'll put pressure on me and encourage people to have somebody go to meetings on the Hill." But, this lobbyist said, he prefers not to be one voice in a big crowd. Presumably, he'd rather spend his time working on issues where he can claim some genuine credit for what he is doing.

The Struggles within Trade Associations

As we've seen, companies pay good money to fund trade associations. For large companies, dues tend to be in the six figures. As a result, they expect to get something out of associations. As an in-house lobbyist for a large company put it bluntly: "Hopefully we use them more than they use us." Part of what companies want is extra lobbying muscle and legitimacy behind a particular policy position. Several company lobbyists talked about this somewhat obliquely.

- "We can use them [associations] to champion issues we might not feel comfortable doing ourselves. . . . We may recommend something, or send a note to a group of people on an issue we should be involved in and say we should get this trade association to advocate more forcefully."
- "On difficult issues, where [our company] doesn't want to be upfront, it's important to have a strong association."
- "It's good to have trade associations to represent the industry, so if there are sensitive issues or members being problematic, it's better to go up and be the face of the industry."
- "We go through the issues and what they're doing, and occasionally engage more heavily if it is particularly important to our business or if there are different perspectives to different firms and I'm concerned that the way legislation is drafted would advantage one firm and not us, or advantage everyone else. I try to keep a close check on that."

In other words, companies recognize the value of having an association take the lead on issues. Companies care about their images and reputations. They don't want to be seen as greedy or too narrowly focused. To the extent they can shape the priorities of the industry behind the scenes, it makes the issues they want to advance seem more legitimate.

The widespread nature of this becomes more clear when we hear the complaints of lobbyists who express the need to stay vigilant of the ways that other companies (not them, of course!) try to use associations to push narrow issues.

- "Some companies aren't shy about using the process to advantage something they're trying to do that would disadvantage you, so you have to be at the table. And you have to be at the table to drive things that are important to your business that other people might not think are important. You need to convince them."
- "[Associations] can be time-consuming, and frustrating because you're dealing with people who would otherwise be your competitors and sometimes people will utilize public policy in an anti-competitive way, and you need to look to the trade association almost as a broker in that context."
- "There is a lot of value in just showing up. You need to participate because others push a narrow agenda."

- "There was a case where one trade association let somebody have a platform to bash us, and so I got the association executive on the phone right away and said, 'what's going on?' But you gotta be careful. Trade associations are a tool, and can be a very strong tool in the toolbox. But there's a problem with trade associations where one person dominates conversations about everything. Some are just not well run."

In some cases, this competition to define the agenda can lead to frustration. Companies jostle back and forth with each other but never quite move forward. And while it might look like a lot of resources going towards inaction, it's also a careful equilibrium in which if any company pulled back, the industry position would shift. Said one frustrated lobbyist (who represents a smaller company): "I go to monthly meetings, and everyone gets together to hear from some Hill staffer on some topic and then we pat each other on the back and go home. You have 60 lobbyists who are concerned about one issue, but can't come to an agreement because everybody has a different opinion."

While there are no guarantees in any form of political engagement, the more effort a company puts into shaping the activities of the trade association, the more the trade association's lobbying efforts are likely to reflect what the company wants. One lobbyist made this point clearly: "You get out of an association what you put into it. It's as simple as that." This lobbyist went on to elaborate how associations are most responsive to the members who pay the most dues and devote the most activity to associations:

- "If you're a small entity paying a small amount of dues, if senior executives are not on committees of real importance and don't come and participate, you're probably going to get poor to negligible service on your own unique issues. If you're a large dues-paying member but not involved, even though you might pay a large amount in dues, if you don't know the people from the head down to the bottom, your ability to influence will be minimal. So the optimal position to be in is you pay a lot of dues and you actually have executives who are very engaged and the trade association knows that you are engaged, and that empowers a good Washington office to maximize the value."

What this means practically is that large company lobbyists often find themselves spending substantial time negotiating policy details with other companies within an industry, playing both offense and defense with each other, well before they even get to lobbying Congress. This provides yet another reason for companies to be active in Washington. They need to keep watch on what the trade associations are doing, lest their interests get undermined.

Ultimately, companies that can spend the most money tend to get the most out of associations. Lobbyists for large companies often spoke about how their companies were happy to play a leadership role in industry lobbying efforts.

- "As industry leader, our CEO would say and has said and has tried to look at his role beyond just heading [our company], really as a leadership role within the industry, to try to take a positive role on issues. He does take seriously representation within the industry."
- "We are traditionally in the top 3, 4, 5, 6 patent recipients each year. Our R&D budget is 3.5 billion dollars. This is a top priority for our senior management. We were told to get [patent reform] done. So we're not going to free-ride on the coalition; we're looking to lead the coalition."

But among smaller companies, the general view towards associations was that while they were useful for general monitoring, some policy development, and the occasional political introduction, there was also a lot of carping about how the associations tended to be far more responsive to the big companies than the small companies. As one small company lobbyist put it, "We can't complain if we aren't there, so at least we get to complain. We pay to complain. But our membership dues aren't that much in comparison to what we spend on other things in the business, so it's not that much to spend for us."

In surveys, I asked in-house company lobbyists to rate both how actively they participated in associations and how valuable they thought associations were. Generally, companies participate very actively and value associations highly. Though not a single company lobbyist rated the value of trade associations at 7 out of 7 (with 7 being the highest), almost half of them (46 percent) rated it a 6. Responses are summarized in Table 5.2.

Not surprisingly, company lobbyists that participate more actively in associations say they find more value in associations. The two ratings are reasonably well correlated (Pearson's correlation is 0.59). Figure 5.1 shows the relationship between the two responses, with dot size representing company lobbying expenditure. Notably, almost half of the company lobbyists listed their participation level at either 6 or 7. Figure 5.2 looks more closely at the relationship between company lobbying expenditures and levels of participation in and satisfaction with associations. As we can see, larger companies do indeed participate more in associations and report greater satisfaction with associations, but there is a fair amount of unexplained variability. The Pearson's correlation between lobbying expenditures and level of participation (0.36) is slightly stronger than the Pearson's correlation between lobbying expenditures and value placed on the associations (0.33).

Table 5.2 **How company lobbyists value and participate in trade associations**

Response	How highly do you value trade associations?	How actively do you participate in trade associations?
7	0%	21.5%
6	46.4%	28.6%
5	28.6%	17.9%
4	7.1%	7.1%
3	0%	7.1%
2	14.3%	10.7%
1	3.6%	7.1%

Source: Author interviews with in-house company lobbyists. Ratings are on a scale of 1 (lowest) to 7 (highest).

How Associations Try to Make Themselves Valuable

Associations, like individual lobbyists, have an incentive to keep member companies politically engaged. After all, individual association employees and lobbyists depend on the association's continued survival for their job. And a

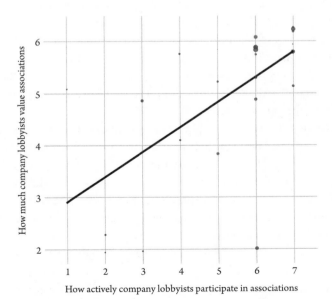

Figure 5.1 How company lobbyists value and participate in trade associations.
Source: Author interviews with in-house company lobbyists. Ratings are on a scale of 1 (lowest) to 7 (highest), LDA reports. Size of dot correlates to how much the company spends on lobbying.

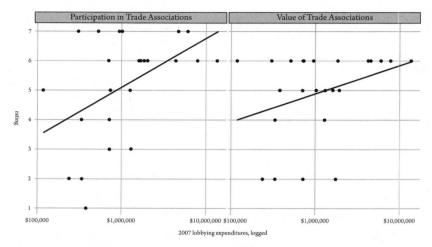

Figure 5.2 How participation in associations and value of associations vary by lobbying intensity. Source: LDA reports, author interviews with in-house company lobbyists. Ratings are on a scale of 1 (lowest) to 7 (highest).

thriving association likely means high salaries for them. As one trade association lobbyist explained, "It's typical, and it transcends this industry. Organizations tend to always want to grow, I think that's what does drive most of them, that desire for growth."

How do trade associations demonstrate their value? For one, they send out regular communications: weekly and monthly newsletters showing all that the association is doing, how it is progressing on issues the industry cares about. Said one lobbyist: "We try to give them the successes. We try to show them we're moving forward on the issues."

Associations also try to develop advocacy niches. They work hard to make themselves indispensable in their particular representation and issue space. Said one association lobbyist: "You kind of have to find your own niche and differentiate yourself. I think different trade associations do have different kinds of characteristics and I think different companies see different values." Or as David Hart notes in an analysis of high-tech trade associations, "Once created, high-tech associations rarely disappear, but they do adapt frequently and significantly as the environment changes and new competitors appear."[10]

Sometimes, organizational survival involves being the go-to association for a particular policy area (some associations get into very targeted issue spaces). Other times this involves being better on the technical and policy details, or being better on providing access. As one lobbyist put it, "We have a director of membership recruitment. It's just a matter of pointing out work we've done and how relevant it is to their policy interests. It's going into the whole niche argument, that we could do something better than other trade associations out there. Definitely there are companies we think would benefit from being members. Our interests as we see it align with theirs."

Associations also have incentives to highlight intra-industry rivalries to get companies to participate (read: pay) more. One trade association lobbyist said his association's sales pitch to companies includes the following: "You can help drive our positions, you can frame our materials, and we have these discussions and we create positions, make statements, you can help drive those, help form our positions, set our priorities."

Importantly, both of these approaches lead to less unity and more particularism in corporate lobbying. Developing niches within an industry highlights differences. So does telling companies why they need to be more active in setting the agenda of the association. Associations implicitly understand the collective action problem. They want to make sure companies don't free-ride on their efforts. A good way to do that is to cast participation itself as a selective benefit.

The Data on Association and Company Lobbying

So far, I've argued that companies actively participate in trade associations for both cooperative and competitive reasons. In part, they value the leadership roles that associations can play in organizing industry lobbying. In part, they view associations as tools to advance company-specific issues, and participate actively to prevent other companies from advancig their issues.

Now we turn to some data. The data will enable us to answer a couple of important questions about associations. First there is the straightforward question of whether association lobbying and company lobbying serve as substitutes or complements. Here the evidence will be clear: they are complements. Industries with more association lobbying also have more company lobbying. We will also see that company lobbying is growing more rapidly than association lobbying across the majority of industries. Finally, we can examine the extent to which the growth of association lobbying and company lobbying in an industry are related. While both are no doubt functions of both history and the larger political economic environment around the industry, we will see that increases in company lobbying correlate with increases in association lobbying the following year. However, increases in association lobbying do not correlate to increases in company lobbying the following year.

The first empirical question is whether company lobbying and trade association lobbying are complements or substitutes. That is, do industries choose either to lobby through associations or through individual companies? Or do industries with more association lobbying also have more company lobbying?

If trade association and company-level lobbying are substitutes, then industries with high levels of trade association lobbying should have low levels of company lobbying, whereas industries with more company lobbying should have less trade association lobbying. If they are complements, industry lobbying and company lobbying expenditures will be highly correlated. Figure 5.1 plots aggregate industry trade association lobbying on the x-axis, and aggregate individual company lobbying within the industry on the x-axis. Again, I continue to use 2007 lobbying expenditures for the sake of consistency.

Industry association and company lobbying are complements. The two measures are highly correlated (Pearson's correlation = 0.78). And this makes sense. Both association lobbying and company lobbying levels are presumably a function of the political environment and the history of lobbying in the industry. Though trade associations are rarely considered in the literature on the determinants of corporate political activity, the two studies that do include a variable for an active trade association both find that this variable is positively associated with increased corporate political activity.[11]

A second and equally important question concerns balance. Is more lobbying done through associations or through companies? This is an important question, because it is a rough measure of the unity vs. particularism of corporate lobbying. If most lobbying is done through associations, it suggests more cohesiveness in the lobbying community. If most lobbying is done through companies, it suggests more divisiveness in the lobbying community, with more companies focused on their own concerns. It indicates a lobbying environment that is more competitive than cooperative.

Again, the empirical evidence is clear. As Figure 5.3 shows, in most industries, the majority of lobbying spending is now done on behalf of companies, as opposed to trade associations. In the median industry, companies spend almost exactly twice (2.01 times) as much on lobbying as associations spend (though as Figure 5.3 makes clear, there is substantial variability across industries).[12] Only 10 (about 20 percent) of 49 industries spend the majority of their lobbying dollars through trade associations.

There is also a noticeable relationship between the overall lobbying intensity of the industry and the balance of trade association vs. company spending: The more lobbying overall in the industry, the greater the share of lobbying spending being done by companies. Put another way, in the most intense lobbying industries, companies are doing the vast majority of the lobbying themselves. Association lobbying appears to have limits. But several industries have many companies who are willing to spend sizeable sums of money on lobbying.

We can see this in Figure 5.4, which plots total industry spending (company + association) on the x-axis, and the share of those expenditures

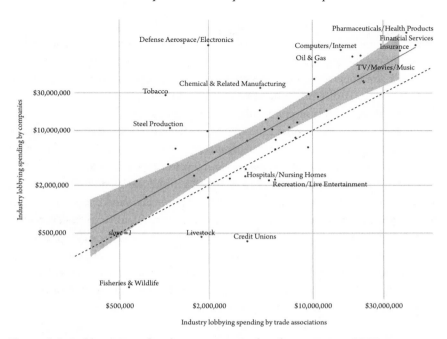

Figure 5.3 Lobbying spending by companies and trade association, 2007. Source: LDA reports.

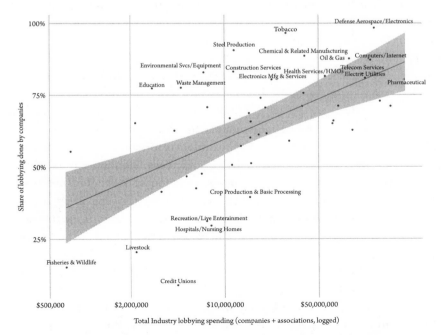

Figure 5.4 Total industry spending (companies + trade associations) and share of spending done by companies, 2007. Source: LDA reports.

coming from individual companies. As overall industry spending totals increase, the within-industry balance increasingly shifts to company-level lobbying.[13] This suggests that the industries with the most lobbying overall are industries where companies are actively competing with each other, and/or where they are also actively seeking selective benefits. This is consistent with the larger story of growing particularism in corporate lobbying.

In both figures, the outlier industries are similar. The industries where the overwhelming majority of expenditures come from companies are either industries where a few large companies dominate (e.g., tobacco, steel production) or industries where the bulk of lobbying is oriented around government contracting (e.g., defense, education). In the first case (where a few companies dominate), a likely explanation is that there is no need for an association because companies can coordinate on their own. In the second case (industries where lobbying is predominantly oriented towards government contracting), there is likely little need for an association because firms are almost entirely competing with each other. The defense industry is the archetype of this arrangement. While defense companies may share similar concerns about procurement rules and the size of the military budget (i.e., the "military-industrial complex"), mostly they are fighting each other to win government contracts. By contrast, the industries that rely primarily on trade associations tend to be industries that don't devote a sizeable amount of money to lobbying generally, and/or industries without many large companies that possess the resources to actively participate.

The Shift Towards More Company Lobbying

While this analysis provides a useful snapshot of the balance between association and company lobbying, that balance has been changing. While companies and associations are both generally devoting more resources to lobbying, companies are increasing their lobbying commitments at a more rapid rate, shifting the balance of lobbying activity more and more towards companies. In 1998, the median industry spent 62.5 percent of its lobbying dollar through individual company lobbying. By 2012, the median share of lobbying done through companies had risen to 71.1 percent—an all-time high in the time series. This trend is visualized in Figure 5.5.

For more granularity, and to better understand the variability in these trends across different industries, I visualize the industry-level changes between 1998 and 2012 in more detail in Figure 5.6. Here, the x-axis represents changes in lobbying spending by industry *associations*. The y-axis represents changes in lobbying spending by industry *corporations*. All calculations are

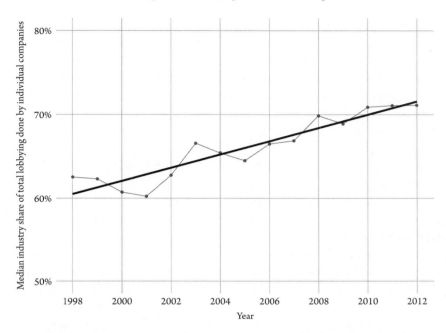

Figure 5.5. Median share of total (company + association) industry lobbying done by individual companies. Source: LDA reports

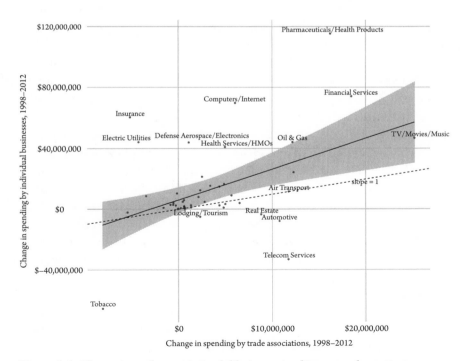

Figure 5.6 Change in trade association lobbying expenditures vs. change in company lobbying expenditures, 1998–2012, by industry. Source: LDA reports

made in inflation-adjusted dollars. The dotted line represents a slope of 1, which would indicate that the levels of spending changed at exactly the same rate. The straight line is a linear regression showing that each $1 change in trade association spending between 1998 and 2012 correlates to a $2.03 change in company-level spending during the same period (in constant 2012 dollars). In other words, individual companies have increased their lobbying expenditures at twice the rate that associations have increased their lobbying expenditures (on average).[14]

In only 10 of 49 industries (about 20 percent) did trade association lobbying spending grow faster than company lobbying spending. In one industry, air transportation, the change was almost perfectly equal (+ $11.74 million for companies, + $11.79 million for trade associations). Industries where association spending has outpaced company lobbying tend to be either extremely concentrated markets (e.g., telecommunications, automotive) or extremely diffuse markets (e.g., lodging/tourism, real estate). In the real estate industry, the National Association of Realtors is a long-established and historically active lobbying operation, and real estate lobbying is largely oriented towards a shared goal of keeping the housing market vibrant (and realtors busy).

By contrast, the outliers on the other side of regression line (where company lobbying has outpaced trade association lobbying) are all highly competitive and active industries where overall lobbying has grown substantially. Interestingly, two industries, insurance and electric utilities, have witnessed small declines in their trade association lobbying while company-level lobbying has increased substantially. Notably, both industries had substantial trade association presences in 1998. Insurance had $40.1 million in trade association spending in 1998 (in 2012 dollars), which fell to $35.0 million in 2012. Electric utilities had $27.4 million in association in spending in 1998 (in 2012 dollars), down to $23.2 million in 2012. Perhaps both of these industries had reached an upper limit in what associations could accomplish on their own.

While it's clear that industry lobbying and association lobbying tend to grow in tandem to some extent, there is the additional question of causality. That is, are both companies and associations responding to the same underlying drivers of political activity (the level of government involvement in the industry, the issue agenda, and the self-reinforcing logic lobbying). Or does an increase in one type of spending lead to an increase in another type of spending?

The results from Table 5.3 show that trade association lobbying increases tend to follow increases in company lobbying, but that individual company lobbying increases do not consistently correlate with increases in trade association lobbying. However, both association and company lobbying levels in each industry exhibit a strong degree of autocorrelation.

Table 5.3. **Predicting annual association and company lobbying from previous year's activity.**

	Model 1 *Assoc. lobbying*	Model 2 *Assoc. lobbying*	Model 3 *Co. lobbying*	Model 4 *Co. lobbying*
Assoc. lobbying (lag)	0.979***	0.997***	0.127*	
	(0.022)	(0.015)	(0.057)	
Co. lobbying (lag)	0.007		0.987***	0.015***
	(0.005)		(0.024)	(0.015)
R^2	0.957	0.957	0.975	0.974
Adj. R^2	0.956	0.956	0.974	0.974
Num. obs.	678	678	678	678

***$p < 0.001$, **$p < 0.01$, *$p < 0.05$
Coefficients computed using OLS with fixed effects for year and clustered standard errors

Source: LDA reports.

The first two models in Table 5.3 estimate the industry's current year spending by trade association lobbying as a function of the previous year's lobbying, with fixed effects for a year. Models 1 and 2 show that trade association lobbying levels are highly persistent from year-to-year, and that the previous year's individual company lobbying level within the industry has no predictive power on the current year's trade association lobbying level. By contrast, individual company lobbying levels (which are also highly persistent from year-to-year) grow in response to more trade association lobbying. Each additional dollar that industry associations spent the previous year is associated with an additional $0.13 in company lobbying in the current year. In other words, more association lobbying appears to stimulate more company lobbying, but more company lobbying does not appear to stimulate more association lobbying. This makes sense, given what we've discussed so far. Associations have an interest in pulling companies into more lobbying (more membership dues!), and more association activity means that individual companies have more issues to jostle over. Of course, as more companies get pulled in, individual companies increasingly take the leadership role in industry lobbying, which may be one reason why the relationship is not reciprocal.

A final piece of evidence for the shift away from associations comes from a 2012 Foundation for Public Affairs survey.[15] The Foundation surveyed 115 public affairs executives on a number of questions, including their reliance on trade associations, business associations, and coalitions. The survey (results are reported in Table 5.4) found 61 percent of companies reporting that their

Table 5.4. **Companies' changing reliance on associations**

	Reliance on Trade Associations	*Reliance on Business Associations*	*Reliance on coalitions*
"we are relying a **great deal** *less*"	48%	59%	45%
"We are relying <u>somewhat</u> *less*"	13%	8%	3%
"We are relying <u>somewhat</u> *more*"	26%	25%	39%
"we are relying a **great deal** *more*"	12%	6%	12%
"Our reliance has not changed."	1%	2%	1%

Source: Foundation for Public Affairs

reliance on trade associations had declined, as compared to 38 percent who said it had increased. And of that 61 percent who had reduced their reliance on associations, the vast majority (48 percent of total respondents) said it had decreased "a great deal." By contrast, only 12 percent of respondents said they were relying on associations "a great deal more."

The survey also found similar declines in the reliance on business associations (65 percent of companies are less reliant, including 59 percent a great deal less). Interestingly, 48 percent of companies lowered their reliance on coalitions, while 51 percent increased theirs. However, of those reducing their reliance on coalitions, the vast majority (45 percent of respondents) said they were a great deal less reliant. By contrast, only 12 percent of the respondents were doing a "great deal more" lobbying in coalitions. To sum up: the Foundation for Public Affairs found a majority of companies relying less on trade associations and business associations, and a solid plurality of companies reporting *significant* declines.

Conclusion

Prior to the 1970s, few companies had Washington offices. Trade associations handled the bulk of business lobbying. Since then, the balance of lobbying has increasingly shifted in the direction of individual company lobbying. However, trade associations continue to play an important role in business lobbying, and understanding them provides valuable insights into the ways in which companies within an industry both cooperate and compete.

In part, associations provide coherence to industry lobbying efforts, helping companies to jointly prioritize issues and strategies, and successfully divide-up-and-conquer. Associations also help move issues forward in ways in which individual companies simply cannot, both because they lack the individual capacity and because key government decision-makers are more likely to take notice when the entire industry says something. But associations can also be a battleground within the industry. Companies compete to shape the industry position. Often this means that the associations take on a "least-common-denominator" position, leaving companies to lobby on their own to advocate the specific details that they most want.

For the period that we have comprehensive data (1998–2012), individual company lobbying has grown, on average, twice as much as trade association lobbying, and in 80 percent of industries, company lobbying expenditures have grown more than association lobbying expenditures. Between 1998 and 2012, the median share of total industry lobbying done by companies grew from 62.5 to 71.1 percent. Trade association lobbying and company lobbying are clearly complements. But the industries with the highest total lobbying expenditures generally do a higher share of lobbying through individual companies.

Trade associations also help foment intra-industry divisions by reminding companies why it is important to participate in setting the agenda of the association, and by sometimes carving out narrow advocacy niches. They do these things to retain and gain membership dues. The changing relationship of companies and associations is both a consequence and cause of the continued growth of corporate lobbying. As companies develop more capacity, they can participate in trade associations more aggressively to try to shape industry positions. But as some companies in an industry do this, so other companies must respond, also participating more. Intra-industry *cooperation* continues to exist, but it is increasingly tinged by intra-industry *competition*.

How Corporations Make Sense of Politics

"The more you are politically engaged, the more likely you are to see issues" – *Corporate lobbyist*

By now, we have a good picture of what corporate lobbying involves. We've seen the tactical diversity, the range of outcomes corporations lobby to achieve, and the diversity of reasons why companies engage in the political process. We've also seen how engagement has increased over time. Now we turn our focus to the internal decision-making within the corporations. This chapter asks how corporate managers make decisions about politics. Answering this question will help us to see how and why lobbying is sticky.

The foundational premise here is that corporations will engage in political activity to the extent that managers believe the benefits of engagement outweigh the costs, but that managers struggle with the cost-benefit analysis of political investments. The basic claim is that the costs and benefits of political activity are difficult to calculate because political developments are ambiguous, the returns to different lobbying approaches are unpredictable, and the connection between political developments and corporate profits is often unclear. Therefore, it is difficult to make good estimates about both costs and benefits. In the absence of clear facts and formulas, managers instead must rely on incomplete information, judgment, experience, and emotions. For this reason, there is a strong cognitive component to corporate political engagement.

The argument in this chapter has four parts.

1. Corporations have a hard time determining their *specific* policy interests. While companies may generally prefer less regulation or lower taxes, translating those goals into workable and realistic policy actions can be difficult.

2. Information is really important. If corporate managers know about political threats and opportunities and have a good understanding of how they might respond, they are more likely to take action.
3. Costs are uncertain. Even if corporations have a specific policy goal in mind, it is difficult to determine how much they need to spend to achieve that goal.
4. The more a company lobbies, the easier it becomes to do more lobbying. Political activity has high fixed start-up costs, but once a company develops its political capacity, additional lobbying activity exhibits decreasing marginal costs.

Collectively, these insights help us to understand how current political activity changes the calculus of future political activity. The more companies lobby, the more information managers have, and the more practice and comfort managers develop with politics. They can establish realistic goals, feel more confident in their ability to affect outcomes, and benefit from decreasing marginal costs of additional activity. Lobbying has both a stickiness and an internal momentum.

The Difficulty of Defining Political Interests

As the previous two chapters have made clear, corporations have many reasons for engaging in politics, and they seek a wide range of policy outcomes. But how do they decide what their interests are? How do they know what they want? Political theory has long wrestled with the concept of "interests." For example, should interests be defined based on objective or subjective concerns? What happens when participants support positions that appear to contradict their material self-interest?[1]

At the most reductionist level, it seems safe to assume that managers want to take political actions that will improve corporate profits, and so, to the extent that interventions in public policy can accomplish this, political engagement is in the interest of a particular company. But what does this mean, specifically? A company manager might say she wants a friendlier regulatory environment, but how exactly does a "friendlier regulatory environment" translate into a specific lobbying task? Is new legislative language needed? If so, what legislative language? Is it a matter of less enforcement? If so, how much less, and how, specifically, is enforcement to be lessened?

Even something as straightforward as a government contract is not as simple as going to a procurement agent and saying: "buy my goods and services." Is there a government agency that might have an interest in the particular product the company produces? Is there an open bidding process? Is the government already buying from another supplier? In other words, how real is the opportunity to secure a contract?

In short, there is a difference between interests in the abstract and actual political interests. As John Heinz and colleagues explain:

> "It is at the intersection of public policy and the wants and values of private actors that we discover interests. What we call the interests of the groups are not simply valued conditions or goals, such as material riches, moral well-being, or symbolic satisfaction. It is only as these are affected, potentially or in fact, by public policy, by the actions of authoritative public officials, that the valued ends are transformed into political interests that can be sought or opposed by interest groups."[2]

In such a way, a corporation may engage in politics with the general goal of maximizing profits, but in the process, managers must somehow figure out how to translate that generalized goal into specific actions and strategies. Agendas shift, windows of opportunity open and close, policy consensus evolves. As Heinz and colleagues write, "groups must decide what to do—indeed, decide whether to play the game or not—under conditions of quite limited information and in a highly dynamic context where the conditions may change very rapidly."[3] In the crazy bazaar of politics, how do corporations know a good opportunity when they see it? And if they do see it, how much should they spend trying to obtain it, knowing that they may pay dearly and still not obtain the good?

The answer is that it depends. It depends on one's experience in this market-place, and on the information that one has about the various uncertainties that must be resolved before making a decision. In politics, interests are always contingent and evolving.

Winning the Influence Game: What Every Business Leader Should Know About Government—a book written to advise corporate executives on how to think about politics—advises that the most common mistake that corporations make in developing a government relations strategy is lacking clear and realistic goals. As one government relations professional said:

> "One of the biggest mistakes any company makes, small or large, is not doing a needs assessment before they approach the government relations concept. They need to take a minute and ask – What exactly do we need? How can we go about it? They really have to spend the time to figure out what exactly they need – and how's the best way to get it. Not enough companies do that."[4]

The book's advice (quoting one Washington insider) is simple: "You have to get to the point where you know what it is you want."[5] At the same time, the book advises companies that they must be flexible. Mistake #2 is "not recognizing when to shift goals."[6] That companies not knowing and/or not being pragmatic about what they want are the most common problems should tell us something: namely, that developing clear and realistic goals is not straightforward. Companies rightly struggle with it.

Several scholars of corporate political activity have come to appreciate that corporate political interests cannot simply be inferred from objective economic factors. Rather, they depend on judgment, which in turn depends on experience and information. Cornelia Woll, for example, argues that "changes in identity, causal and normative beliefs, and strategic environments" are all important influences on the "policy stances communicated by economic actors."[7] Similarly, Peter Hall describes "preference formation as a political process,"[8] pointing to the way in which internal narratives inevitably evolves as organizations try to make sense of an ever-changing political world.

Scholars who have looked more closely at how corporations come to their positions on issues have found substantial variation across similarly situated firms. Cathie Jo Martin argues that business managers "struggle to locate their interests in a world of imperfect knowledge."[9] She argues that much depends on what she calls "corporate policy capacity." There is a strong "cognitive dimension in preference formation."[10] Internal resources, historical legacies, and information processing channels and networks all help to explain how corporations come to their political positions far more reliably than the alternative hypothesis, which Martin calls "economic determinism."

Similarly, Kathleen Rehbein and Douglas Schuler offer a theory of "the filtering role of the firm" to explain how firm histories and internal mechanisms can explain variation in firm political activity: "Although external political, economic, and industry factors affect corporate political activity in a general way, an individual firm's behavior is mediated by its organizational structures, procedures, experiences, and resources."[11] Firms have different processes and routines in place for dealing with politics. These shape how they respond.

All of these theories argue that determining a firm's political interest is not a straightforward objective calculation based on some set of economic factors and/or exogenous conditions (like shifts in the policy agenda). Rather, such determinations rely much more on the resources companies have to acquire and process information and the biases and networks of key decision-makers within the organization.

Locating interests is even harder for multi-divisional firms. Bauer, Pool, and Dexter's *American Business and Public Policy* found many large firms struggling to define their position on trade policy, since different divisions in the firm often had different perspectives. In general, they found that simple "economic determinism" could not explain the positions companies took on tariffs. Rather, the positions depended much more on the information available, and how the political communications that the firms received framed the issue. The difficulty of how companies identify their political issues resonated with some of the lobbyists I interviewed.[12]

- "Part of my job is to unite different sides of company, which frequently have different viewpoints on very big issues. It's not that differences aren't resolvable. But I have to go into every conference call having prepped everybody on different sides."
- "A company as big as ours will sometimes have different positions within different parts of the business . . . We go to those people and bring them together and ultimately figure out a position that works for everyone."

These quotes show how lobbyists are important in identifying the "benefits" that company managers see in political engagement, a point that Chapter 7 will cover in more detail.

The key point here is that political interests are neither objective nor exogenously-determined. Corporate managers may wish to maximize profits, but how that maps onto a political strategy is often unclear. As one contract lobbyist I interviewed put it bluntly, "Very often clients don't know what they want."

This is important. Motivation is a key driving force behind any action. If corporate managers don't know how to define their political interests, they are going to have a difficult time seeing benefits in political engagement. And if they don't see the benefits to engagement, they are unlikely to engage.

Absent a government affairs department, managers are likely to have a difficult time locating their political interests. They need somebody to connect their general wants (e.g., lower taxes, less regulation, or more profits) to specific policy possibilities. They need a government affairs department to sit down with them and help them to see how different policies could potentially affect them, and what the possible threats and opportunities might be. Doing this requires both an understanding of public policy and an understanding of a company's business. Lobbyists occupy this unique middle ground. As we will see, this puts them in a very powerful position. But for now, let us stick with the basic observation that political interests are not always obvious and, thus, political benefits are not always easy to discern. One must be educated in the ways of what politics can offer.

The Importance of Information

A second foundational point is that even if companies have figured out their political interests, in order to see the benefits of political engagement, corporate managers must know what is going on in Washington that connects directly to those political interests. In other words, they must have information.

Organizational leaders make decisions largely based on the information that is available to them and the structures by which information is organized and processed internally.[13] The world is an information-rich place. To make a decision, managers need to first decide what information they need to seek out to make a good decision. Generally, they do this by seeking out information that they already think is important. William Starbuck and Frances Milliken, for example, describe the prevalence of "processes that amplify some stimuli and attenuate others, thus distorting the raw data and focusing attention." They call these processes "perceptual filters."[14]

In other words, there are powerful feedback loops inherent in information processing. Once you start paying attention to something, you notice it. Once you notice it, you are more likely to see it as something important. Once you determine it is important, you pay it more attention. And so on. As Jeffrey Pfeffer and Gerald Salancik note, "The fact that certain information is regularly collected focuses the organization's attention on it. The collection of certain information occupies the time and attention of the organization, which necessarily restricts the time and attention devoted elsewhere."[15] Starbuck and Miliken plainly conclude, "If events are noticed, people make sense of them; and if events are not noticed, they are not available for sensemaking." They provide an example of an outbreak of Seattle drivers suddenly reporting small pits on their windshields. This was not a new phenomenon. But what *was* new was that drivers had begun paying attention to the possibility of small pits, and upon looking for the pits, discovered that they were, in fact, there.[16]

Our hunches and biases matter, especially in information-rich environments where we must constantly make judgments about what to ignore and what to value, and these biases shape perceptions.[17] As a result, management scholars have noted that even within the same industry, different executives often have fundamental disagreements about the characteristics of the industry.[18] These variations in interpretation are highly consequential in accounting for different firm responses to the same objective conditions.[19] What one set of managers might see as signal, another set sees as noise. What the second set of managers sees as noise, the first set might see as signal.

Richard Daft and Karl Weick argue that because organizations are incredibly complex, the most important task of top management is creating a "thread of coherence" to understand the external environment.[20] Daft and Weick model the process in a three-stage cycle: first organizations scan their environment for information; then they interpret it; and finally they learn as part of a "process of putting cognitive theories into action."[21] In many cases, there is no such thing as "the answer"—the answer depends on the questions that are asked. "The basic raw materials on which organizations operate are informational inputs that are ambiguous, uncertain, equivocal," writes Weick. "The activities of organizing are directed toward the establishment of a workable level of certainty."[22]

Management scholars generally find that the more ambiguous the environment, the more likely it is that qualitative data, judgment, and intuition will dominate.[23] More uncertain environments are also associated with more information processing.[24] When the world is viewed as complicated, companies are motivated to spend time and energy figuring things out. When objective measures are inadequate, subjectivity becomes more important. A complicated world is open to many interpretations. As W. Richard Scott writes in summarizing the literature on information processing, "The environment of an organization is as much, if not more, a function of the organization, the cognitive work of its participants and their structure of attention, and its information system, as it is of the external situation."[25]

This has obvious consequences for corporate political activity. At the most basic level, it means that if corporate managers have put in place a government affairs division to report to them about political developments, then corporate managers are more likely to be aware of political developments. But more broadly and more importantly, the narratives that emerge around political activity matter. Corporate managers without active government affairs departments may keep up with political news and even donate personally. But without a government affairs department and a history of political engagement, managers are likely to categorize political developments as interesting things going on the world, but not necessarily actionable developments.

On the other hand, at a company with an active government affairs department, the narrative is likely to be that politics is important to the company, and a source of both threats and opportunities. This will lead managers to be more aware of public policy. And as managers become more aware of public policy, they will likely see more reasons to be engaged, creating a positive feedback cycle.

As we will see in more detail in the next chapter, this process requires some steering. Company lobbyists spend a good deal of time engaging with corporate managers and departments to get them to see why government affairs should matter to the company, and how and why it can contribute to the corporate bottom line. As we will discuss in some detail, this is not as obvious to managers as popular accounts of corporate influence might lead a casual observer to suspect. Many corporate managers struggle with questions of why their company should hire a lobbyist. And although they are not as common as they used to be, knee-jerk anti-government attitudes still run deep in the business community, perhaps keeping some companies from being more engaged than they might otherwise be.

For corporate managers to value political activity, they must have confidence that there are specific outcomes that will improve or maintain corporate profitability, or that there are real threats that could hurt the bottom line. Government affairs departments connect the dots by translating both political opportunities and threats into corporate benefits, by posing public policy solutions to corporate problems, and by demonstrating that politics is a good use of the company's capital (or at least, better than other possible investments).

More information also helps managers to better understand the cause-effect relationship of their actions.[26] In general, people are hesitant to act if they don't know the possible results of their actions. Knowing more about the possibilities for action and the political landscape can give managers more confidence that they are at least making an informed decision. The more managers (and people in general) understand cause-effect relationships, the more they tend to perceive their environment as controllable.[27] Increased information use also increases the likelihood that managers will see issues as potential gains.[28] Thus, more information can buoy managers' confidence that political action will lead to success. While it may not be possible to know anything for certain, managers can feel more confident that they are making a good decision if they know more about the political situation.

In other words, information matters. Corporate managers that know more about politics are more likely to see the benefits, because they are both aware of the potential opportunities and far more keen to the ever-present threats. With a government affairs department to help crystallize the connections, they are more likely to see political developments as things to potentially impact, and they are more likely to seek out public policy solutions to existing market problems.

The Problem of Cost

Even if corporate managers have achieved clarity on a policy outcome they want, they face another question: can they obtain that outcome? And, how much will it cost? Corporate managers may wish to change many policies, or protect against any number of potential threats. But there is always a cost. Lobbyists do not provide their services pro bono to corporations.

How much to spend in part depends on what a company wants to achieve. As we've seen, there are many different outcomes companies might want, and different outcomes require different levels of effort and resources to achieve. Does the company want to preserve the status quo or change it? How visible is this issue? Is there opposition? If so, how much opposition? And who are the opponents? And how well-funded is that opposition? Are there allies? If so, how well-funded are they? How powerful are they politically? And if there are allies, why not just free-ride on their efforts and save the money? What do members of Congress and other decision-makers know or think about this issue? Is it a partisan issue? And at a higher level: how much capital does the firm have available to spend? And are there other higher-yield uses of capital? If they engage politically, corporate managers might also need to think up front about the range of alternative policy outcomes they might be willing to accept. The answers to these and other questions will determine how much a company might need to spend. Magnify this across multiple policy goals, and one begins to see the difficulties in allocating political resources.

As Chapter 4 demonstrated, corporate lobbying strategies come in different types. There is a basic ("bronze") strategy of contacting members of Congress and working with allies that involves limited resources. There is a more deluxe ("platinum") version of lobbying that involves talking to everyone, and actively shaping the intellectual environment. Companies can merely preserve the status quo, or they can more aggressively try to change it. But the more they do, and the more aggressively they engage, the more it will cost them.

Much political science research has come to the conclusion that resources don't translate to policy outputs in any predictable manner.[29] As I argued in Chapter 2, this makes sense, given the uncertainties and unpredictabilities of politics and the constantly shifting scopes of conflicts. Thus, it should not be surprising that Baumgartner and colleagues' *Lobbying and Policy Change,* the most comprehensive study of the effect of lobbying on outcomes, finds no systematic relationship between lobbying resources and the likelihood of success. Mostly, the authors conclude, it is just really, really hard to change the status quo. Lobbyist-driven changes do sometime happens, but there are no lobbying inputs bring success with anything resembling certainty.[30]

This leads Baumgartner and colleagues to pose an excellent question: "If there is so much stalemate, why then do some lobbyists get so concerned about the threat of policy change (and why do those seeking change even bother)?"[31] After all, if there are no reliable predictors of influence, and thus no way for rigorous social science to meaningfully show that the billions of dollars spent on lobbying make a whole lot of difference, aren't companies just wasting their money? Wouldn't they just be better spending $24 for the paperback edition of *Lobbying and Policy Change?*

"The answer," write Baumgartner and colleagues, "is uncertainty about outcomes and the threat of significant change when it does occur." Their research finds that when policy change happens, 70 percent of the time the change is far more major than it is marginal.[32] This important issue of uncertainty is also a theme in another comprehensive survey of lobbying, *The Hollow Core*. As Heinz and colleagues write, "Despite historically unparalleled levels of investment in attempts to shape national policy, the return on that investment is highly uncertain and often intangible."[33]

Politics is a complex and dynamic system, full of multi-stage causality and countless interaction and feedback effects. To reduce it to a stable statistical relationship between a particular set of inputs and a particular set of outputs is Sisyphean, at best. Sometimes small amounts of activity, well-timed and well-strategized, can make a big impact. Sometimes large amounts of activity have no effect. Sometimes two sides are locked in an arms race that looks like Newton's third law of motion, with each action producing an equal but opposite reaction from the other side. A good part of political engagement may be wasted. The problem for managers is that it is often impossible to know which part. Certainly some situations are more amenable to influence than others. But the only reasonable conclusion to draw is frustratingly unscientific: Sometimes lobbying pays off; sometimes it doesn't. And it's almost impossible to know *a priori* what will work and when.

Yet all it takes is an occasional big payoff to justify the importance of political engagement. Take the 2004 American Jobs Creation Act. What began as a simple fix to resolve a subsidy dispute with the World Trade Organization eventually evolved into a 633-page bill with $140 billion worth of changes to the U.S. tax code, helping everybody from tobacco growers to film producers to NASCAR track owners to manufacturers of archery equipment, sonar fish finders, and tackle boxes. Starbucks got coffee roasting qualified as manufacturing. Companies and industries whose lobbyists were well-placed were able to get their favored provisions into a bill that *The Economist* magazine dubbed "No lobbyist left behind."[34]

And because one never knows when such a "Christmas tree" bill will come along, it pays to be always in the game. Bills like this serve as powerful reminders for the value of engagement. As David Lowery and Kathleen Marchetti suggest, lobbying can exhibit a "combination of lumpiness, rarity, uncertainty and large payoffs might make lobbying operate as a partial or variable reinforcement schedule." They point out that "under such schedules, rats will continuously press a lever in hopes of a reward of a food pellet and gamblers will stay at slot machines long after it is reasonable to do so. This characteristic of some policy goods may feed cognitive biases that make lobbying addictive, with the lobbyist as the enabling pusher."[35]

Likewise, since there is always the lingering threat that some favored policy benefit might be removed (especially in a competitive lobbying world), it pays to have lobbyists on hand keeping watch at all times, ready to douse anything that looks like the threat of a conflagration with plenty of cold water. As the old Washington saying goes, "if you are not at the table, you are probably on the menu." It is always better to have a seat at the table. The proverbial menu is an unhappy place to be.

We might certainly expect corporate managers to be able to make rough estimates of how likely a company's lobbyists are to influence any particular issue or set of issues. And while there are certainly situations with higher and lower probabilities of success, any decision ultimately involves guesswork based as much on hunches as on data.

Thus, any corporate lobbying portfolio is likely to be no more than a series of guesses that the estimated sum of all benefits of lobbying across all issues will exceed the sum of costs. Perhaps the only certainty in political engagement is that if you *don't* participate, you have *no* chance of wielding influence over outcomes. The only way to guarantee failure is to not be there at all. And since you never know when an issue might blow up, there's always an argument to be made that it's better to be there at the beginning, rather than jump in at the end. It's always easier to take advantage of an opportunity before everybody knows about it, to get your provision in a bill before everybody else is clamoring for inclusion, or to stop a bill from going forward by talking to the right people before it gains any momentum.

Of course, there are also circumstances where it might be perfectly rational not to engage politically: if a company's interests are uncertain, and/or the probability of success is low, and/or the likelihood that the company can free-ride on the efforts of other similarly oriented companies is high, managers might conclude reasonably that any effort to influence politics is wasted effort.

The Declining Marginal Cost of Political Engagement

Cost calculations are different for companies with established government affairs departments and those without such departments. Political engagement has high fixed start-up costs (hiring a lobbyist, setting up an office, and building relationships all take time). But once a company establishes a lobbying presence, it benefits from a decreasing marginal cost of additional activity. A company with a history of political experience is likely to be savvier and have better relationships with government decision-makers, as well as more ability to build and navigate coalitions, and work with and sometimes lead industry associations. All else equal, managers at companies with a history of political involvement will be more confident in their ability to be successful on a broader range of issues. Companies will become more ambitious in their lobbying as their capacity and comfort with Washington both increase—especially if a company has had some success in the past.

A corporation that wishes to influence policy outcomes must first set up a government affairs division and hire a lobbyist. In order for that lobbyist to be an effective advocate, that lobbyist must learn about the company's issues, and company executives need to learn at least a little about Washington and establish some relationships. A company that sets up a Washington office faces even higher start-up costs. Matidle Bombardini argues that the "lump-sum nature" of set-up costs benefits large firms over small ones.[36]

In interviews, numerous company lobbyists stressed the importance of having long-term relationships with members of Congress as a key to being effective in Washington:

- "With a long-term presence you build relationships, so people who are making the laws understand your business."
- "If you aren't in the arena, elected officials don't know you. We have a good reputation and want to have a good reputation. It's all about relationship building."
- "We want you [member of Congress] to understand who we are, what we do, and why we do it before we ever go to you with an ask on an issue, partly out of respect, because your vote is important, and it should be important to you that when you support us that we want you [member of Congress] to feel confident and able to defend it and that you have a good sense of who we are."

Company lobbyists must cultivate friendships with congressional offices. Often this involves attending fundraisers and supporting candidates. It takes time to develop the kind of comfort and trust that lobbyists say their effectiveness depends on. While companies can certainly hire "access" lobbyists to speed up this process, it is not quite the same as having a long-term relationship.

A good example of the way in which existing political capacity alters the cost-benefit analysis of lobbying is provided by William Kerr and colleagues. They studied the lobbying in response to the decline in H-1B visas that occurred in 2004. Many firms rely on the highly skilled immigrant labor that is made available through the program and thus might have been expected to lobby in response to the sudden change in policy. Kerr et al. found that among companies that would benefit from more skilled labor, only those with existing lobbying resources took up the immigration issue. Those without existing lobbying resources did not suddenly get in the game. After all, without existing resources, the start-up costs of lobbying would be high. And besides, they would probably prefer to free-ride on the efforts of companies already doing the lobbying. But for companies who had lobbying resources, the additional marginal cost of lobbying on an additional issue was small. The authors note "the existence of significant barriers to entry in the process of lobbying." For companies who have not already entered the lobbying arena, "These costs can substantially limit the extensive margin response by firms to changes in policy environments."[37] Timothy LaPira finds a similar pattern in the emergence of the Homeland Security policy domain, showing that groups with an existing lobbying presence quickly jumped into the new policy space: "large-scale attention-shifts inside the government produce an equivalent shift in attention in the existing interest group system." Politically active organizations simply devote existing capacity to the hot issues.[38]

Corporate managers may also view existing political capability as a strategic asset. Numerous scholars have explored how, once organizations invest in a particular capacity or competency, these existing capabilities often drive their future strategic investments (above and beyond market conditions). This is known in the strategic management literature as the "resource-based view of the firm".[39] As Jay Barney explains, "strategic choices should flow mainly from the analysis of [a firm's] unique skills and capabilities, rather than from the analysis of its competitive environment."[40] He also notes that new strategies are often costly to implement, which can provide a brake on firms imitating each other. This suggests that otherwise similar firms may, in fact, do very different things in similar situations because of their unique cultures, histories, experiences, capabilities, reputations, and so on. Or, as Richard R. Nelson put it, "The ultimate reason why firms differ is rather superficial. Implicitly, they differ because some chance event, or some initial condition, made different choices profitable."[41] Similarly, David Teece and colleagues explain, "From the resource-based perspective, firms are heterogeneous with respect to their resources/capabilities/endowments. Further, resource endowments are 'sticky:' at least in the short run, firms are to some degree stuck with what they have and may have to live with what they lack."[42]

Moreover, as Hebert Simon observed, managers (like most people) can become emotionally attached to favored solutions. He called this "identification with the means."[43] Once managers decide to favor political solutions, they may have a tendency to default to those solutions. In a similar vein, Richard Cyert and James March envision the firm as a series of "standard operating procedures"—a set of routines that tend to resist change. In this way of thinking, if political engagement becomes a routine, companies are likely to stick with it.[44]

Like most strategic assets, political engagement becomes more effective with use. The more a company invests in politics, the better its relationships become. The more times lobbyists spend explaining the company's interests and relevant policy details to staffers, the more elected officials and their staffs come to know and trust the company's representatives. And the more working relationships a company has in Washington, the easier it becomes for a company to feel confident in its ability to shape outcomes. All this leads to more lobbying.

Sunk costs and investments in capacity can also explain ongoing commitments to specific issues. For a company, it takes a certain initial investment to learn about a particular issue or policy, and to build the necessary relationships around that particular issue. Each issue, after all, has its own policy community, its own set of congressional staffers and members who work on those issues. It also has its own complicated infrastructure of existing law. But once a company's managers and lobbyists understand the particular intersection of a company's business and that particular policy issue (and the high upfront cost has been paid), the cost of continued activity on that particular issue declines. Moreover, having already decided that an issue is important to a company, corporate managers are likely to keep paying attention. Their lobbyists will be active in associations and coalitions and working groups. They will be informed about all the opportunities, and their connectedness will give them an advantage in participating. There is a stickiness to engagement on particular issues for many of the same reasons that there is a stickiness to lobbying in general. Once managers start paying attention to an issue, they understand why it matters, and what they have at stake.

Companies that have a longer history of involvement in the political process can also think more ambitiously about the kinds of policy outcomes they'd like to achieve. Major proactive changes require substantial resources. They require large networks of allies who are comfortable with the company and have some affinity towards the company. But these kinds of changes become more possible when a company has invested in all of these long-term relationships.

Moreover, as companies build up their political networks, they are more likely to hear about both threats and opportunities in advance. They are more likely to know of proposals circulating that would come as unwelcome developments. They are more likely to know when windows of opportunity to advance a favored provision might occur.

Finally, the experience and information that come with a highly active government affairs department are likely to reduce uncertainty among corporate managers. When a company has little to no experience with political activity, its managers have little way of knowing what works and what doesn't, and how likely they are to succeed. Washington feels unfamiliar and uncertain. But as

the company engages more widely, as its managers develop experience overseeing political activity, and as its lobbyists develop more and better channels
of information, company managers can feel less immobilized by uncertainty.
Of course, they can never eliminate uncertainty entirely. Nothing is certain in
politics, but as organizational theory has taught us, more information improves confidence in decision-making, and confidence in decision-making is
more likely to lead to action.

Conclusion

Political engagement is path dependent. Absent a political operation, corporate managers have a hard time locating their interests and a hard time making
accurate cost-benefit predictions about political engagement. Without internal advocates, without experience, without capacity, without ongoing issues in
which they are already invested, political engagement can seem at best an uncertain gamble. And without existing capacity, there is a barrier to political
engagement.

But getting involved politically changes the cost-benefit analysis. Most fundamentally, managers gain more information about politics, which helps them
to see what is at stake, and how they might participate. Knowing more makes
politics seem more familiar, and potentially more pressing (especially given
lobbyists' incentives to push companies towards more lobbying). With more
information and experience, managers can better develop more realistic policy
goals. And as they build capacity, they can feel more confident in their ability
to achieve those goals. Political activity has high fixed start-up costs. But once
companies invest, there are decreasing marginal costs to additional political
activity.

Just as individual citizens who become politically engaged build networks
and political capital, which increases their internal sense of efficacy and in turn
makes future participation more likely,[45] so do companies and the key actors
within them. As one lobbyist put it, "The more you are politically engaged, the
more likely you are to see issues."

How Lobbyists Perpetuate Lobbying

"I do a lot of work to educate the higher-ups. My purpose is to communicate what we are doing, so the dots are being put together and they get why we're doing this." – Company lobbyist

In the previous chapter, I argued that becoming politically active changes the cost-benefit calculus behind political engagement. As corporate managers begin to pay attention to politics, they learn to sharpen their political interests. They also start paying attention to political developments, becoming more aware of both threats and opportunities. More information about politics means more reasons to participate. Having paid the start-up costs to establish a Washington presence, a company now has existing capacity on which to draw, reducing the marginal costs of additional lobbying. When a company's representatives have built up relationships with congressional offices and other decision-makers, companies can be more ambitious in their political engagement. All of this makes the costs seem lower and the benefits seem greater.

Now we turn to the key drivers of the process: the lobbyists themselves. This chapter argues that lobbyists benefit from informational asymmetries that allow them to push corporations towards continued and expanding political engagement.

Certainly, others have observed that lobbyists shape the decision environment of their clients and bosses in ways that tend to be favorable to the lobbyists by taking advantage of information asymmetries.[1] Others have also observed that lobbyists are entrepreneurs who must communicate information to *both* politicians and clients.[2] The analysis here expands on these observations. First, I focus on the ways in which lobbyists use their position to *perpetuate lobbying*. Second, I focus on the ways that lobbyists push corporate political engagement towards *more particularistic and more competitive lobbying*.

This chapter will proceed as follows. First we will look at the structure of lobbying, and the different types of lobbyists, in-house vs. contract (outside).

We will then more closely investigate the principal-agent problem between corporate managers and their in-house lobbyists, and examine the ways in which in-house government affairs departments can push companies towards more lobbying. Then we will look more closely at how lobbyists communicate information about political developments. We will observe some of the challenges they face in making the case for political involvement. The same ambiguities and uncertainties that give them room to push for more lobbying can also make it difficult to show the value of lobbying. Then we will see how lobbyists work hard to educate corporate higher-ups about the value of lobbying, and how they focus on bottom-line and particularistic issues in demonstrating their internal value. Finally, we will narrow our attention specifically to the role of contract lobbyists.

In-house vs. Contract Lobbyists

Companies use two types of lobbyists: in-house lobbyists and contract (or outside) lobbyists. In-house lobbyists work only for one company. They are company employees. Contract lobbyists work for a Washington, DC lobbying firm and contract with different clients to provide lobbying services, typically working on a retainer fee that serves as a baseline of activity.

The most politically active companies all have their own in-house lobbyists, which form a "government affairs" team in the company. Typically, this government affairs department is based in one of the many office buildings in and around the K Street corridor in downtown Washington, DC. Sometimes, a company with a small government affairs team will have its lobbyists split time between corporate headquarters and Washington. Most companies with their own government affairs department gain additional representation by contracting with Washington lobbying firms. They do so because contracting with outside firms expands a company's lobbying reach by providing expanded access, policy expertise, and/or intelligence gathering and monitoring. Additional lobbyists also help with strategic planning.

The majority of companies that are active, however, rely only on contract lobbyists. For a company with a limited political objective, it often makes much more sense to contract with a Washington lobbying firm. That firm can essentially act as the company's in-house lobbyist, providing representation before Congress and helping the firm's managers understand and think about Washington. Hiring a firm on a contract basis gives a company flexibility. If an issue heats up, the company can increase the size of its contract, or even add additional lobbying firms. If an issue dies down, the company can decide to not renew its contract with the firm. As we will see in more detail at the end of this chapter, lobbying firms also vary. Some are very large, with sometimes more than 100 lobbyists and a similar number of clients. Others are very small, with only a few lobbyists and clients. There are even many sole-proprietor lobbyists.

Figures 7.1 and 7.2 show that the more committed a company is to politics, the more reliant the company will be on in-house lobbyists. As I do elsewhere in the book, I use 2007 data. Here are some key findings from Figure 7.1:

- Among companies spending at least $1 million on lobbying ("major" lobbying companies), 89 percent (284 out of 320) had both in-house lobbyists and outside lobbyists. Of the remaining 36, 34 relied only on contract lobbyists.
- Only 31 percent (212 of 695) of the companies spending between $25,000 and $1 million ("big" lobbying companies) had both types of lobbyists. By contrast, 61 percent (426 of 695) had only contract lobbyists. (The remaining 8 percent had both types of lobbyists.)
- Among the companies that spent the least, the vast majority relied only on outside lobbyists. I found that 94 percent of the "medium" companies

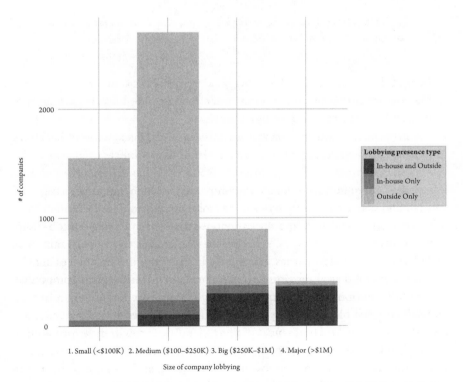

Figure 7.1. Type of lobbying presence, by company lobbying size, 2007. Source: LDA reports.

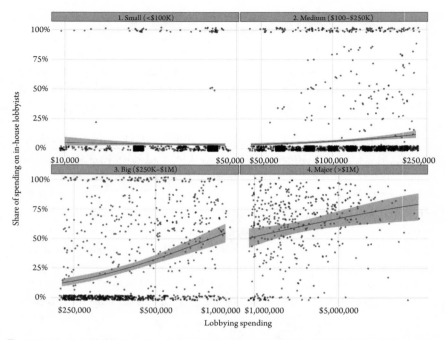

Figure 7.2 Total lobbying spending and share of spending on in-house lobbying, 2007. Source: Author calculations from LDA reports.

($100,000 to $250,000 in lobbying) and 96 percent of the "small" companies (under $100,000 in lobbying) only used outside lobbying firms, and did not have any in-house lobbyists.

- The rarest arrangement is having only in-house lobbyists. Only 140 of companies total—just 3 percent—have only in-house lobbyists.

We can better see how the balance of in-house vs. outside lobbying changes as companies get more involved by looking closely at Figure 7.2. Each dot represents a company. The darkness corresponds to the density of observations. The lines are fitted smoothing lines. What we see is that while there is a fair amount of variation in how companies balance their lobbying, the balance shifts towards more in-house lobbying as companies spend more. The companies spending $1 million and up spend (on average) half of their lobbying in-house, and half through contract lobbying firms. On average, the companies that do the most lobbying tend to do most of their spending through their own lobbyists. This makes some sense, since companies that spend the most are most committed to politics, and can benefit from economies of scale in having a large government relations staff. However, even the largest companies have reasons to go beyond their in-house capacity. We will spend some time discussing why this is the case later in this chapter, and what this tells us about modern corporate lobbying.

Principal-agent Theory and the Lobbying Information Asymmetry

Principal-agent theory provides a helpful analytic framework to understand the relationship of the government affairs department to corporate management. The world is full of principal-agent relationships once you start looking for them. For example, every time you hire a car mechanic or an accountant or a doctor, you (the principal) are hiring an agent (the mechanic/accountant/doctor). These relationships tend to be characterized by the fact that you (the principal) are relying on the agent's expertise. And the agent wants you to pay large sums of money for her labor. You (not being the expert) have a hard time evaluating whether the agent's work is worth her requested fee. Say you know little about cars. Your car makes a strange noise. You take it to the mechanic. Your mechanic tells you he has to order a special part that is difficult to install, and it will be $500 for parts and labor. Who are you to judge?

Much work in economics describes and sometimes tries to solve the manifold mismatches in knowledge and incentives between principals and agents, often focusing on the problem of workplace contracts. In general, in the timeless struggle between employees and employers, employers are at an advantage when the job is technically simple, which makes it relatively easy to both observe and evaluate the work effort and its connection to output. Managers can set the terms of employment and effectively dole out punishments and rewards. On the other hand, when a task is highly specialized, and it is difficult for a non-specialist (say, a generalist manager) to effectively evaluate the work effort and its connection to the output, the employees (agents) are in a better position to dictate the conditions of their employment.[3] The canonical principal-agent model is built around six basic assumptions.[4] Of these, the first three—"Agent impact," "Information asymmetry," and "Asymmetry in Preferences"—are most relevant here.[5]

The first and third assumptions are rather straightforward as applied to lobbying, so we need only discuss them briefly. The first assumption, "Agent impact," states simply that "the principal relies on the agent to accomplish a task that will benefit the principal." In our case, a profit-maximizing company hires a lobbyist because it wants to bring about and/or prevent changes to public policy as so to improve the company's bottom line.

The third assumption is that there is "an *asymmetry in preferences*." The lobbying preference asymmetry is that lobbyists (agents) want to earn more money and have more stability in their jobs. Corporations (principals) want to keep their costs down. So the basic tension involves lobbyists asking for more money and more resources, and corporate managers wanting to spend as little as possible without sacrificing results. In interviews, for example, several lobbyists explained that management viewed them as a "cost center"—that is, they were a line in a budget.

Lobbyists' ability to pull corporations into more lobbying comes from the second assumption of the canonical principal-agent model: *"there is an information asymmetry."* This lobbying information asymmetry springs from five primary factors:

1. Political developments are ambiguous and unpredictable;
2. Corporate managers are not particularly savvy about politics;
3. Managers are far away;
4. Lobbying is tactically varied; and
5. Much lobbying is done in coalitions.

We will discuss each of these five factors in more detail in the pages to come. As we will see, these information asymmetries can cut both ways. While these asymmetries can help lobbyists to make the case for more lobbying regardless of the actual political circumstances, the difficulty managers have in observing what lobbyists do can also make managers altogether skeptical of why they should even spend money on lobbying in the first place. This can put pressure on lobbyists to look for, clarify, and discover the bottom-line benefits of political engagement—the more particularistic, the better. Lobbyists want to be able to claim credit for their efforts. It is easiest to claim credit for outcomes that only affect one company.

Political developments are ambiguous and unpredictable

Like the practitioners of the ancient art of extispicy (in which animal entrails were used as signs of future events), Washington "experts" fill newspapers and television programs, peddling their analysis as to what will happen next and why, often based on nothing more than a desire to be provocative. A wide variety of predictions often emerge out of the same raw material. There are many ways to spin the same basic set of facts. In politics, ambiguity and uncertainty are everywhere.[6] Lobbyists must pick and choose what to send to their busy corporate bosses, who presumably only want to have to read through a few highlights from the endless fire hose of political news. This gives them the ability to pick and choose only those developments that either make them look good or make the case for more spending on lobbying.

Of course, the ambiguity and unpredictability of politics can cut both ways. "The hardest part is trying to communicate the completely unpredictable nature of DC," noted one contract lobbyist. "Clients are more comfortable with precise results. It's hard trying to explain why you didn't get something done, because the chairman of the committee was mad at somebody for something unrelated."

But while lobbyists are prone to complain about the difficulties of their work, these ambiguities and unpredictabilities do provide ample opportunities for lobbyists to pick and choose the facts and narratives that they report to the companies, shading the pictures they paint in ways that make them look as good as possible, and making politics seem as important to the companies as it possibly can.

Corporate managers are not particularly savvy about politics

If corporate managers were careful observers of politics with intimate knowledge of Washington, there would be less opportunity for lobbyists to take advantage of any potential information asymmetry. But most corporate managers pay much closer attention to their company and their industry than they do to politics.

While most managers may read the news and have a rudimentary sense of what is going on in Washington, it is not surprising that they would maintain a level of "rational ignorance"[7] about politics. The work of a corporate manager is a demanding job. Few can spend their day culling through the endless haystack of inside-the-Beltway rumors and gossip to find the occasional needle of an actionable item. Managers hire lobbyists to do this. As one survey of Fortune 100 companies found, "Most senior managers are *woefully ignorant* about the workings of government."[8] The survey quotes one consultant who said, "If there is a group of people in America who don't really understand the political system, it is corporate executives."[9] Of course, most Americans have at best a rudimentary grasp of politics,[10] so perhaps it shouldn't be such a surprise that corporate executives tend to know little about politics.

Even at some of the largest and most politically engaged companies, lobbyists I interviewed reported a substantial disconnect between Washington and corporate headquarters. Part of that disconnect is cultural. In interviews, lobbyists frequently described themselves as translators and interpreters.

- "What lobbyists spend a lot of time doing is there's sort of a government speak and the way people talk in Washington and we translate that to business, and there's a business talk and we translate that to the Congress."
- "I always described my job more as interpreter than anything, I interpret Washington for Wall Street and Wall Street for Washington. It's a lot of an education process of misperceptions . . . they tend to talk over each other."

- "We use a chart with Washington culture points, and [company] culture points. When you go into meeting at [company], you talk about first, what is the problem, what is the proposed solution, and then the reasons for the approach, and then, at the end, if there's time, you talk about personal things, like how are you doing, how are your kids? In DC, you start with how are you doing, how are your kids, business is going well, we employ this many people, and then at the end of the meeting you make the ask. It's a real challenge—this is a business where they report numbers quarterly, and there is immense pressure on them to deliver on a quarterly basis, whereas our strategies stretch out over course of a Congress or several."

The role of the translator is a powerful one. Lobbyists sit at the intersection of two worlds, and have the ability to translate between them. As a means of influencing Congress, this allows them to play the role of expert on a particular industry or set of business issues for a congressional office. As a means of influencing the decisions of corporations about how much to spend on politics, what issues to care about, and what positions to take, they are in an even more influential position. After all, while a congressional office can hear from multiple lobbyists representing different viewpoints, corporate managers have only one government affairs team to translate the developments of Washington for the consumption of busy managers.

Corporate managers, especially those at publicly traded corporations oriented around quarterly earnings reports, are results-oriented and impatient. They often don't intuitively understand the loose-jointed, hurry-up-and-wait nature of the policy process. Two more quotes from lobbyists further elaborate on this point:

- "There are people within the business who want to get something done and they'll come forward and say 'let's just have a congressional resolution'."
- "Sometimes executives and headquarters people don't understand that it could take years and years to get something done and getting a bill through committee is a huge victory for us, but it doesn't get them cheering . . ."

This mismatch between the slowness of government and the demands of quarterly earnings can make it difficult for lobbyists to prove their worth. I will have more to say about that later in this chapter.

Managers are far away

Few corporate headquarters are in Washington, which makes it difficult for managers to observe what lobbyists and government affairs offices are doing with their time. While lobbyists do send regular reports and make the rounds in corporate headquarters from time to time, they work remotely, which makes it impossible for managers to really know what they are doing. This means an enterprising lobbyist can find plenty of ways to overstate her role as a key player, a mover and shaker with privileged access. As one lobbyist put it, "The joke in this town is that you have these breakfasts with 100 people there and [then Ways and Means Committee] Chairman Rangel speaking, and then in the hall you have 20 people on the phone saying they just had a conversation with Chairman Rangel."

For this reason, the corporate lobbying advice book *Winning the Influence Game* warns corporate managers to beware of lobbying consultants reporting on a steady stream of conversations with politicos: "Do not let consultants cite meetings with decision makers as a measure of their effectiveness. When hiring consultants, press them for examples of situations in which they have had a measurable impact."[11]

Again, this can cut both ways. As one in-house lobbyist noted: "We are physically isolated, so we don't see people in the elevator or the parking lot where you might engage in chit-chat, so we have to be proactive in reaching out . . . making sure they know who we are. In many ways we are like a salesperson. We have to be seen as proactive and visible and be on their radar screen and educating them about the value that we add."

Still, all else being equal, distance probably gives lobbyists more flexibility and freedom and more ability to overstate what it is they're doing and how much time it takes them to do it. While managers do sometimes come to town or talk to politicians directly, they mostly leave it to their lobbyists, who are, after all, much more deeply steeped in the cultural mores of Washington.

Lobbying is tactically varied

As Chapter 4 demonstrated, lobbying is far more of an art than a science. The proper lobbying strategy on any issue is highly subjective, and what works in one case may not work in another. The potential diversity of tactics gives lobbyists the opportunity to argue that there are many more things a company could be doing, if only it was willing to spend the money. Lobbyists can point to a broad toolkit of possible advocacy tactics and strategies, some of which can be quite expensive. Lobbyists have every reason to want companies to go beyond the basic approach of contacting congressional offices and mostly working with allies (what I called the "bronze" strategy in Chapter 4) to purchase the "platinum" strategy—aggressively shaping the intellectual environment, building large coalitions, going after opponents as well as supporters, and expanding to the executive branch.

If lobbying were cookie-cutter and straightforward, it would be easy for managers to evaluate what lobbyists do, and what is necessary for success. But the tactical diversity of lobbying makes it difficult for managers to determine what the right mix of strategies is on any given issue. Even lobbyists will often disagree. Certainly, managers are perfectly capable of judging lobbying campaigns by their success or failure. But the larger constellation of informational asymmetries gives lobbyists many ways to explain away failures. Lobbyists can also spin events to make it look like they came very close, and that if only the company does more next time around, it might get the policy outcome it wants.

Most importantly, it is a lobbyist's job to advise on political strategy. They have every reason to recommend companies do as much as possible. It means both more money for them and a greater chance that they will deliver a result that will make their clients happy.

Much lobbying is done in groups

Finally, a substantial amount lobbying occurs as part of larger coalitions.[12] In Chapter 5, I showed how trade associations play an active role in organizing industry lobbying efforts. A persistent issue in principal-agent theory is that when work is produced jointly, it is often difficult to determine what contribution any one member of the team has made.[13] This gives agents more flexibility to both claim credit and deflect blame. This issue came up repeatedly in interviews. As one lobbyist (unhappy that others had claimed credit for work he had done) noted, "Success has a thousand fathers." Here are two other similar observations from lobbyists:

- "Some people . . . report on big battles that a lot of people are working on, so like the Internet tax bill, or the R&D tax credit, they are determined by large forces. You just feed back to people, here's what's happening in Washington, and that's what a lot of people do. It's very easy if you can get away with it."
- "With so much of work . . . so many people are working on it. It's a challenge sometimes to apportion credit or blame on any issue. Most of it is perception."

If something good happens, lobbyists can tell corporate headquarters how instrumental they were in making that happen. If something bad happens, lobbyists can tell corporate headquarters how hard they worked, but how there were other, bigger factors at play. Again, they might choose to emphasize how close they came, and how if only the company would do more lobbying next year, they might have a real shot. Lobbyists are always trying to communicate the "unpredictable nature" of Washington (as one lobbyist put it). The more successful they are at communicating this perspective, the more autonomy they can buy themselves.

And again, this cuts both ways. If politics is seen as too unpredictable, companies might not bother. It has to be just unpredictable enough. Moreover, because there are so many different actors on many issues, lobbyists can sometimes struggle to distinguish their unique contributions to public policy outcomes. For this reason, again, lobbyists have incentives to find particularistic policy outcomes that can be traced directly to their effort. But, still, the coalitional aspect of much lobbying does allow flexibility in claiming more credit (and deflecting more blame) than perhaps they deserve.

Taken together, these five factors—the ambiguities of politics, combined with the relative political ignorance of most managers, plus the distance of managers from Washington, plus the tactical diversity of lobbying, plus the widespread nature of group lobbying—all give lobbyists an informational advantage. These factors make it hard for managers to know exactly what their lobbyists are up to, and how exactly to make sense of what is going on in Washington. It us up to the lobbyists to communicate all of this. So then, let us now turn to the communication aspect of lobbying.

The Mechanisms of Communication

Providing information and analysis to corporate headquarters is a central part of a lobbyist's job. While there is often a tendency to focus on how lobbyists influence congressional understandings of policy, equally important are the ways in which lobbyists influence corporate managers. Both, presumably, require a similar set of persuasion skills. So it makes sense that if lobbyists are good at influencing public policy, they might also be good at influencing how corporations see public policy.

The basic idea is that since lobbyists are hired by companies to advise them on politics, lobbyists do exactly that. As Rogan Kersh writes (drawing on interviews with contract lobbyists), "Whatever policy knowledge . . . clients do have is obtained largely from their lobbyists themselves through memos, e-mail exchanges, and telephone conversations."[14] Kersh goes on to quote a company executive who claimed to be "essentially blind here without [my lobbyist]. You could say that she is my eyes, ears, and other senses here in the capital." When Kersh asked corporate clients for their top priorities in Washington, he reported that they generally responded with some version of "Whatever our firm's lobbyists say they are."[15] Kersh also reported that lobbyists spent 30 percent of their time explaining issues to clients ("a duty that involves much *creating* of preferences and interests"), and an additional 13 percent of their time preparing their clients for their occasional Washington visits—as compared to only five percent of the time taking directions from clients. He also found that lobbyists were "wholly or primarily responsible" for identifying 74 percent of specific client policy interests.[16] Similarly, lobbyist Nicholas Allard writes that: "Lobbyists play a critical 'intermediating role' by enabling people and businesses to understand how government works and what government is working on, and then helping these people and businesses identify and communicate their interests to the government in an effective manner."[17]

Lobbyists typically send back regular reports and often make regular visits to corporate headquarters to provide updates. In interviews, lobbyists described a range in the frequency with which they report.

Out of the 31 in-house lobbyists I interviewed, five claimed to be in touch with corporate managers on a daily basis. One bragged: "I'll probably talk to [the CEO] a couple of times a day. I'll be in 15 minutes of a management call. Government affairs is very involved in the day-to-day management of the company. Not that I am making decisions on our HR policy, but I understand all the issues they're dealing with, what manufacturing and marketing people are dealing with, regulatory affairs, and I have a voice in decisions. I say, this may not be a good time to do such and such because of policy changes. I certainly have the ear of the chairman."

The amount of CEO interest also varies. Said one experienced lobbyist: "If you have a CEO, and I've had several who are very active in Washington, who wants to be engaged in the public policy debate, there's a lot more to do . . . Then there are those CEOs who periodically come but it's not high on their agenda."

In general, the larger the company, the more layers there are between government affairs and senior leadership. As one lobbyist for a large company said, "Large companies can be very bureaucratic. They just don't know that they are."

Two thirds (20 of 31) of the in-house lobbyists said that they generally communicate on a weekly basis. Five report on a monthly basis. Generally, lobbyists' regular memos and communications are designed to give corporate managers the lay of the land: what the lobbyists have been up to, what the company should be attending to, etc.:

- "Our way of communicating is a weekly report, and it goes to the top brass and it's widely distributed throughout the company. It says, here's what we're up to. It also alerts people to various issues. We rely on people in the company to read this thing . . . We also get e-mails all the time: "I read this article and I need more information on x.""

- "What we've done is keep a pretty close eye on the issues, and send monthly updates to higher level people, let them know what we're doing: "We're having a hearing we plan to attend, we've done meetings and issues on this." When something passes that's good for us, we let people know about it, and when something looking bad for us we let people know about it.""

Since lobbyists get to curate the information, what they choose to include and exclude is important. In interviews, lobbyists commonly discussed the importance of "managing expectations." This was particularly important to for-hire lobbyists, who much more commonly work with companies with limited political experience who hire them to be their Washington office. The below quotes all come from contract lobbyists, but they do speak to the broader issue of lobbyist autonomy.

- "You *manage expectations*, and a cliché we often use is, it's a marathon and not a sprint. . . . The way our practice works is we are very good at making sure people have realistic expectations. . . . Sometimes you get skeptical people, but usually by the time you are talking to them about an engagement you've either brought them into the notion or they are willing to take a risk."
- "How do you establish that you made the difference? You have to have close communication with your clients and engage them in the lobbying process . . . It's all about *managing expectations*; deciding what the metrics are; helping them appreciate threats and opportunities. You need to think, what would be appropriate benchmarks? You need concrete things to evaluate every six months. You need to stay in close touch."
- "We *manage our expectations*. We're all professionals in this office. Everybody has had a long career in government and Washington, and I think we know what to expect. We don't oversell, and we never right out front sell any kind of results. We sell our expertise in the process . . . You can never, in my view, promise results. A lot of it is outside your control."

In-house lobbyists discussed the ability to set their own goals and select their own priorities, which is essentially a form of expectations management. While several lobbyists complained about managers at corporate headquarters making politically ignorant requests and/or responding to news stories with the occasional (though usually misplaced) panic, these kinds of events seemed more like a nuisance than an ongoing problem. Mostly, lobbyists felt that they had adequate license to operate, within reasonable expectations.

- "There's a comfortable amount of deference given to us. I think we certainly run things through the board. So if wanted to hire a new person, that would be significant action to get their approval. But basically we're on the ground, so we see everything happening, and then we let them know what's going on. We set our priorities, but we run those priorities by them so they're familiar with them."

- "We have a strategic plan, and you are evaluated on that, but you get to help determine what the goals are . . . And this is pretty typical of companies our size now."
- "We have our own budget and some latitude. [name omitted] heads the office, and he's a former cabinet secretary so he has very good access, and he's very well regarded, so that has helped."
- "[We] play a major role in determining what we're going to work on."

Across companies, the basic pattern is that government affairs departments propose and set priorities, contingent on management and/or board approval. While there is some variation in how this works, not a single lobbyist complained about a lack of autonomy, though several complained about not having the budget they would have liked.

The Lobbyists' Challenges

In general, the information asymmetries we've discussed help lobbyists advocate internally for bigger lobbying budgets. But these asymmetries can also make it difficult for lobbyists to clearly demonstrate the bottom-line value of lobbying. Just over half (16) of the 31 in-house company lobbyists I interviewed described serious pressure to prove to managers that the lobbying they do is worth the cost. Here are some representative quotes:

- "We're overhead, right? We're not selling things. We're a cost center. They're [management] always eager to get a sense of the return on investment."
- "You have to justify yourself. On a daily basis we have to point to something that benefited the company in a way you can quantify."
- "The metric objective is tough. In a traditional corporate sense, you can't show X number of dollars brought in or X number of costs saved."
- "We are constantly justifying our existence to the board and the shareholders."

In interviews, lobbyists described three main challenges in demonstrating value. The following section will take us through each of these problems. It will also walk us through the solutions that lobbyists use to overcome these problems. As we will see, these solutions make lobbying more aggressive, more long-term, and more particularistic. It is under these three conditions that lobbyists get the most revenue from lobbying. So they have every incentive to steer lobbying in this direction. Here are the three problem-solution pairings:

Problem 1: Much lobbying involves being there to stop things from happening.
Solution 1: Lobbyists seek out issues to demonstrate bottom-line benefits.
Problem 2: Lobbying is a slow process.
Solution 2: Lobbyists educate companies to see it as a long-term benefit
Problem 3: "Why not just leave it to the trade associations?"
Solution 3: Lobbyists show what companies have at stake *differentially*.

Problem 1: Much lobbying involves being there to stop things from happening.

Probably the most difficult challenge for lobbyists in justifying the value of lobbying is that by nature, a lot of lobbying involves simply monitoring developments and keeping certain issues off the agenda. It involves just being there to make sure that proposals that would harm corporate profits are squashed before they ever even make it to a committee hearing or get floated in a *Politico* op-ed. As we saw in Chapter 4, the top reason why lobbyists said their companies were politically active was "to protect against changes in government policy." However, in interviews, lobbyists commonly lamented the difficulty in quantifying the work they do into preventing things from ever happening in the first place.

- "It is hard to translate what you do into profitability for the company. But a lot of what you do is preventative so you never see the benefits in terms of something happening."
- "A lot of what we do, too, is risk mitigation and that's difficult to quantify."
- "I'm keeping a major asset of the company in good shape, and making sure the Department of Commerce has no concerns about what's going on, that people are happy, and that we're in a good trusted partnership."

Showing what you've kept off the agenda is a difficult problem because it involves counterfactual reasoning: "If only we hadn't been there, x would have happened!" This, of course, is impossible to prove. But in interviews, lobbyists frequently used the example of Microsoft as the constant reminder of why companies need to hire lobbyists. Microsoft, many lobbyists argued, got slammed with an antitrust lawsuit because it didn't take Washington seriously. The implication is that if the software giant had hired lobbyists, the

Department of Justice would have left Microsoft alone. By extension, companies that ignore Washington will find that bad things happen to them. Ergo, they need to maintain a lobbying presence.

Solution 1: Lobbyists seek out issues to demonstrate bottom-line benefits.

All in-house company lobbyists I interviewed said that they were able to furnish examples of how their presence in Washington contributed to the company's profits. Lobbyists representing companies in different industries had different strategies. Pharmaceutical lobbyists seemed to have it the easiest, given that Medicare and Medicaid reimbursements for specific drugs have multi-million, and in some cases multi-billion-dollar, impacts on the company. Here's what some of the pharmaceutical lobbyists said:

- "We informally try to be a profit center. We have a new product coming out in two years. For that product, the Medicare program pays for only three years of drug coverage. It's an anomaly in Medicare, so one of my tasks is to change the policy so these particular drugs are treated like all other drugs, so instead of three years of government paying for them, there will be indefinite payments. And we can quantify how much money that means."
- "If you're dealing with a Medicaid rebate, you can quantify the impact it will cost, $10 million more, $100 million more."
- "Medicare reimburses a significant portion of our products. I am making sure products are available, covered by Medicare, reimbursed by Medicare. I want to make certain I maximize coverage. To make certain they are reimbursed at the proper level, that's absolutely critical to [company]'s future."
- "Earlier this year CMS [Centers for Medicare and Medicaid Services] bundled our code for [drug omitted] with [competitor's drug omitted] as a blended reimbursement, so they're way underpaying for our drugs and way overpaying for [competitor's drug omitted]. We're trying to fix it so the government can save money. It's actually a saver. It's a drug that costs about 10 cents, government is paying like a buck ten for it."

Decisions on patent exclusivity also have clear bottom-line issues for drug makers. A lobbyist for a generic drug manufacturer, for example, was able to point to not one but two 9-figure policy decisions: "We would argue that for example, by keeping substitution open for [drug omitted] 10 years ago, that made $100 million for company, and that probably paid for government affairs alone, and we're still working off of that. Or when we made sure it was clear that our 180 days of exclusivity for having a generic for [drug omitted] did not run at the same time as [competitor's drug omitted] pediatric exclusivity. That was another $100 million there."

Companies that sell directly to the government can also very easily quantify the value of having a Washington lobbyist to help make the sale:

- "When I was at [pharmaceutical company omitted] we had some very targeted focused things we could point to and say that means X dollars. We had a drug, and we knew when the government bought it, it had an impact on the company. So I could say, I went into HHS today, we got the appropriation for [drug], we signed the contracts, here's the impact."
- "You start producing meetings with people related to federal procurement, you start producing opportunities for the company to get greater visibility, and if [managers] see that coming, they say 'I understand it, I like it.'"

Other lobbyists pointed to tax legislation. The R&D tax credit renewal was a lingering issue at the time of interviews (as it perpetually is in Washington), and many companies had much at stake in its future. Trade deals were also of interest to companies that sold abroad, since expanding markets mean more profits. One lobbyist explained it this way: "Tax bills are more easily quantifiable, because we can actually run the numbers. With trade we can look at market opportunities, tariffs, and the like."

Retail chains were particularly interested in trade issues. For them, lower tariffs meant they could buy goods more cheaply. One retail lobbyist for a major retail chain said, "We can say, here is a piece of trade legislation worth $100 million for the cost of goods."

A lobbyist for a major retail chain described one particular narrow benefit he was able to win for his company: "Several years ago, I found an opportunity through reduction in the tariff on ceiling fans. Even though there were no domestic manufacturers of ceiling fans, there was still a legacy tariff of 4.7 percent. We went to Congress and said, since there are no domestic manufacturers, there should be no tariff. It took a lot of time and a lot of effort but that tariff was removed." The lobbyist later in the interview said, "the ceiling fan provision equates to this office operating for 10 years." (this ceiling fan tariff termination, by the way, was a provision in the aforementioned American Jobs Creation Act of 2004). This lobbyist also boasted that he had also successfully lobbied to allow the company to open a store on Native American tribal land. "That's a $40 million store, and the store would not be there if not for legislation."

As we saw in Chapter 4, taxes tend to be one of the most important issues for the largest companies. Roughly 10 percent of their lobbying budget goes to this single issue. Trade policy is also consistently important. However, as I argued in Chapter 6, corporate managers might have generalized interests in lower taxes or less regulation, but turning these into specific "benefits" often requires lobbyists. In interviews, lobbyists frequently talk about the time that they spend working with corporate managers to identify these "benefits."

- "Half of my job is internal lobbying, letting the internal clients know we're here, that we have a Washington office . . . It's telling our tech guys that there's money here, helping us to identify particular needs so we can identify champions and construct programs, meet some agency need, see if we might have answers. It's an iterative process that goes back and forth . . . For example, the Department of Defense needs light-weight batteries. We have a thin film that could reduce weight. We could get a contract to do that."
- "We constantly are advocating for ourselves. Government relations for us is all about our internal stakeholders. If our tax or HR or finance department comes to us and says this is a huge hit for company we then take that and turn it to government relations. We're constantly making people aware that there is a government relations office and we can help."
- "[Company omitted] has a DC office that's consistently been shown to add value. But when they started, [management] thought government relations did something else. They thought it was to manage public relations crises, hearing inquiries . . . My boss told me, you've taught us to do things we didn't know could ever be done."

Of course, when all else fails, a looming congressional investigation can always provide a good reminder to any company doubting the importance of a Washington office. At the time of interviews, Sen. Chuck Grassley (R-IA) was conducting investigations into whether pharmaceutical executives were intimidating medical researchers.[18] One lobbyist noted: "When you have Grassley call in 15 CEOs, they get it. They fully understand why you have to be in politics."

It is worth noting that a growing number of studies do find that lobbying is, on average, good investment. Recent published studies find that:

- The more firms lobby, the lower their effective tax rate.[19]
- Compared to non-lobbying firms, companies that lobby are substantially less likely to be detected for fraud, and even when they are detected for fraud, the fraud detection comes later (117 days, on average).[20]
- Stock markets reward companies with politically connected board members when the party they are connected to is in power.[21]
- "Lobbying also has a positive effect on the firm's equity returns relative to the market and, to a lesser degree, relative to its industry."[22]

In 2011, an investment research firm called Strategas created a rolling index of the 50 firms that lobbied most intensely—that is, that spent the most on lobbying as a percentage of assets—and compared those firms to the entire S&P 500. Since 2002, this index of firms outperformed the S&P 500 index by 11 percent annually.[23]

Problem 2: Lobbying is a slow process.

One key difference between the corporate boardrooms and the halls of government institutions is that in Washington, things happen at a much slower pace. This is not always easy for results-oriented corporate executives to understand, and it can present an obstacle for lobbyists who recognize that effective lobbying requires a long-term approach.

This is perhaps most difficult for contract lobbyists, who represent companies who often have very little understanding of how Washington works. Said one: "Clients can get discouraged. You need to keep them going. It takes much longer than they think. Clients who don't know Washington require more hand-holding. You need to say over and over: I told you this is what happens."

In-house lobbyists struggled with this as well. Part of it, as we discussed already, is cultural. Businesses work on a quarterly earnings schedule. Government works on a much slower time-frame. Ideas and policies sometimes need to circulate for years before they gain the necessary momentum. Here's what some lobbyists had to say:

- "I don't know we could show the bottom line on biologics [a type of drug]. We recognize the industry is changing and sometimes you have to do things now to make a difference in the company 10 years from now. But every year it doesn't happen is several years that our company and consumers won't have the ability to take advantage of lower-cost products."
- "You need people who have been here for a long time who have been involved in government in some way or another or are astute enough to understand that the founding fathers set up a very slow process."
- "I think the slowness of the solutions is a headache, to come back [to headquarters] and say, 'I've been to Washington, this is what I worked, on this is where I'm going.' Sometimes change is so incrementally small, or the commitments are great but getting things done takes so much time. I'm amazed that I've become pleased that someone will write a letter or hold a meeting. When I first went I just wanted change, and that goes back in the learning column. It's slow, and sometimes the things you ask for are real, small incremental steps to getting where you really want."

Solution 2: Lobbyists educate companies to see it as a long-term benefit.

The policy process is indeed full of twists and turns. Without a long-term view, managers can easily get discouraged. For this reason, lobbyists expend substantial resources educating managers to be patient, to view lobbying as a long-term investment. As we've already discussed, lobbying is most effective when companies have long-standing relationships with members of Congress. But lobbyists must educate companies to value politics as a long-term investment.

In interviews, I found a split among in-house lobbyists. Roughly half (15) reported still needing to educate company executives about the value of a Washington office; the other half (16) reported that managers at the company were adequately convinced of the importance of a Washington office.

In interviews, lobbyists talked about their constant efforts at internal company outreach—getting to know lots of different people in the company, making sure that they all know that the company has a government relations department.

- "I do a lot of work to educate higher-ups. My purpose is to communicate what we are doing, so the dots are being put together and they get why we're doing this."
- "It's a constant process just building and cultivating relationships within the firm, and making sure a dialogue is going on. It's kind of making phone calls, e-mails—we don't want something to happen and people in the firm to say you didn't tell me, so we send a lot of e-mails and memos."
- "An interesting challenge is educating [other people in the company] that we're here. Some think it's really cool that we exist. Others ask us why we even need one [lobbyist]. We explain what we do and they say, 'why would any company not have one?' Some people who understand what we do use us a lot, and others don't even know we exist . . . it's a constant battle to prove your value to people within the company."

Such a process helps managers to get more familiar with political involvement, and to start paying attention to politics generally. It also helps the individual lobbyists to get to know the company better and to find opportunities to highlight issues that would be of interest to managers. Even some lobbyists at companies where managers generally seem to get the value of a Washington office say that they continue to do internal outreach.

- "Fortunately, the right people who make decisions are very aware of the value we deliver, but it's an ongoing process, we're always looking for opportunities to let people know that we're here and we're able to help."

- "I think some people get it, but different people have different perceptions of government affairs, so they require a tiny bit of education as to how the group functions and why it's beneficial, but it doesn't take a whole lot to realize."

Over time, though, lobbyists report that these conversations make a difference. After all, one of the key qualities of an effective lobbyist is being a good persuader. If lobbyists are hired because they are good at persuading government decision-makers, we should also expect them to be good at persuading corporate decision-makers. Indeed, lobbyists who have been around a while generally report that they have been effective at internal persuasion:

- "People reach out to me now, and I used to always have to reach out to them, but by having been here a while and shown the value of using what I do in different ways internally, I get calls as a resource and as an advocate and as a political officer and as a trade association liaison. So, I think we've kind of broadened what government affairs can do; how it can add value. More people appreciate what we can do, and we've increased what we've done."
- "The longer we are here, the easier it is. Our challenge is that so many people are so busy just doing their job that they kind of do their job with their head down. They do what they need to do. They get their job done, but they don't always see what's around them and affecting their environment. It's easy for people to overlook us, which is why we have to be so vocal, we have to be proactive in educating. I could sit here when Congress is out of session and have a six-hour day, but that's not helping me advance my profile in the company. We all want to add the value we know we can add."

Lobbyists play an important role making managers aware of the value of lobbying. The combination of clear, traceable bottom-line examples and ongoing educational efforts about the long-term value of lobbying helps managers to value political engagement.

Problem 3: "Why not just leave it to the trade associations?"

For a company to have its own lobbyists, managers must be convinced that there is some reason that the company has a unique interest that won't be covered by the trade association. Otherwise, why wouldn't they just free-ride on the lobbying efforts of the association and other companies in the industry? As one lobbyist put it, "The new CEO is wondering, 'Don't we get it all from trade associations?' My answer is there are times when want to be a voice in the choir, but you always want to be positioned to sing solo."

Solution 3: Lobbyists show what companies have at stake differentially.

Lobbyists often must not only convince corporate managers that they have something at stake politically, but also that they have something at stake *differentially* from other companies in the industry, and/or that what they have at stake is so important that they can't merely leave it to the trade association. Most lobbyists had at least one or two issues that they could point to that were specific to their companies. Here are a few examples:

- "One thing we will be working on is that we make what is going to be our most profitable vaccine . . . it's been extremely effective on market for 8 years, and it's coming out with a second generation for the developing world and for adults. What we have worked on as a company and an industry is an advanced marketing agreement where entities like the Gates Foundation partner with NGOs to purchase and distribute vaccines to developing countries, and a provision in tax law allows corporations to have charitable contributions for up to 10 percent of their income. But the quantities of this stuff are so great that we would quickly exceed that. There are exceptions to that for food, computers, and special categories for obvious reasons. This is a vaccine that is so important that it may also merit that kind of treatment. *That's something very specialized to us.*"
- "Pensions are an important issue for us, and every company's pension is different. *We can't do it in a group,* everyone has to be working on their own."
- "Say, for example, the R&D tax credit. We are a company that was very much benefited by the old 20 percent credit.. We didn't have a big research budget in the early to mid Eighties when that credit was first enacted. But we had a very linear increase in research budget and really liked that old credit. But as an economy, we've changed over last 15 years, and more and more companies were not benefiting from the credit as much as they had been. They sold off divisions, research went down . . . and there was growing philosophical objection to the 20 percent credit. People just didn't believe that it really was promoting additional research. So we worked to preserve that credit for as long as possible, even though, quite honestly, as a matter of tax policy, it became harder to defend. As of last session, Baucus put a bill on table that would have eliminated the old credit, and *we've worked hard to make sure there is significant transition relief for our company.*"

Lobbyists have clear incentives to shade towards particularism in the information and narratives they share with corporate managers. If the company has nothing at stake that affects it differentially than other companies in the industry, there is less reason for it to be involved politically. But if there are changes to policy that would affect the company uniquely, that means more work (and more resources) for in-house company lobbyists. It is clear from my interviews that lobbyists can make a case why their companies have unique needs in Washington. Moreover, as we saw in Chapter 5, corporate lobbying budgets are increasing faster than trade association budgets, which is also consistent with the story of growing particularism, which also shows up in other historical accounts of lobbying.[24]

The Role of Contract Lobbyists

The discussion has so far focused largely on the relationship of in-house corporate lobbyists to the companies they represent. However, a substantial number of Washington lobbyists work for lobbying firms, which represent multiple clients, including many small companies. Their incentives and operations are slightly different, so it's worth spending some additional time understanding how they contribute to the growth of lobbying.

A little descriptive data will be helpful to get the lay of the land. In 2007, 1,820 different lobbying firms represented clients in Washington. Of these, 840 (46.2 percent) appear to be single-proprietor firms (in that they had only one registered lobbyist), and 1,357 (74.6 percent) had three or fewer registered lobbyists. The top 20 firms, which account for barely 1 percent of all lobbying firms, took in 25 percent of the reported lobbying revenue, and the top 40 firms took in 41 percent of the revenue. Of the 1,820 lobbying firms, 505 (27.8 percent) reported representing a single client, and just more than half (923, or 50.7 percent) represented three or fewer clients.

Table 7.1 lists the top 20 firms, as ranked by revenue, in 2007. Even in the top 20, there is some notable variation. For example, the PMA Group (now defunct after a federal investigation into whether it wielded inappropriate influence through its close connections with former Rep. John Murtha [D-PA]) specialized heavily in defense lobbying, focusing most heavily on corporate clients. Ernst & Young, not surprisingly, specialized in taxes. Others devoted significant resources to the appropriations process, while others had a more diverse issue base. Some are lobbying firms that are connected with law firms. Others are pure lobbying firms.

We can also observe the population of lobbying firms over time (Figure 7.3). Here, I break down lobbying firms into three sizes, based on annual revenue. As with individual companies, we see a steady increase in the number of lobbying firms of all sizes over time. In 2008, the smallest firms were the first to start declining, then the medium-sized firms. The population of firms with more

Table 7.1. **Top 20 lobbying firms in 2007, as ranked by revenue**

Firm	Lobby revenue (MM)	Clients	Industries	Lobbyists
Patton Boggs LLP	$42.3	398	63	145
Akin, Gump et al.	$32.1	202	59	78
Van Scoyoc Assoc	$25.2	282	45	58
Cassidy & Assoc	$24.5	145	42	48
Barbour, Griffith & Rogers	$22.3	109	45	20
Ogilvy Government Relations	$22.2	105	49	17
Dutko Worldwide	$22.1	245	54	65
Hogan & Hartson	$18.7	197	56	64
Quinn Gillespie & Assoc	$18	73	35	24
PMA Group	$16.5	139	29	39
Williams & Jensen	$16.3	125	43	31
Holland & Knight	$16	196	46	87
K&L Gates	$13.8	193	48	79
Ernst & Young	$13.8	71	37	24
Brownstein, Hyatt et al.	$13.1	90	39	30
DLA Piper	$12.9	99	44	61
Carmen Group	$12.7	89	34	37
Covington & Burling	$12.5	72	38	62
Ferguson Group	$11.2	150	30	36
Podesta Group	$11	80	38	26

Source: LDA reports.

than $1 million in revenue (adjusted for inflation) rises the most steadily, and declines the most gradually.

Perhaps the most salient takeaway is that between 1998 and 2009, the number of unique lobbying firms grew by 73 percent, from 1,204 to 2,080. However, that number fell to 1,797 in 2012. The biggest percentage increase was in the small firms (less than $100,000 in lobbying revenue), from 390 to 781 in 2009 (almost exactly doubling), though down to 678 in 2012. Medium firms ($100,000 to $1 million in revenue) grew from 641 in 1998 to 997 in 2010 (up 55 percent), down to 845 by 2012. The population of the largest lobbying firms, those doing over $1 million in lobbying, grew from 173 in 1998 to 326 in 2008 (up 88 percent), only to fall down to 274. The number of

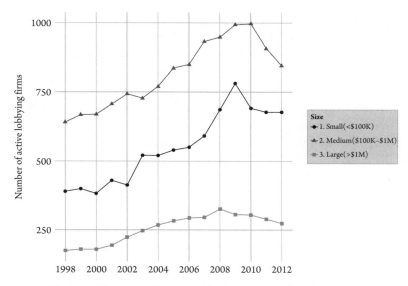

Figure 7.3 Number of contract lobbying firms by revenue, 1998–2012. Source: Author calculations from LDA reports.

individual registered lobbyists at these firms grew from 4,543 in 1998 to a high of 7,490 in 2008, falling down to 5,654 in 2012. Some of this decline, presumably, is because of individuals who de-registered in response to the Obama administration rules.

Lobbying is a competitive business. It represents at least several thousand individuals across almost 2,000 different lobbying firms, all of whose livelihoods depend on them retaining existing clients and/or acquiring new ones. Almost certainly, there are many more individuals employed (possibly twice as many) in similar capacities who have not registered.[25]

It is both misleading and instructive to bring up Jack Abramoff, the disgraced one-time contract lobbyist whose very public trial and later attempts at public redemption have perhaps made him Washington's most famous lobbyist. Abramoff built friendships with a few key members of Congress (most notably, then-Republican Majority Leader Tom Delay) through food and trips and tickets, dangled prospective jobs to staff, and urged his clients to contribute generously. He cultivated a reputation for connectedness by spending $1 million a year on sports skyboxes and famously instituted an all-members-of-Congress-eat-free policy at his upscale DC restaurant, Signatures. These appurtenances of influence allowed him to charge unsophisticated clients substantial sums of money. He went to prison for, in effect, defrauding four Indian tribes of $25 million. In one choice e-mail about the tribes, he wrote: "those moronic Tiguas . . . I'd love us to get our mitts on their moolah." In another e-mail, he wrote about his clients: "I think the key thing to remember with all these clients is that they are annoying, but the annoying losers are the only ones that have this kind of money and part with it so quickly." He openly talked of his ambition to make "a million a day."[26]

Abramoff's approach was more a throwback to the Gilded Age (when lobbyists commonly moved votes with food, drink, and the occasional prostitute) than a window into the machinations of modern lobbying. Several lobbyists brought up Abramoff in interviews to denounce him as not at all representative of the profession.

But Abramoff is instructive in one way. His case provides an insight (albeit, an exaggerated one) into the simple fact that lobbying is a business, and lobbyists are selling themselves as fixers. Abramoff cultivated a sense of his own importance and connectedness so that he could market that to clients. That he largely represented unsophisticated clients either tells us that more savvy clients could quickly see through his puffed-up self-creation of a super-lobbyist, or that he didn't even bother to sell his services to Washington-savvy clients in the first place.

One way to understand this salesmanship is to observe the copy that populates lobbying firms' websites. It tends to hit on three basic themes: that the firm's lobbyists are very well connected in Washington; that the firm has proven to deliver value for a range of clients; and that it is capable of conducting a comprehensive lobbying campaign. Here is a snapshot sampling of prose from the websites of top lobbying firms:

> **Van Scoyoc Associates:** "VSA's original specialties were appropriations and taxation, but the firm quickly developed practices in more than 20 different areas, ranging from agriculture to water resources . . . Such institutional capacity is necessary today, when Federal Government affairs are more complicated than ever. A successful government relations campaign often requires effort across a wide front and entails much more than shepherding a request through Congress."[27]
>
> **Ogilvy Government Relations:** "All of our partners have served in senior-level positions throughout the legislative and executive branches of the federal government. In addition many have played key roles in presidential and congressional campaigns. Our hands-on experience, coupled with a long-standing belief that intelligence, strategy and dedication can solve virtually any problem in Washington, enables us to successfully represent clients on a wide range of issues."[28]
>
> **Quinn Gillespie and Associates:** "QGA has a bipartisan team of roughly 20 seasoned government relations and public relations specialists. Our

team represents decades of experience in the legislative, political and communication arenas. With a roster that includes former senior White House and congressional staff, attorneys, journalists, TV producers and public relations executives, we are uniquely qualified to help clients navigate the intricacies of the legislative process, craft compelling narratives and deliver full-scale public affairs campaigns for the Washington, D.C., market and beyond. In addition to the rich experiences in policy and the private sector, our experts have a long track record of political engagement. Firm members take a continued, active role in government and political campaigns – from serving as members of steering committees, volunteers, advisors and strategists. This diversity of experience provides our team with a wider range of contacts and our clients a 360-degree view of policy issues."[29]

Lobbyists and lobbying firms are selling a product: themselves and their services. Like law partners, lobbyists tend to be compensated based on the clients that they bring in. Some for-hire lobbyists report that they find new clients by looking at what's happening in Washington and asking: who might need representation who doesn't have it already? What companies might be well-positioned to bid for a particular contract, or might qualify for a particular subsidy or tax break, if only they knew about the opportunity?

- "When we recruit companies we see what's happening. For example, we'll see what needs to be re-authorized, and keep track of what happens. August is a good month for client development. We send them letters, proposals. Sometimes we use connections, other times we just send them out cold."
- "Since we know what the government is looking for, we can find firms who do that and pitch to them."

One contract lobbyist said his firm works to build a public reputation by speaking and writing on the issues they cover: "The way we approach things, people usually come to us and either they'll know about us through reputation or through referrals or through our speaking. We speak at a lot at conferences. It's not just marketing, it's also we're experts in this area, so the same way that an academic would perfect their expertise, we write on the issues, we lecture on the issues. Companies come to us, we'll come to them."

One in-house company lobbyist, relatively new to Washington and exhausted by the pitches he had received from multiple lobbying firms, joked, "Everybody around here knows everybody, and everybody here is all things to all people. It's just amazing. You never find anyone who says they don't know everyone or can't do everything."

Other more veteran in-house lobbyists also described the constant sales pitches they received:

- "Rarely a day goes by that somebody is not wanting to demonstrate to you how they think they can be of value to the company, and it's hard because they're people you've worked with. You know them from the Hill or from a trade association or just around the Washington community and everyone has value or something to bring when they open their own consulting group or go to a consulting group."
- "[We get pitched] all the time. I know a lot of these people, and a lot of them are soft, some are hard . . . People know our profile. In the last couple weeks, we've heard from 2 or 3 people. We get some e-mails. One guy just e-mailed me said he's starting a coalition to promote the interests of sovereign wealth funds. Would we be interested in joining, for $15,000 a year? I turned them down. But it's always interesting to see what people are doing."
- "Usually you get calls from people you know at least slightly, who used to work with you or know you have particular problem, and may be able to help out."

Contract lobbyists have similar goals as in-house lobbyists. They would prefer their contracts to be renewed and increased, and for companies generally to do more (rather than less) lobbying.

When they are working for less politically engaged companies without a Washington office, these lobbying consultants essentially play the role of Washington office. The principal-agent relationship is similar to what I've covered already, though in general, the less politically engaged companies have both more specific political goals and less political savvy. Typically, lobbyists are representing multiple clients simultaneously, so they simply cannot devote as much attention to any one company. Yet, this does not stop them from being entrepreneurial. One lobbyist who Kersh interviewed told him that instead of doing what his client wants done right away, "What I'll do is dig around some on that issue and get back to him and say, Well, this isn't moving for a few months, though I'll keep working on it behind the scenes. But in the meantime, you ought to be aware that all these other issues are coming down the pike and these could really affect your business."[30]

At companies with their own Washington offices, it is generally the in-house government affairs department of the company that selects the contract lobbyists, which means that the contract lobbyists are at least one degree removed from the company managers who have the ultimate say over the political budget. It makes most sense to think of in-house lobbyists and contract lobbyists as co-agents in the shared production of lobbying. After all, Washington remains a very big small town, where everybody often really does know everybody (or least pretends to when they see them). All lobbyists share a common interest in a thriving lobbying economy. The more contract lobbyists hired by a company, the more resources the in-house lobbyists have. And the more resources they have, the more issues they can take on; and the more activity they take on, the more information they can feed back to corporate headquarters about all the important and valuable things they are doing in Washington.

In interviews, in-house lobbyists describe three primary uses for contract lobbyists:

1. access;
2. process and issue expertise; and
3. extra intelligence-gathering.

Access

All lobbyists have their own sets of contacts, but Congress is a big place, full of overlapping jurisdictions and 535 individual members. The executive branch is also a big and sprawling place, with more than 1,000 federal agencies. A company with only few lobbyists will have a limited set of contacts. These lobbyists can certainly build new relationships by getting to know new members of Congress and their staff. But if a company wants to have an impact on a particular office, sometimes it helps to be able to hire a contract lobbyist to facilitate that contact.

One study found that between 2001 and 2011, almost 5,400 former congressional staffers had registered as lobbyists.[31] Lobbyists tend to earn a premium for their experience and their connections, with well-connected aides earning on the order of $300,000 a year.[32] As Conor McGrath argues, "There are three important things to know about lobbying: contacts, contacts, contacts."[33]

These relationships are valuable not just because of the ability to get meetings and make phone calls, but also because lobbyists who have worked in particular member offices or on committees or in administrative agencies know the procedural and personality idiosyncrasies and informal power relationships that are key to understanding how things really work. They know how to package policies, what issues will appeal to whom, and even how different decision-makers like information and issues presented to them. They can identify the key moments in the process. In-house lobbyists were quite straightforward that they were hiring lobbyists because of the access they provided:

- "You hire consultants because there is no way you can reach all 535 members, all the committee staff, and all the agencies, with the small staffs that we have. You bring in consultants that have more relevant experience on a particular issue or have better access to certain parts of the government."

- "I view consultants as a tool to expand our influence beyond what it should naturally be, to take into account the vagaries of who is chairman, whether or not our home state members are on the right committees where a lot of our legislation tends to be written. So for very long time, until this Congress, there were no members from our state on the Ways and Means Committee, so we'd look for consultants who would help us on a committee that's really important to us, give us relationships, contacts, strategic advice about how to approach the committee."
- "We use them to work with us on a certain committee or subcommittee. We largely recruit them while they are still in the Congress. When they come out, all but one of our consultants, we were their first client."

Additionally, as Washington has become more partisan, access has become more partisan. Several lobbyists said that they had made specific hiring decisions based on needing partisan access. When I interviewed lobbyists in 2007 and early 2008, many had recently hired more Democratic lobbyists in response to the Democrats' electoral successes in 2006.

- "We needed to beef up our Democratic consulting base, so right off the bat, we hired two Democratic consultants. That got us started to make sure we're doing the things we needed to do. Then we hired another Democratic consultant."
- "Certain consulting firms have better connections in certain offices. We now have one lobbying firm with lot of Republican contacts; now we need one with lots of Democratic contacts."
- "A year or two ago it was clear to me I was weak on being able to deal with the Republican side of the Energy and Commerce Committee, so I just made some inquiries to find out who was actually relatively well-respected in those circles. When [Rep. Jim] Greenwood [R-PA] was there, it was pretty clear to me we were not going to have a lot of luck at that point of time. Greenwood was never going to be a large supporter of ours, so I was not going to go out and find somebody who would sway that particular individual. I'd rather have somebody who can help me in a more general way and help me to figure out who on the Republican side is likely to be an ally, who is likely to show some leadership."
- "It's become so specialized, that somebody is hiring for a shop now, and they're looking for a Democratic lobbyist from the House to deal with the Ways and Means Committee only. When I joined nobody was that

narrowly targeted, and now almost everybody has a committee staff they served on and have better relations there."

So, at the most basic level, companies that are hiring multiple lobbyists are buying access. They are buying introductions. They are buying advice on who is likely to be sympathetic to them on a particular issue, how best to win the support of particular member. And in some cases, they are buying themselves an insight into what their critics and opponents think, and how they might best neutralize such opposition.

Issue expertise

Some lobbyists are hired for their access, but others are hired because they know certain policy issues really, really well. As one lobbyist explained, "There are access lobbyists. If you want to see Harry Reid, who do you go to? You go to Tom Daschle. But if you have to explain the complexities of licensing for follow-on biologics, you can't go to Tom Daschle." Sometimes you want the policy expert who can break down a complex issue—not just for government decision-makers, but also for the company.

In-house company lobbyists tend to know the core concerns of the company very well, and thus build up good expertise on the issues related to those core concerns. But frequently, new issues and concerns arise. When they do, in-house government affairs departments need to be able to move into those new issue areas quickly and nimbly. That is another reason why they hire contract lobbyists. Said one in-house lobbyist: "Most of us in the office are generalists. On new issues like energy, we didn't know the concerns, so we need specialized talent. We're a lean shop here, and we're not going to hire an energy expert, so we go to the consultant who can offer a percentage of time for issue expertise. One of our consultants knows the Energy and Commerce Committee very well, so we hire them to explain what the issues are."

Sometimes companies pool together resources to jointly hire firms with expertise on a specific new issue that the companies care about, a sort of mini-coalition organized by the lobbyist. Said one lobbyist: "There was an issue on executive compensation and deferred compensation. I don't know anything about that. This is very specialized stuff, I hired [a consultant] along with half a dozen companies – he had a partner, who was very good benefits lawyer in Atlanta, and we worked on putting together a response to stuff coming out of the committee."

Other times, it's just easier and more efficient for a specialist in a particular policy to handle those issues. Said one lobbyist: "If there is a tax issue over a certain provision in the tax code, I don't need to listen to every conference call on that – I'll have a consultant and an internal person get together and figure out what they're doing." Often, access and policy expertise go together:

- "[name omitted] came to us over tax matters. He is very close with a number of Republican senators, and when I have a problem on an issue and we have to talk to a Republican senator, he probably has 10 or 12 close friends who are Republican senators, so I will call him and we'll go talk to Senator X. And we have seven or eight consulting arrangements on that basis. Some came out of the Ways and Means Committee and some came out of the Finance Committee and some came out of the Energy and Commerce Committee and it goes on and on."
- "We need somebody with CMS expertise or somebody who has wide range of expertise in the FTC, FDA, and CBO. There's a lot of agency work. My consultants are really more about understanding issues and being able to tell me who can I talk to at FTC to see if they'd be willing to weigh in on that."

Intelligence gathering

A third reason that companies turn to additional lobbyists is intelligence gathering. Any individual company lobbyist can only hear so much, and can only be plugged into so many channels. If a company wishes to increase its likelihood of getting valuable gossip at a time when it is able to do something about that gossip, it helps to hire additional lobbyists to be on the lookout for issues affecting the company, wherever they may arise.

For instance, one company lobbyist described hiring one consultant for issue expertise, and a second for intelligence gathering. The lobbyist said: "One we have for legislation having to deal with tax law because that's too big a spectrum of potential issues for me to cover. The other is a small operation that gives me information on things because I'm only focusing on [my company], but they have lots of other clients. They might hear information about things that might affect us."

Another said: "We have one consultant, we knew her from Capitol Hill when she went out on her own, and we get a daily monitoring from her for all of the tax stuff, on any matter affecting [the] pharmaceutical industry..."

In general, contract lobbyists are a way for a company to expand its networks and its knowledge. It can know more key people and facts in a relatively flexible and cost-effective way. A company typically wants an in-house staff that will know the company and its core issues really well, but Washington is a big sprawling place, with many people and issues. Additionally, rather than

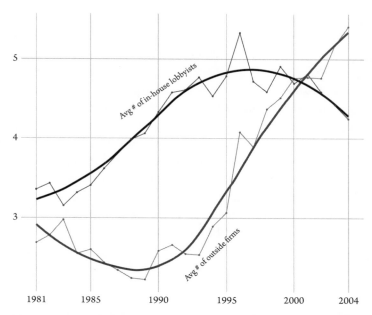

Figure 7.4 The shift from in-house lobbyists to outside firms among companies with at least one Washington lobbyist. Source: Author's calculations based on lobbyists listed in the *Washington Representatives* directory for companies in the S&P 500 sample.

committing to a full-time person, a company can hire or fire a firm on a much shorter notice. "Using consultants allows you more flexibility. You can shift around more."

In my sample of S&P 500 companies, we can observe a shift towards more use of outside lobbying firms starting in the mid-1990s. Figure 7.4 looks at companies who have at least one in-house lobbyist to better understand this shift. Throughout the 1980s, the average number of in-house lobbyists grew at a steady clip, while the average number of outside firms retained by companies remained roughly flat. But starting in the mid-1990s, this changed. All the growth in lobbying presence among firms with Washington offices occurs in the number of outside lobbying firms, while the growth in the number of in-house lobbyists flattens out and then starts to decline. The companies that are the most active—those with their own Washington lobbyists—are exhibiting a clear shift.

The preceding discussion helps us to understand this shift. As we've seen, companies turn to outside lobbying firms when they want to expand beyond their core issues—when they want to reach out to new members of Congress, get involved in new issues, and just generally be more plugged in. To rely only on in-house lobbyists is to be limited to the core issues of the company, and therefore to be mostly reactive. To rely more on Washington lobbying firms is to go beyond a company's natural allies in Congress, and to go beyond its natural issues.

In other words, Figure 7.4 is another piece of evidence of corporations' increasingly aggressive and proactive approach to lobbying. It is also consistent with the growing professionalization of lobbying. Contract (outside) lobbyists have the strongest identity with the Washington lobbying community. While in-house lobbyists are company employees, contract lobbyists are not. They are first and foremost oriented towards Washington lobbying. Their increasing importance even among the most active companies is an observable implication of the larger shift in corporate lobbying: from defensive and reactive to aggressive and proactive; from protecting the company from politics to using politics to help the companies to be more profitable.

Conclusion

Corporate lobbyists straddle two very different worlds: business and government. Lobbyists are hired for their ability to persuade government decision-makers. But if lobbyists are so persuasive, why should corporate managers be immune to their charms? Lobbying is a business, and lobbyists have a very personal stake in companies doing more lobbying. The more corporate managers value political engagement, the more issues on which they will want to engage; and the more aggressively they will pursue these issues, and the more they will spend on lobbying.

Corporate managers are not typically political junkies. Companies hire lobbyists to tell them what is going on in Washington and what they should do about it. The uncertainties and ambiguities of politics give lobbyists room to operate and room to spin. Lobbyists choose details and narratives to persuade managers why the maximalist approach to politics makes the most sense, taking advantage of the informational asymmetries inherent in their position.

Over time, lobbyists teach corporate managers why politics is important, helping to shape the cognitive biases and information-processing mechanisms of key corporate decision-makers. They make sure that corporate managers understand the long-term value of engagement, even as they struggle with the culture of quarterly earnings reports. To demonstrate the value of politics, lobbyists seek out bottom-line issues, especially those narrow benefits for which they can claim credit. They make sure that corporate managers understand why the company has unique interests in Washington, and why those interests cannot simply be left to trade associations. Lobbyists benefit from a competitive universe of corporate lobbying.

All of this contributes to both the stickiness and the growth of corporate lobbying. Lobbyists are powerful internal advocates for continued lobbying, and once government affairs takes hold within a company it rarely lets go. Once companies start lobbying, they tend to keep lobbying. And the more companies lobby, the more they orient towards proactive and particularistic policy outcomes. Lobbyists are the key actors in this process.

Testing Alternative Explanations
for Growth

This book argues that lobbying is sticky. To recap very briefly: Companies hire lobbyists. Lobbyists teach managers about the value of political engagement. Lobbyists help to highlight reasons why companies should be politically active. This leads companies to maintain (and often increase) their commitments to politics. This suggests a straightforward explanation for the growth of corporate lobbying in Washington: Over the years, a growing number of companies have been pulled into lobbying. Once they come to Washington, political engagement begets deeper political engagement. Lobbying has a self-reinforcing logic.

I believe that this process offers the best explanation for the growth of lobbying over the last several decades. There are, however, other possible explanations. In this chapter, I deal with three alternative hypotheses: (1) lobbying grew because government got bigger; (2) lobbying grew because government devoted more attention to issues companies care about; (3) lobbying grew because companies got bigger. As we will see, all three explanations have something to contribute but are limited in what they can explain. Of the three, the growing size of companies probably explains the most. But as we will see in Chapter 9, all three pale in comparison to the explanatory power of the stickiness of lobbying.

Explanation 1: It's Big Government

If a folk theory emerged from the interviews I conducted, it was that companies are lobbying more because government is getting "bigger." This argument came in two varieties. One is that a bigger government means more regulation, and more regulation means more reasons to lobby. Another variety is that

lobbying is about trying to get contracts and subsidies, and a bigger government is a government with more benefits to distribute.[1]

Certainly, comparing time trends might lead us to think that the growth
of lobbying and the growth of government are linked. Between 1981 and
2004, non-defense discretionary spending[2] increased from $339 billion to
$460 billion (held constant for inflation). And as we've seen, the average
company lobbying presence (in-house lobbyists plus outside firms) increased
from 1.9 to 4.1 during this same period. Moreover, looking at Figure 8.1, we
can see that both grew faster starting in the mid-1990s after a more sluggish
period in the 1980s (and in the case of non-defense discretionary spending,
actual decline).

However, we might ask a few additional questions to better understand
whether these trends are linked. While the data on lobbying are somewhat imprecise prior to the 1980s, we do know that corporate lobbying investments
were pretty flat in the 1960s, and then jumped in the 1970s. Figure 8.2 shows

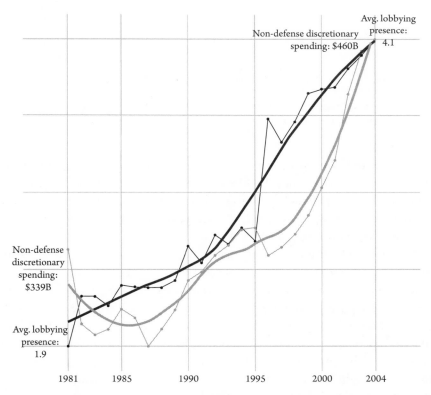

Figure 8.1 Lobbying presence and non-defense discretionary spending, 1981–2004.
Sources: Author's calculations based on lobbyists listed in the *Washington Representatives*
directory for companies in the S&P 500 sample; Office of Management and Budget.

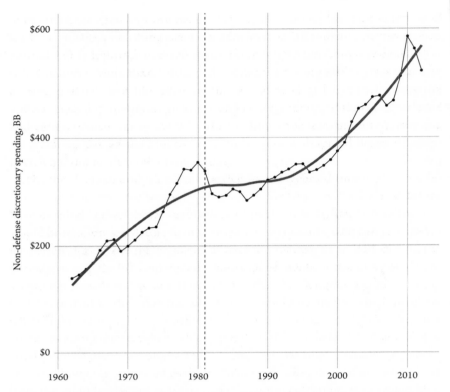

Figure 8.2 The steady increase in non-defense discretionary spending, 1960–2012.
Sources: Office of Management and Budget.

that the growth of non-defense discretionary spending is nothing new. It has been growing steadily since the 1960s, and in fact, grew at a good pace in the 1960s when corporate lobbying investments were stable. If the size of government drives lobbying investment, why didn't the growth in federal spending corporate lobbying investments in the 1960s?

We can also look at the annual changes in both measures. Does corporate lobbying grow more/less in years when the government grows more/less? Does corporate lobbying grow more/less in years *after* the government grows more/less? Figures 8.3 and 8.4 investigate these two hypotheses. In both graphs, there is a very slight positive relationship between the annual change in government and the annual change in lobbying, but a significant amount of variability that is unexplained. The conclusion from these graphs is straightforward: lobbying increases are not direct responses to increases in the size of the government (at least as measured by discretionary spending).

Certainly, these are broad-brush correlations. As we saw in Chapter 3, different companies and different industries have expanded their political activity

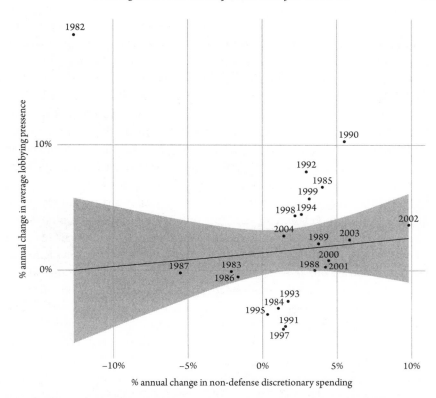

Figure 8.3 Year-to-year changes in average company lobbying presence vs. year-to-year changes in non-defense discretionary spending, 1982–2004. Sources: Author's calculations based on lobbyists listed in the *Washington Representatives* directory for companies in the S&P 500 sample; Office of Management and Budget.

at different rates, and this macro-level correlation can't really address that variability. For now, let's consider this a background condition. A larger government probably exerts a diffuse and weak pull on lobbying activity, expanding the reasons and opportunities for lobbying. But this is very imprecise and general. We can almost certainly do better.

Explanation 2: It's Government *Attention*

Several scholars have argued that the key variable in explaining lobbying activity is not necessarily the size of government writ large, but rather government *attention* to a specific set of relevant issues. That is, when government attends to issues, organizations with something at stake on those issues attend to government by mobilizing and lobbying in turn. David Truman's *The Governmental*

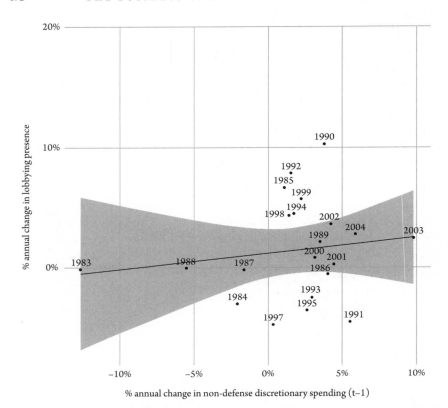

Figure 8.4 Year-to-year changes in average company lobbying presence vs. year-to-year changes in non-defense discretionary spending *(lagged)*, 1983–2004. Sources: Author's calculations based on lobbyists listed in the *Washington Representatives* directory for companies in the S&P 500 sample; Office of Management and Budget.

Process argues that groups form in response to "disturbances"—socioeconomic change leads to government activity. Government activity threatens interests in society. Interests in society mobilize in response.[3] John Mark Hansen extended this work by showing the importance of threats specifically in mobilizing interests.[4]

Beth Leech and colleagues make the case for a "demand theory of lobbying." They argue that, "Government activity acts as a magnet, pulling groups of all kinds to become active." In other words, organized interests devote their attention to areas where the government is already devoting attention: "A government decision to become involved in an issue area sets the agenda for existing and potential organized interests, who are thus encouraged to come to the capital and defend their interests and advocate particular solutions to perceived problems . . . Groups do not automatically form and come to Washington; there must be a demand for them. Government creates that demand."[5]

Leech and colleagues find that more committee hearings and more government spending were associated with more lobbying activity for 56 of the 74 issue areas they studied.[6]

Virginia Gray and David Lowery make similar claims about government attention in their "population ecology" theory of interest groups.[7] Comparing interest group populations across states, they conclude that, "The likely sources of recent growth of organized interest populations are long-term changes in the size of latent constituencies and the resources of government activity and interest certainty."[8] Their theory is based on a conceptual framework out of population ecology known as energy-stability-area. In population ecology, a species needs all three to survive. In their model, *energy* is government attention. *Stability* is the consistency of that government attention. They define *area* as "the number of potential constituents the group may serve . . . If, for example, there are no business firms in a state, there will be no one for the aspiring business lobbyist to represent."[9] The first two features predict government attention, particularly sustained government attention, will be a key determinant of lobbying activity. The third predicts that a bigger economy, with more companies, will lead to more lobbying. In more recent work, Gray and Lowery (and colleagues) argue that legislative agendas and related lobbying activity wax and wane concurrently.[10]

I will approach the government attention hypothesis in two ways. First, I will draw on my interviews to assess government attention as a cause of mobilization. These interviews will show that while government activity sometimes brings companies to Washington, almost as often it was not a factor in the decision to mobilize. Second, I will look at the lobbying time trends of companies in six industries (five growing, one declining) and compare those trends to the changes in government attention. If the government attention hypothesis is correct here, we would expect lobbying levels of the industry to respond to the levels of government attention to the industry. I find at best sporadic support for the hypothesis. Levels of lobbying seem to follow a similar trajectory across all growth industries. That lobby growth trajectory is occasionally responsive to government attention. But mostly, it appears to have its own dynamic.

Attention and mobilization

Let's start with mobilization. In interviews, I asked company lobbyists if they could tell me the story of how their company became involved in Washington lobbying. Among the company lobbyists I interviewed, 18 of 31 could do so. Seven different types of reasons emerged and they are listed in Table 8.1.

Table 8.1. **Reasons why companies came to Washington**

Reason	#	Starting Years
Involved in some sort of legislative battle	4	Pre-1981 1999, 2001, 2002
Resolving specific problem or concern with government policy	3	2001, 2002, 2006
To handle government contracting	3	1985, 1999, 2004
Reached certain size and so it made sense	3	1996, 2002, 2005
Seeking government help to deal with private sector problem	2	2005, 2006
CEO decided it was a good idea	2	1998, 2001
To handle increased trade association activity	1	1993

Source: Author interviews with in-house company lobbyists

Among those responding to a particular legislative battle, one was a pharmaceutical company that first opened its office in 1986 during the consideration of the Orphan Drug Act ("I wanted to make sure the definition and benefits of the Orphan Drug Act could be realized by companies like [us]," the company's lobbyist told me.) Another was an Internet services company that came to Washington in 1999 to have a say in the creation of ICANN (the Internet Corporation for Assigned Names and Numbers). A third was a retail chain that wanted to have a say in discussions of international trade in 1999. A fourth was a large diversified financial services company that decided to set up a lobbying shop in 2003 following the Enron blow-up and the passage of the Sarbanes-Oxley Act. ("I watched all these different evolving rules and regulations being imposed on the financial services industry," the company's in-house lobbyist told me.)

Among those responding to a particular problem or concern, two were pharmaceutical companies concerned about Medicare reimbursement rates for their company's drugs, both in 2006. A third was a retail chain whose decision to lobby in Washington in 2002 stemmed from compliance issues that required more "relationship-building" to handle.

All three companies that had set up a Washington office when they reached a certain size were technology companies that had previously relied on outside lobbyists or trade associations. As one of the company's lobbyists put it, "It was time we grew up . . . there was no single crystallizing issue." Another company's lobbyist said that, "The company was getting bigger and bigger, and more and more of the issues impacting the company were coming from Washington, like export control issues and appropriations." These two companies set up their current offices in 2002 and 2001, respectively.

The two companies that came to Washington to resolve a private-sector problem were both small companies who were trying to seek relief for what they felt was manipulation of their stock price by investors; they wanted the Securities and Exchange Commission to change the rules regarding short selling. These companies came to Washington in 2005 and 2006.

Among the two companies who acted on the impetus of the CEO, one was a large retail chain whose new CEO had come from a company with a large government affairs office. "His feeling was that a company as large as [ours] needed a presence in Washington," said a company lobbyist, who added that there was "nothing going on in DC that was affecting us." This was 2001. The other was a large financial services firm whose chairman and CEO had always been active in political circles, and in 1998 decided to have a formal government affairs office.

Finally, one company, another financial services company, hired a lobbyist in 1994 to make sense of all the information the company was receiving from trade associations: "General counsel hired me as a subset of the legal department. They got a pound of paper from various trade associations and didn't have any place for it to go, and nobody to act on it, to be at the table representing us."

In total, slightly more than half (10 of 18) mobilized in response to specific government activity. Among those companies responding to government activity, 6 of 10 were responding to a very narrow company issue. Among the remaining four, two companies (the pharmaceutical company and the retail company) had company-specific stakes in the particular legislative outcomes.

Among the eight company lobbyists whose mobilization appears to have had nothing to do with government attention, two turned to government for help resolving a private sector problem. The other six seem to have just decided that having a government affairs department made sense, given the size of the company.

In conclusion, the stories of these 18 companies provide only mixed support for the claim that political mobilization is a response to government attention. There are multiple reasons for companies to start lobbying. Sometimes companies mobilize in response to external events. Sometimes new managers come in and decide it is time for a company to open a Washington office. Sometimes mobilization is the culmination of an internal process—something executives in the company have been thinking about for a while. Sometimes it is to seek government help to resolve a private-sector problem.

Industry case studies

Now let us examine how well changes government attention correlate to changes in the level of lobbying. What follows are time series of lobbying and relevant congressional activity for six industries, plotting lobbying presence alongside measures of industry-relevant hearings and bill introductions, based on the relevant set of topic codes from the Policy Agendas Project.[11] For both hearings and bills, I use a two-year trailing average, combining the current and previous year into one measure. There are two reasons to do this. One is to deal with the fact that both hearings and bill introductions tend to occur more often in the first year of a two-year congressional session, and so taking a two-year window smooths this out. The second reason is because if lobbying responds to government activity, both the current and previous year's activity should be relevant.

The analysis in this section makes two assumptions: The first is that at least some company-level lobbying is oriented towards industry issues, which are far more likely than company-specific issues to be the topic of congressional hearings. Chapter 5 provided evidence that large companies in an industry devote a substantial amount of lobbying attention to industry-level issues, although they may all have their own take on those issues. So, this seems to be a reasonable assumption. The second assumption is that congressional hearings and bills are appropriate measures of relevant government attention. While it is true that companies are also concerned with the executive branch, considerable evidence, both from my interviews and lobbying scholarship in general, shows that companies care about congressional activity and lobby to influence it. Also, it is worth noting that Baumgartner and colleagues find that presidential actions do not appear to stimulate additional lobbying activity.[12]

The measures of bills and hearings come with the obvious caveat that there is no perfect one-to-one match from topic codes to industry interests. In some industries, the fit is better than others, though the industries I have chosen all have relatively clear crosswalks since government has a clear interest in all these sectors. Another possible caution is that hearings and bills don't tell us anything about how important the bills or hearings are to the companies in the industry. They also don't tell us about the hearings and legislation never introduced because they were scuttled by behind-the-scenes lobbying.

It is also quite likely that once companies in an industry build up a lobbying presence, their attention spills out into additional issue areas that don't match as closely with the core industry issues, and thus will not be counted in these measures of government attention. For example, this measure will link telecom companies with hearings specifically about the telecom industry. But telecom companies increasingly have an interest in intelligence hearings (since much surveillance is conducted over their wires). This measure doesn't capture that.[13] For this reason, it is helpful to think of these as measures of government attention in a company's primary regulated industry.

In the pages that follow, I will focus on five industries where lobbying presence has increased (pharmaceuticals, telecommunications, financial services, tech [computers/Internet], and defense). I will look at one industry—automotive—that started out relatively high in lobbying intensity, but actually declined over time.

The scales vary, but the basic trend seems to be consistent among the growth industries: slow but stable growth through the 1980s, followed by a period of faster growth starting in the 1990s, with plateaus here and there, and the very rare short dip. Only the auto industry has any sustained periods of decline. While it is conceivable to link particular growth spurts to particular periods of government attention in three of the industries (pharmaceuticals, telecom, and finance), there is little evidence that the annual changes in industry lobbying are intimately tied to changes in the government agenda, at least as measured by bills or hearings.

These thumbnail policy histories also show that, to the extent that there are major policy battles that affect these industries, they are almost always policy battles that industry lobbyists have initiated and welcomed. If government attention appears to matter during this period, it is largely government attention driven by corporate lobbyists.

Thus, there are two key themes that will emerge out of the analysis to come:

1. While government attention to industry (measured by bills and hearings) has peaks and valleys, industry attention to government (measured by lobbying) has peaks and plateaus (it is either increasing or stable, but almost never decreasing except in one industry). Thus, industry lobbying is largely independent from government attention.
2. To the extent that government does devote attention to these industries to enact major public policies, the public policies are largely favored by the industry, especially in the later years of this time series.

The basic time trends for all six industries are represented in Figure 8.5, again using average company lobbying presence within industry as the measure of corporate political activity. While lobbying in the automotive industry is on the decline, the other five industries grow at very similar rates. Knowing that government attention on issues tends to ebb and flow, this cross-industry similarity is our first empirical clue that government attention is not the key driver of industry lobbying growth.

Pharmaceutical

The time trends of government attention and company lobbying for the pharmaceutical industry appear in Figure 8.6. (Again, the measures of hearings and bills are a two-year trailing average [current and previous years].) The

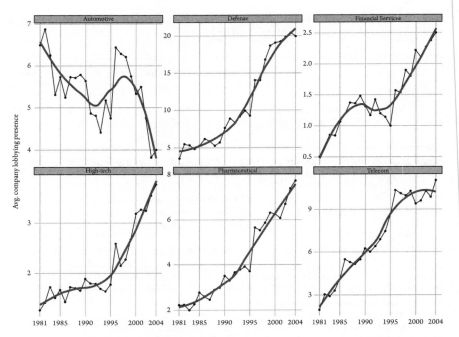

Figure 8.5 The changing lobbying presence of six select industries. Source: Author's calculations based on lobbyists listed in the *Washington Representatives* directory for companies in the S&P 500 sample. Lobbying presence is the average for industry companies.

basic storyline of the growth is that while government attention waxes and wanes, industry lobbying only increases. Moreover, as I detail in the thumbnail policy history that follows, almost all of the major public policy issues related to the pharmaceutical industry were issues raised by the industry. There has been a general expansion of government financial support for the industry, and legislation over the years has made the Food and Drug Administration (FDA) much more industry-friendly. During this time series, the one major potential challenge to the industry, Clinton's proposed healthcare reform, never became law.

The government has long played a role in the pharmaceutical industry, since all drugs must be approved by the FDA. Prior to the start of this time series, President Carter signed the Bayh-Dole Act of 1980. This allowed for the commercialization taxpayer-funded university research, which has generally been viewed as a big victory for the drug industry.[14] However, only a limited amount of major legislation affecting the industry was passed in the 1980s. The Orphan Drug Act passed in 1983, giving drug companies an estimated $75 million in tax breaks over five years to develop drugs that treat rare diseases.[15] In the mid-1980s, there was some attempt by the pharmaceutical industry to ease bans on exporting drugs to the Third World and

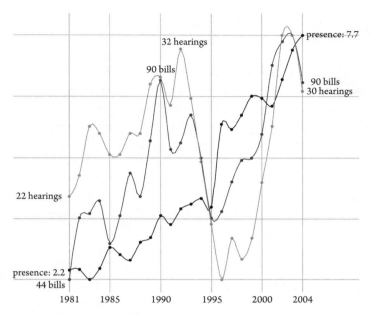

Figure 8.6 Pharmaceutical company lobbying and government attention. Source: Author's calculations based on lobbyists listed in the *Washington Representatives* directory for companies in the S&P 500 sample. Lobbying presence is the average for industry companies; Policy Agendas Project.

reduce liability for vaccines. A growing concern for the industry in the 1980s was the slowness of the FDA drug approval process.

In 1992, the Prescription Drug User Fee Act (PDUFA) helped to speed up the process, though it did mean that drug companies would pay more to fund the FDA. This was a welcome and sought-after law, since pharmaceutical companies found that delays in bringing drugs to market were eating up their profits. The president of the Industrial Biotechnology Association called the legislation, "a landmark in cooperation between a regulatory agency, lawmakers in Congress and the private sector." The president of the Pharmaceutical Manufacturers Association, said that, "a concerted effort over the past several months has enabled Congress to enact into law this historic agreement."[16] In 1992, an active year of government attention to the pharmaceutical industry, Congress also held hearings on misuses of drugs in nursing homes for the elderly, HHS regulation of infertility services (which resulted in legislation), and regulation of human tissue transportation. Congress also proposed changes to the Orphan Drug Act.

More broadly, the federal government began devoting substantial attention to healthcare issues around this time, and the pharmaceutical industry had obvious interests in the debate over nationalized healthcare. Said one pharmaceutical lobbyist:

- "Up until 1994, I think the pharmaceutical industry was just sort of drifting along. The industry was selling to private payers, and even though there was support in regulating the products, Congress wasn't as involved in that process. But there was a sense that the Clinton healthcare plan was going to demonize two industries primarily, and that included pharmaceutical companies."

The healthcare debate served as a wake-up political moment for the healthcare industry, and the number of healthcare companies with a Washington lobbying presence almost doubled between 1992 and 1994.[17] Interestingly, pharmaceutical companies made major investments in Washington *after* attempts to enact major healthcare reform died. Congress moved on to other issues. Pharmaceutical companies moved into Washington. In 1996, Congress held only five relevant hearings, two on the need to look at the effectiveness of FDA regulation, plus a hearing to, "Consider an act to permit manufacturers to give doctors peer-reviewed information about prescription drug and medical device off-label uses, involving the use of products for purposes other than those listed on their label"—a proactive approach by the industry to weaken FDA regulations on off-label drug usage.[18] In 1997, congressional Republicans succeeded in passing FDA reforms that allowed for off-label drug use and faster approvals of medical devices, along with a reauthorization of PDUFA despite consumer group objections.[19]

The industry won its biggest victory, however, with the passage of the 2003 Medicare Modernization Act. The bill created a new government-funded prescription drug benefit, which the pharmaceutical industry had pushed very hard to enact into law.[20] As I learned from talking to pharmaceutical company lobbyists, the industry had for years been opposed to a prescription drug benefit. They were convinced that such a benefit would mean government bulk purchasing. But at some point industry leaders realized they could push for a prescription drug benefit *without* bulk purchasing. Once it passed, the prescription drug benefit made government more important to the pharmaceutical industry, since now government Medicare pricing decisions mattered even more. This created additional reasons for pharmaceutical companies to devote attention to politics.

Drug companies continued to look for government support. In 2004, for example, the industry won the passage of Project BioShield, which allocated $5.6 billion in federal funding to stockpile drugs to combat a potential bioterrorism attack.[21] Yet, even after the bill was passed, drug companies were not entirely satisfied; they wanted protection from loss in developing bioterrorism vaccines.[22] It was a telling sign of just how emboldened the industry had become.

Of course, this period doesn't cover the passage of the Affordable Care Act (ACA). But it is worth noting that the ACA was crafted with the drug industry on board. President Obama and congressional Democrats made a decision early on that they needed to have drug industry support if they were going to pass healthcare reform. It was a very clear signal of the industry's political power.

High-Tech

It is often said of the high-tech industry that it has had a long-standing aversion to Washington, DC, as many Silicon Valley entrepreneurs were imbued with a technology-oriented libertarianism that made them indifferent and perhaps even disdainful towards politics.[23] However, as the data show, technology companies eventually overcame this aversion. Of all the industries this section examines, the high-tech industry's lobbying growth hews most closely to government attention. During the 1980s, the industry didn't lobby much, and the government devoted less attention. Government attention grew in the 1990s, as did the industry lobbying. However, once government attention to the industry declined after 2000, industry attention to government continued. This is the familiar theme: government attention goes up and down; industry attention goes up. Figure 8.7 describes the time series in the tech industry.

The first significant political fight for the industry involved gaining protection for computer chip patterns. The semiconductor industry wanted help fighting back against counterfeiting of its chips. The industry got that protection in 1984, when Congress passed the Semiconductor Chip Protection Act.[24] In the late 1980s, the industry pushed for $320 million to promote technology programs and got some attention in Congress, but it didn't quite have the political muscle to get such support through. In the early 1990s, high-tech companies were pushing for a relaxation on technology export controls, trying to do away with what they felt were antiquated national security concerns that were hurting their ability to sell abroad. But while President Clinton supported this relaxation, legislation to accomplish this ultimately floundered, as concerns about "rogue regimes" overwhelmed industry's hopes of expanding markets and compromise failed to emerge.[25] In 1997–98, software companies were involved in efforts to reduce export controls, and Internet companies succeeded in maintaining an Internet tax moratorium. Congress also passed a law extending digital copyrights, including for computer software (though some Internet service providers were unhappy about the extension of digital copyrights in movies and music).[26]

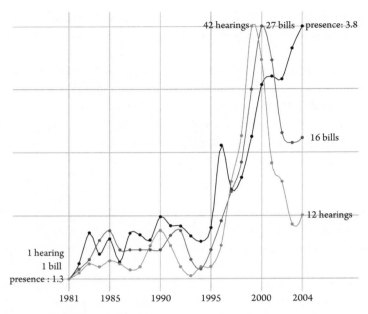

Figure 8.7 High-tech (computers/Internet) company lobbying and government attention. Source: Author's calculations based on lobbyists listed in the *Washington Representatives* directory for companies in the S&P 500 sample. Lobbying presence is the average for industry companies; Policy Agendas Project.

The turn of the century was marked by extensive federal interest in what to do about the Y2K problem, though it was never clear that this posed any particular threat or opportunity to the industry. The two-year trailing average of hearings peaks at 42 in 1999, and the two-year trailing average of bill introductions peaks at 28 in 2000.

In the 2000s, the Internet tax moratorium continued to be a major issue, as did the ability to export potential "dual-use" technologies. The high-tech industry was also able to fight off regulations regarding privacy and confidentiality of personal information, preferring to self-regulate. By 2007–08, when I was conducting interviews, industry companies were working very hard to reform the patent laws (in order to make it more difficult for so-called "patent trolls" to hold up technology companies) and to increase H-1B visa quotas to attract top talent from around the world, both proactive changes to public policy. Immigration has continued to be an issue on and off in the years since.

So what brought technology companies to Washington? In interviews, industry lobbyists frequently cited the 1998 Microsoft antitrust suit as a wake-up call. The lobbying time series is consistent with this. The two years following 1998 (1999–2000) mark the biggest two-year growth period. However, many lobbyists also described the politicization of the industry as more of a gradual education, one that is very consistent with my theory that lobbying has its own internal momentum. Here's what these lobbyists had to say:

- "I think it's just a maturation of the industry . . . a lot of companies used to have someone out in California and then they'd hire somebody from the Hill who'd educate them, and they'd say this is why it's important, and over the years you see things change . . . The people in Washington were able to speak to issues in much more intelligent and meaningful way than someone just in the general counsel's office. Over the last 10-15 years, it's just a gradual process of education. You get the CEOs more involved, testifying on the Hill, they get a little more familiar with process and understand why it's important."
- "Traditionally, like most high-tech companies at the time, we were very entrepreneurial in very fast-moving markets. Understanding that we are sort of opposed to unnecessary regulation in industries, it's the sort of thing that happens to companies, and they go, oh, okay. Then you ask, how do you make sure you make the right investments to get your message out to inform people so when people do start to ask questions you've got the right people on the ground, and that's the process that a company goes through. Now we are more proactive. We're now a resource and a partner with many facets of the government in many areas and I think it's because we've become more mature as an industry in sitting down and talking on a range of issues."

Telecommunications

Telecommunications also follows the by-now-familiar trajectory: steady growth of lobbying presence alongside ups and downs in hearings and bills (See Figure 8.8). There are really two key political moments for the telecom industry. The first came in 1984, when the Department of Justice forced the AT&T to break up into the seven "Baby Bells." The second came with the Telecommunications Act of 1996. This law marked the culmination of more than a decade of lobbying by the seven Baby Bells, who wanted to repeal or significantly amend the Communications Act of 1934 so they could expand into manufacturing and information services.

The push for telecom deregulation picked up speed in the early 1990s. By 1992, the industry won passage of the bill in the Senate. In 1994, the House passed two different telecom deregulation bills. In 1995, the House and the Senate both passed different bills, and in 1996, the Senate and House finally passed the same bill, which re-wrote the rules of the telecommunications

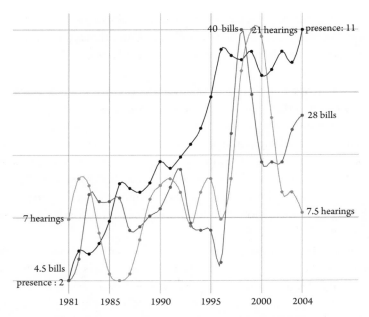

Figure 8.8 Telecom company lobbying and government attention. Source: Author's calculations based on lobbyists listed in the *Washington Representatives* directory for companies in the S&P 500 sample. Lobbying presence is the average for industry companies; Policy Agendas Project.

industry. The Telecommunications Act of 1996 forced incumbent local exchange carriers to open up their networks and attempted to create new competitive markets in local, long distance, cable, and broadcast services. The basic logic of the bill was that by allowing companies to enter other markets, the discipline of market competition would accomplish what regulation had previously attempted to accomplish directly. At the time, critics worried that the bill did not give federal regulators the tools to ensure this competition, a concern which has been vindicated by the evolution of the telecom market in the years following the bill's passage.[27]

Telecom deregulation was a major legislative battle, and the concurrent increases in lobbying leading up to the bill's passage reflect this. Telecom companies put substantive resources into this proactive effort. After the bill's 1996 passage, the industry only slightly reduced its lobbying efforts. No doubt there were good reasons to stay active. The bill delegated many decisions to the Federal Communications Commission (FCC), and not surprisingly, companies had strong interests in making sure the law was implemented in they ways they wanted it to be implemented. For example, in 1997, SBC Communications sued the FCC and claimed the law was unconstitutional. Consumer advocates argued that the phone company was just unhappy about the FCC's attempts to require SBC to open some of its markets to competition.[28]

Hearing titles from 1997 remind us that political battles do not end with the passage of legislation:

- "To review FCC implementation of Telecommunications Act of 1996"
- "To examine consumer protection issues related to unauthorized switching of telephone carrier to another"
- "To examine need for additional regulations to protect privacy of cellular phone use and other wireless communication devices"

And again, in 1998:

- "Examine implementation of Telecommunications Act of 1996 section 271, which provides that regional Bell operating companies (RBOCs) may enter into the long distance telephone service market"
- "To examine whether FCC mandatory charges on telecommunications constitute administratively imposed taxes"
- "To examine FCC Common Carrier Bureau implementation of Telecommunications Act"

And again, in 1999:

- "To review FCC implementation of Telecommunications Act of 1996"
- "To review issues related to competition among telephone, cable, and other communications providers"
- "Examine issues relating to FCC present and future roles in regulating the telecommunications industry"

The four years after the passage of the bill were the most active for congressional hearings in my time series: 15 in 1997, 21 in both 1998 and 1999, and 20 in 2000. But by 2001, the number of hearings was back down to 9. There is also a dip in telecom lobbying at this point in the time series. But that dip is temporary, and lobbying picks right back up. In 2001, the Bells were fighting to enter Internet service markets on equal footing with the cable companies without having to open up their own services to competition.[29] In 2002, President Bush signed legislation allowing the FCC to auction off airwaves to the highest bidder, as large telecom companies had requested (as opposed to doing it by lottery).[30] Certainly, in the years since this time series ends, telecom issues have remained important, as the industry has continued to consolidate and battles over net neutrality have taken up considerable Washington bandwidth.

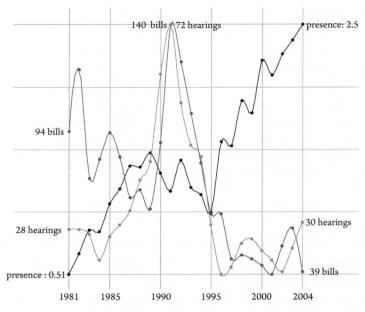

Figure 8.9 Financial services company lobbying and government attention. Source: Author's calculations based on lobbyists listed in the *Washington Representatives* directory for companies in the S&P 500 sample. Lobbying presence is the average for industry companies; Policy Agendas Project.

Financial Services

Again, the time series presents the same pattern: ups and downs in government attention, but primarily ups in lobbying (though there is one slight dip in the mid-1990s). Likewise, the policy history describes the industry seeking and getting favorable policy changes. (See Figure 8.9)

Hearings activity in the financial services industry peaks in the early 1990s in response to the savings and loan banking crisis and subsequent bailout. Congress held an impressive 74 hearings on banking issues in 1990 and another 70 in 1991, largely dealing with the fallout from the crisis and the subsequent problems with the Resolution Trust Corporation, the government-owned organization charged with resolving the assets of failed thrift banks.[31] Interestingly, the financial services industry actually slightly reduced its lobbying presence between 1989 and 1994, during this time of intense industry scrutiny.

However, this congressional scrutiny did not stop large banks from pushing their top priority: the passage of legislation that would put an end to all limits on interstate banking. Even as late as 1994, a dozen states still required national banks to own subsidiaries in their state. But in 1994, Congress passed (and

President Clinton signed) the Riegle-Neal Interstate Banking and Branching Efficiency Act, which eliminated all remaining barriers to a fully nationalized banking system, allowing big banks to set up national branch networks.[32]

During the next few years, the finance industry threw its effort into a push for major financial services industry deregulation. While hearings and bill introductions declined, major financial institutions worked towards a repeal of the 1933 Glass-Steagall Act, which had separated commercial and investment banking in an attempt to make banking safer and more stable. In 1999, Congress passed the Gramm-Leach-Bliley Act, which allowed commercial banks, investment banks, securities firms, and insurance companies to enter each others' markets, and paved the way for the financial conglomerates of the 2000s. However, as a *New York Times* article describing the bill's passage explained, "The opponents of the measure gloomily predicted that by unshackling banks and enabling them to move more freely into new kinds of financial activities, the new law could lead to an economic crisis down the road when the marketplace is no longer growing briskly."[33] That criticism seems almost prophetic, given the financial crisis that followed. (Intriguingly, Deniz Igan and colleagues found that the financial companies that lobbied the most aggressively on mortgage lending and securitization issues in the 2000s subsequently engaged in the riskiest lending practices and were most likely to be bailed out after the crisis.[34])

In 2000, the finance industry succeeded in the passage of the Commodities Futures Modernization Act, which "shielded OTC [over-the-counter] derivatives from virtually all regulation or oversight."[35] This lack of oversight allowed the unregulated derivatives market to boom. Many believed that this booming derivatives market led to the increasingly leveraged positions that large banks took on, which were a key factor in the financial crisis of 2007–08.[36] While the financial crisis and subsequent Dodd-Frank Wall Street Reform and Consumer Protection Act happened after this time series, it is worth briefly noting that despite deep public ire towards the banks, the political response was basically to buoy the existing financial institutions and then enact a massive bill that did nothing to directly challenge the fundamental structure and size of the largest financial institutions. When given the choices to repeal Gramm-Leach-Blilely or to put size limits on banks, Congress chose not to do so.

Defense

The defense sector provides another insight into the relationship between government attention and lobbying (See Figure 8.10). Throughout the 1980s, Congress continually held hearings on defense issues, typically numbering in the low 20s annually. After all, there was a Cold War on, and a major defense build-up taking place, yet the industry didn't engage in a major lobbying build-up during

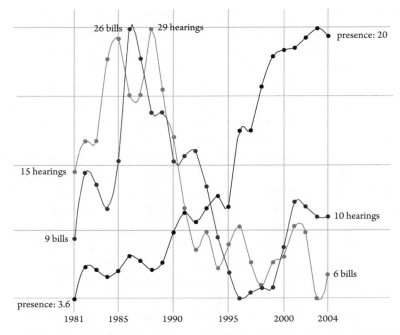

Figure 8.10 Defense company lobbying and government attention. Source: Author's calculations based on lobbyists listed in the *Washington Representatives* directory for companies in the S&P 500 sample. Lobbying presence is the average for industry companies; Policy Agendas Project.

this period. Congressional attention to defense issues dropped off the radar in the late 1990s at the same time that the industry's presence was growing rapidly. Perhaps the industry increased its presence not in response to government attention, but in response to a lack of government attention, trying to combat the post–Cold War lack of interest in a strong military defense and declining spending on defense. Or perhaps industry lobbying increased because less spending meant more competition for fewer contracts. Either way, it's clear that the defense industry's lobbying does not follow government attention.

Automotive

The automotive sector offers the rare opportunity to look at a sector that has reduced its overall lobbying presence in Washington (See Figure 8.11). It certainly appears that Congress had more interest in the automotive sector in the early 1980s. Between 1981 and 1985, Congress averaged 12 hearings a year. Since then it's averaged just under 4 hearings a year that were relevant to the industry. Likewise, between 1981 and 1985, Congress averaged 39 bills of

Figure 8.11 Automotive company lobbying and government attention. Source: Author's calculations based on lobbyists listed in the *Washington Representatives* directory for companies in the S&P 500 sample. Lobbying presence is the average for industry companies; Policy Agendas Project.

relevance to the industry per year. Since then, it's averaged only 19. Yet interestingly, the automotive sector had some increases in lobbying presence in the late 1980s not associated with an increase in government attention. The mid-1990s, when everybody, it seems, was devoting more to lobbying, also marked an increase in automotive lobbying. But it does not appear to be associated with any particular increase in government attention.

Putting it all together

What have we learned? The five growth industries, despite being in different issue areas, all demonstrate a very similar pattern: Steady growth through the 1980s, followed by a bigger growth spurt in the mid-1990s, with a few plateaus here and there. Once an industry engages politically, it tends to stay engaged, regardless of the ebb and flow of government attention.

How well does government attention explain levels of industry lobbying? Figures 8.12 and 8.13 describe the correlations between the annual percentage changes in industry-relevant hearings/bills and annual percentage changes in

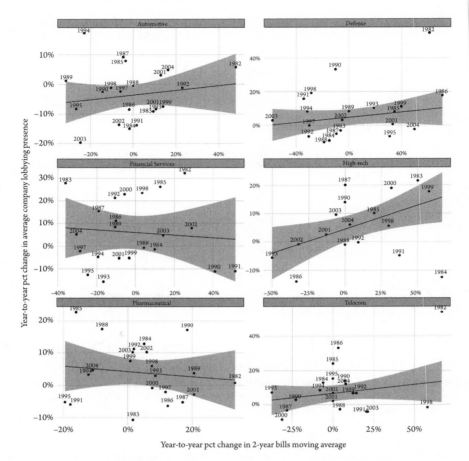

Figure 8.12 Annual percent changes in two-year moving average of industry-relevant *bills* and annual percent changes in average company lobbying presence in industry. Source: Author's calculations based on lobbyists listed in the *Washington Representatives* directory for companies in the S&P 500 sample. Lobbying presence is the average for industry companies; Policy Agendas Project.

average industry company lobbying presence.[37] Changes in government attention and changes in industry lobbying are statistically independent. Only one industry (high-tech) shows a positive correlation in the relationship between government attention and lobbying presence. Looking at Figures 8.12 and 8.13, a clear conclusion emerges: at the industry level, companies are not predictively responsive to changes in government attention (at least at the level of the primary regulated industry). In Chapter 9, we will see that there is also no relationship at the company level, either.

To be sure, if the goal here were simply to explain variation in political activity *across* industries (rather than explaining change over time), it would be

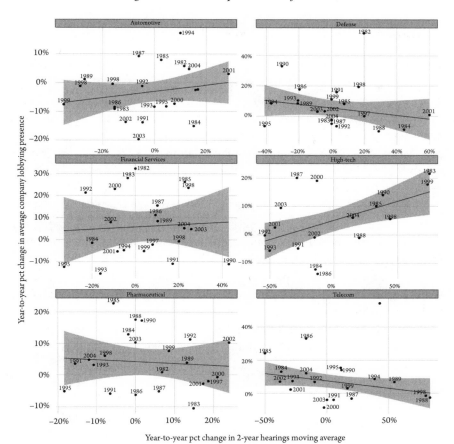

Figure 8.13 Annual percent changes in two-year moving average of industry-relevant *hearings* and annual percent changes in average company lobbying presence in industry. Source: Author's calculations based on lobbyists listed in the *Washington Representatives* directory for companies in the S&P 500 sample. Lobbying presence is the average for industry companies; Policy Agendas Project.

easy to determine why telecom, banking, defense, and pharmaceuticals are among the most politically active industries. Government regulations and/or purchases are critically important to these industries. Government devotes substantial attention to the rules and regulations governing these industries. But this has been the case for decades. Government was also an important player in all of these industries four decades ago. And companies in these industries were not nearly as active then. What these data reveal is that the ups and downs of industry-relevant government attention do not correspond with the ups and downs of industry lobbying activity. Mobilization has a stickiness that is independent of measures of government attention.

Explanation 3: Companies Are Getting Bigger

It is also possible that the growth of corporate lobbying is merely a consequence of companies getting bigger. The literature on the determinants of corporate political activity finds size to be the most consistent and reliable predictor. Numerous studies have shown that the bigger the company, the more likely it is to be politically active. [38] As we will see in Chapter 9, company size does explain some of the variability in company lobbying levels. But for now, we can ask a narrow question: Are companies lobbying more simply because they are getting bigger?

Again, we can start with the 30,000-foot view, tracing the 1981 to 2004 trajectory of both company lobbying presence and company size among my sample. Here, my measure of company size is sales, which is the most common measure of size in the literature on corporate political activity. [39] And, at first glance, Figure 8.14 would provide some initial support for this hypothesis, since the median size of companies in my sample has grown at the same rate as their average lobbying presence.

However, macro-level correlations might not necessarily translate into company-level correlations. And since I have company-level data, we can test

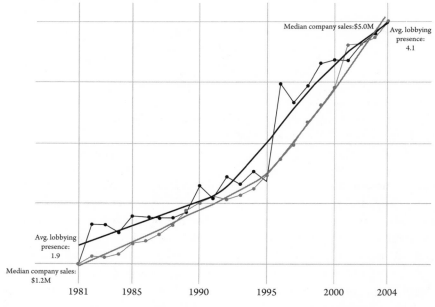

Figure 8.14 Are companies lobbying more because they are getting bigger? Source: Author's calculations based on lobbyists listed in the *Washington Representatives* directory for companies in the S&P 500 sample; Compustat

how well company size (measured by sales) and changes in company size predict changes in company lobbying presence. To do this, I estimate a few fixed-effects OLS regression models.

For purposes of this and forthcoming analyses, I will employ some variable transformations. For lobbying presence, the key variable of interest in both this chapter and Chapter 9, I employ a square-root transformation. This accounts for the fact that while going from no lobbyists to one lobbyist is a major change, going from one to two lobbyists is less of a change, and going from two to three lobbyists is less of a change than from one to two, and so on and so forth. This transformation also resolves the heavily left-skewedness in the lobbying presence variable—most companies who lobby only have a few lobbyists; a few maintain a substantial lobbying presence. From herein, I will call this variable "marginal lobbying presence." I will also log-transform the variable for company sales, also reflecting the left-skewedness of the variable.

The regression results are reported in Table 8.2. The results suggest that increasing company size explains a small fraction of the growth of lobbying.

Table 8.2 **Predicting changes in marginal lobbying presence from changes in company size**

	Model 1	Model 2	Model 3	Model 4
Change in log(Sales)	0.178^{***}		0.102^{***}	
	(0.008)		(0.011)	
log(Sales)		0.023^{***}	0.013^{***}	
		(0.003)	(0.003)	
Change in log(Sales) × log(Sales)			0.022^{***}	
			(0.003)	
Change in log(Sales) (t–1)				0.011
				(0.006)
R^2	0.051	0.024	0.056	0.020
Adj. R^2	0.047	0.020	0.052	0.016
Num. obs.	16422	16422	16422	16421

$^{***}p < 0.001, ^{**}p < 0.01, ^{*}p < 0.05$

Coefficients computed using OLS with fixed effects for year and industry and clustered standard errors

Source: Author's calculations based on lobbyists listed in the *Washington Representatives* directory for companies in the S&P 500 sample; Compustat.

On average, the more a company grows from year-to-year, the more it will expand its lobbying presence, on average, but the effect is pretty small.[40] Bigger companies are more likely to expand their lobbying presence than smaller companies, but the effect is tiny.[41] Model 3 shows that the interaction between company size and change in company size is positive and statistically significant, indicating that bigger companies that are growing more rapidly also grow their lobbying more (though again, these effect sizes are tiny). Model 4 shows that the previous year's increase in company size doesn't do much to explain the current year's growth in lobbying. There is a very tiny lag effect of change in sales.

Overall, these results indicate that some of the growth of lobbying can be explained by companies getting bigger. Company increases in lobbying correlate with company increases in size generally. But at the company level, changes in size explain only a small piece of the overall variability. Something else is clearly going on.

Conclusion

This chapter has addressed three possible explanations for the growth of lobbying: the size of government, changes in government activity, and the size of companies. Government has gotten bigger, and the growing size of government may exert a diffuse pull on corporate lobbying activity. Government has also shifted its attention. However, in some of the key growth industries, changes in government attention (as measured by congressional hearings and bill introductions) do very little to explain the growth patterns. Rather, industry-level lobbying seems to have an internal logic of growth. Regardless of the ebbs and flows of industry-specific government attention, the growth patterns across several industries are similar: steady but slow increases throughout the 1980s, and faster increases starting in the early 1990s. Companies have also gotten bigger over the last several decades, and changes in company size can explain a small amount of the increases in lobbying activity.

The existing theories give us some insight into the larger patterns of corporate lobbying, but even collectively they leave a significant amount of the variability in corporate lobbying activity unexplained. In short, none of these explanations can offer a theory of why corporate lobbying has expanded and grown as it has. We need a better explanation.

The Stickiness of Lobbying

In Chapter 8, I argued that three possible reasons for the growth of lobbying—bigger government, more government attention, and bigger companies—were limited in what they could explain. Now, I turn to my theory: that lobbying grows because it has a self-reinforcing stickiness. Put simply, lobbying begets more lobbying.

This chapter will make the case for the stickiness of lobbying by detailing three observable empirical implications:

1. Once companies invest in Washington, they rarely leave;
2. Company-level lobbying is very consistent from year to year; and
3. Lagged lobbying is by far the best predictor of current-year lobbying.

This is a data-heavy chapter, and the goal of all this data analysis is to provide convincing evidence both that lobbying is very sticky and that this stickiness provides the best explanation for the observed trends in lobbying activity.

Observable Implication 1: Once Companies Invest in Washington, They Rarely Leave

My theory argues that once companies come to Washington, they tend to stick around. Figure 9.1 offers the most straightforward descriptive visualization of this observation. For all years of my S&P 500 lobbying time series (1981–2004), I break down companies by the size of their lobbying presence. (Again, "lobbying presence" measures the sum of in-house lobbyists plus the number of outside lobbying firms retained.) Then I look forward into the future and ask: among all companies in each grouping (for all appropriate years), how many companies still have lobbyists, one, two, three years out, and so on, up to nine years into the future (assuming, of course, that

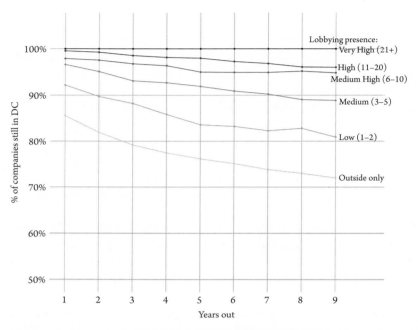

Figure 9.1 The persistence of lobbying, by size of lobbying presence. Source: Author's calculations based on lobbyists listed in the *Washington Representatives* directory for companies in the S&P 500 sample.

they are still in business)? The simple answer is that the vast majority are still lobbying.

Among companies with the most sizeable baseline lobbying presence (greater than 20), the answer to how many are still lobbying is: all of them. Even nine years out, not a single company with a lobbying presence of at least 21 ever gave up on politics. Among companies in the "high" group (lobbying presence of 11 to 20), departure from Washington happens only very occasionally. One year out, 99.5 percent of companies were still lobbying; five years out, 98 percent were still in politics; nine years out, 96 percent were still paying a lobbyist. Companies with a lobbying presence of between 6 and 10 look similar. Five years out, 95 percent of these companies are still lobbying. The same percentage are still lobbying nine years out.

Moving down to the companies in the "medium" category (lobbying presence of 3 to 5, and at least one in-house lobbyist), their one-year persistence rate is 97 percent. Five years out, 92 percent are still in Washington, and nine years out, 90 percent are still paying a lobbyist. Even companies in the "low" group (lobbying presence of 1–2, with at least one in-house lobbyist) rarely depart. Of these companies, 93 percent are still around one year later, 84 percent are still around five years later, and 81 percent are still around nine years later.

Finally, even the companies we might expect to be most likely to get in and out of lobbying—those who don't have any in-house lobbyists and rely only on contract lobbyists—usually stay in. One year later, 86 percent were still lobbying; five years later 77 percent were still lobbying; and nine years later 73 percent were still lobbying.

In short, once a company starts lobbying, and especially once it hires its own lobbyist, and even more so once it hires a few of its own lobbyists, that company is going to keep lobbying.

How many companies are in each of the categories in Figure 9.1, and how has this changed over time? Figure 9.2 visualizes the categories as a percentage of all companies in the sample. A few things are worth noting. First, a plurality of companies have only outside (contract) lobbyists. The share of companies with only a contract lobbyist hovered around 20 percent throughout the 1980s and into the mid-1990s. After that, it comes closer to 30 percent of all

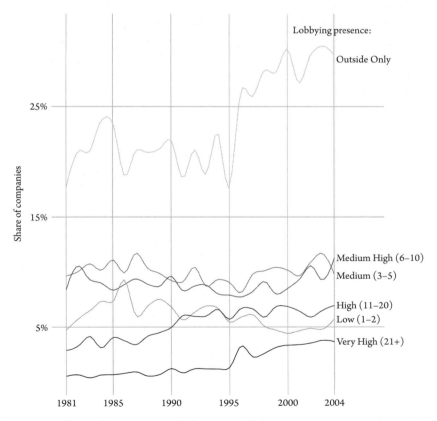

Figure 9.2 Share of companies in different-sized bins. Source: Author's calculations based on lobbyists listed in the *Washington Representatives* directory for companies in the S&P 500 sample.

companies. For most of the period, the "medium" group (presence of 3–5) has been the next most common, averaging 10 percent of the companies. Next is the "medium high" lobbying group (presence of 6–10), averaging about 9 percent of all companies. The most notable changes have taken place in the "very high" group (presence of 21+), which grew from 0.05 percent of all companies in 1981 to 3.6 percent in 2004; and the "high" group (presence of 11–20), which grew from 2.8 to 7.3 percent of companies during the time series. This is consistent with individual companies increasing their lobbying presence.

Observable Implication 2: The Year-to-Year Consistency of Company Lobbying Presence

The second important observable implication of my theory is that companies should be very consistent in their year-to-year lobbying commitments. They are. One way to visualize the consistency of lobbying presence is by plotting each company's current-year lobbying presence against the company's previous-year lobbying presence. If most of the observations sit on or near a 45-degree (1:1) line, this is evidence that year-to-year lobbying is very consistent. Figure 9.3 plots the current year's lobbying against the previous year's

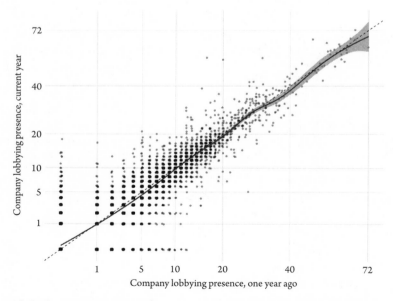

Figure 9.3 Current year vs. previous year company lobbying, all years combined (1981–2004). Source: Author's calculations based on lobbyists listed in the *Washington Representatives* directory for companies in the S&P 500 sample.

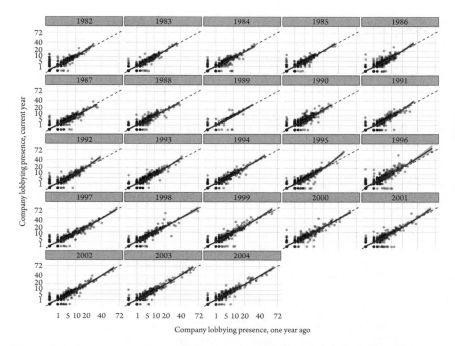

Figure 9.4 Current year vs. previous year company lobbying, separated by year (1981–2004). Source: Author's calculations based on lobbyists listed in the *Washington Representatives* directory for companies in the S&P 500 sample.

lobbying, combining 24 years of observations into one graph. Figure 9.4 includes separate scatterplots for each year. This allows us to examine whether there has been any change in the relative stickiness of lobbying over time.

In both figures, I plot a dotted 45-degree line that represents a perfect one-to-one correlation. I also plot a local smoothing line that estimates the changing relationship between previous-year and current-year lobbying. I show the confidence interval for the predicted values in gray. The darkness and density of the dots correlates to the number of observations. The darker and denser the dots, the more observations.

The local smoothing line in all cases hews very closely to the dotted (1:1) line, which makes clear that lobbying in the previous year is a very good predictor of lobbying in the current year. There are very few outliers. But for the vast majority of observations, companies do what they did last year, plus or minus a small change.

Another way to visualize these changes is to bin them. As we begin to get into more advanced data analysis, I will move to a transformed version of the lobbying presence variable. As I did in Chapter 8, I use "marginal lobbying presence," which is the square root of lobbying presence. Again, there are two reasons for this transformation. The main reason is that it reflects the declining marginal importance of additional lobbyists and/or outside lobbying firms. Going from no lobbyists/outside firms to one is a big deal, from one to two is a slightly less big deal, and from two to three slightly less of a big deal, and so on. In practice, this treats the shift from zero to one lobbyists/outside firms as the equivalent of the shift from one to four lobbyists/outside firms, and equivalent of the shift from four to nine, and so on up the ladder of perfect squares. The second reason is methodological. Lobbying presence is heavily "left-skewed": Most companies have only a few lobbyists; a few companies have many lobbyists. As I will be using regression analysis, I want my key variable to follow a relatively normal distribution.[1]

To start to understand the persistence of lobbying, Figure 9.5 visualizes the annual changes in the square root of lobbying presence, across all years, among

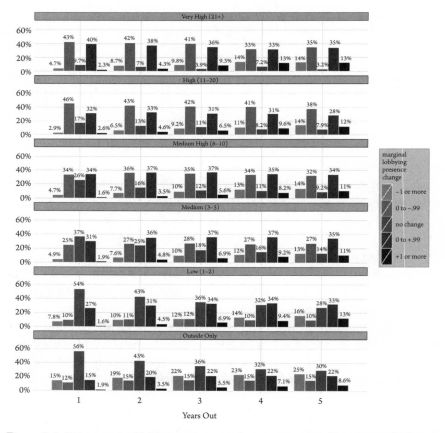

Figure 9.5 How marginal lobbying presence changes over time, by company lobbying presence. Source: Author's calculations based on lobbyists listed in the *Washington Representatives* directory for companies in the S&P 500 sample.

companies that lobbied in the previous year. Again, I'll break active companies into the same six categories as before, based on the size of their lobbying presence. Across all size categories combined, the most common one-year change is no change. Almost half (44 percent) of the active companies experienced no change. The vast majority of one-year changes in marginal lobbying presence (90 percent) are between −0.99 and +0.99. These patterns are generally consistent across different size categories. Major changes are rare.

Even five years out, the majority of changes in marginal lobbying presence are still within the −0.99 to +0.99 range. Again, this is true for all six size categories. Certainly, the share of companies in all categories making big changes in either direction increases as the time horizon increases. But even five years out, roughly 70–75 percent of companies in each category have changed their marginal lobbying presence by less than 1. To put this in more precise terms for those who might not think intuitively in terms of square roots: 75 percent of companies with a lobbying presence of 16 (4 squared) in year 1 will have a lobbying presence of between 10 (3 squared + 1) and 24 (5 squared − 1) in year 5; similarly 75 percent of the companies with a lobbying presence of 9 (3 squared) in year 1 will have between 5 (2 squared + 1) and 15 (4 squared − 1) lobbyists in year 5.

It is also worth noting that within both the "low" and "medium" categories, companies are a bit more likely to increase their presence than to decrease their presence. By contrast, in the "medium high" category, there tends to be rough parity in the increases and decreases. The "high" category has consistently more decreases than increases, the most intense lobbying category—"very high"—contains slightly more declines one to three years out, but the declines and increases are pretty much even at five years out. This implies that growth may not be unlimited. Companies with a smaller lobbying presence are more likely to increase than decrease. Companies with a larger presence are a little more likely to stabilize their lobbying presence.

Observable Implication 3: Lagged Lobbying is by far the Best Predictor of Current-Year Lobbying

Now we turn to the regression analysis. By now, we have seen clear evidence of the importance of lagged lobbying as a strong predictor of current-year lobbying. Readers who are either convinced of the stickiness of lobbying by now, or who have little interest in heavy data analysis, may wish to skip ahead. They can trust that lagged lobbying is by far the most important predictor of current lobbying, that government attention has no explanatory power, and that company size has, at best, only moderate explanatory power. In short, the data strongly support my theory of the stickiness of lobbying.

Other readers, however, may be interested in the effect sizes, or simply enjoy wading into a deeper statistical analysis. Some readers may also think that my prediction of strong serial autocorrelation (the more technical term for stickiness) is actually a low bar, since many political phenomena experience serial autocorrelation—that is, what happened last year is usually a pretty good predictor of what will happen this year.[2] Moreover, from an analytical perspective, it is common for lagged observations of an outcome variable to "dominate" regression models, diminishing the apparent statistical importance of other variables.[3] Those who are skeptical of these kinds of coefficients may want to know just how big the effects of lagged lobbying are, and how far back into the data they go. The following pages, then, are for these readers.

The goal of these regressions is to explain the current-year, company-level marginal lobbying presence. Again, my theory has suggested that lobbying is sticky, and so we will expect to see a high degree of serial autocorrelation. These regressions will help us to see just how sticky lobbying is, and how far back in time that stickiness goes. These regressions will also provide additional tests for the two alternate hypotheses discussed in Chapter 8—that lobbying activity is a response to the congressional agenda, and that lobbying grows because companies are getting bigger. I will also add some additional control variables from the larger literature on the determinants of corporate political activity.

The main variable of interest is "marginal lobbying presence," which is the square root of lobbying presence (as discussed earlier). Again, lobbying presence is the sum of the number of in-house lobbyists and the number of outside firms. I will also separately test the effects of in-house lobbyists and outside firms on total lobbying presence, with the same square root transformation.

I also include a government attention variable, which is a combined measure of bills and hearings relevant to a company's primary industry. Since the two measures are highly correlated (Pearson's correlation = 0.87), it makes more sense to combine them into a single measure.[4] The way I combine them is slightly complicated, but there are very good reasons for the complications. First, I take a moving two-year average for both bills and hearings. As I argued in Chapter 8, there are two reasons to take a two-year average. One, Congress moves in two-year cycles. The first year tends to have more activity. The second year is generally more electorally focused. Therefore, a certain averaging is necessary for consistency. For another, we should expect that lobbying activity is both a response to the current year's potential agenda and the previous year's agenda. A two-year moving average takes both of these considerations into account. However, the measures are slightly uneven. For a given company in a given year, the median number of bills is 2.1 times more than the median number of hearings. To bring the two measures into rough equality, I multiply the number of hearings by 2.1. Next, because the measure is somewhat left-skewed, and because there is presumably a decreasing marginal impact of additional hearings and bills (there is often a pile-on effect), I then take the square root of the two measures.[5] Finally, I sum them into a single measure of government attention. The same caveats about the measures of bills and hearings that I raised in Chapter 8 apply here as well. These are only measures of government attention of the company's primary industry (and thus cannot account for government attention to issues that may be of interest to companies beyond their primary industry). They also rely on the imperfect mapping between industry categories and policy agenda categories. Still, despite these imperfections, this is the most comprehensive measure I have of government agendas.

To measure company size, I use company revenues (sales). This variable is also extremely left-skewed (even more than the other variables), so I log transform it. There is also some evidence in the literature that companies who do more R&D are more likely to be politically active,[6] and there are also important questions as to whether more profitable companies are likely to lobby more. For this reason, I also include variables for R&D expenditures and profit margin. Since R&D expenditures are heavily left-skewed, I log transform this measure as well.

I also include a dummy variable, "government purchase," that is coded as "1" if government is a major purchaser of goods from the industry, and "0" otherwise.[7] The literature shows that companies that sell more to the government tend to lobby more. However, unlike many studies on the determinants of corporate political activity, I do not include a variable for industry regulation. There are two reasons for this omission. First, regulation is very difficult to collapse into a single dimension. There is no agreed-upon approach to measuring regulation, and all of the measures in the literature on the determinants of corporate political activity have significant limitations.[8] Moreover, the hypothesis of interest here is whether companies respond to changes in government attention, and the key independent variable is my measure of government attention. Since we can expect government attention to be correlated with government regulation of industry (presumably government devotes more attention to industries it regulates than those it doesn't), controlling for regulation runs the risk of biasing this coefficient of interest downward.

Two short methodological notes before we proceed. In these regressions, I include fixed effects for year.[9] Including fixed effects for year controls for the secular growth trend generally, as well as the other possible factors that might be unique to a given year (such as, for example, the fact that 1996 appears to have witnessed a robust increase in reporting). Fixed effect models generally perform well in accounting for unobserved, unit-specific heterogeneity in cross-sectional data.[10] As Nathaniel Beck and Jonathan Katz note in their widely cited article on time-series cross-section data, "Fixed effects present no special problems for TSCS [time series cross section] models, because the number of unit-specific dummy variables required is not large."[11] Though time-series cross-sectional data can raise issues of panel heteroskedasticity, clustered standard errors are generally seen as a way to address these concerns.[12]

I also limit the analysis to only observations in which the company lobbied in the previous year.[13] There are a few reasons to limit the sample in this way. The primary reason is because this allows us to more directly answer the question that is at the heart of my theory: given that a company is currently lobbying, how much is its current year's lobbying presence determined by its previous year's lobbying presence? As I've argued, there are significant transaction costs in setting up a political office. Companies with Washington lobbyists have a very different decision process than companies without Washington lobbyists. Therefore, these processes should be modeled separately. At the end of this chapter, I will model the decision to start lobbying.

Table 9.1 summarizes the descriptive statistics for all the variables.

We can begin with Table 9.2. Model 2.1 shows that both company sales and the "government purchase" dummy variable are significant predictors of marginal lobbying presence, as we would expect, and with fixed effects for year, this model explains a reasonable percentage of the variability in company marginal lobbying presence (Adjusted r-squared = 0.35). The coefficient for logged sales in this model is 0.53.[14] The exact parameter estimates are not that important, and they dance around depending on the model. The important thing to note is that company size is a robust predictor of company lobbying, but that even a 50 percent increase in sales is only going to add one or two extra lobbyists/outside firms, depending on a company's existing lobbying presence.

In Model 2.2, I add a few variables. Most importantly, I add my measure of government attention. Again, this is a two-year moving average of the number of bills and hearings relevant to companies in the industry. The coefficient is tiny, and intriguingly, slightly negative. It appears that more industry-relevant government attention is associated with marginally less lobbying. But the coefficient is too small to be substantively interesting or worth trying to explain. Additionally, neither R&D expenditures nor profit are statistically significant predictors of marginal presence. Also note that this model, with the additional variables, doesn't explain much more variability than the much more parsimonious Model 2.1.

Model 2.3 introduces the variable for lagged lobbying, which is the variable of key theoretical importance in my model. As my theory predicts, the coefficient for lagged marginal lobbying presence is substantial and highly significant, and its inclusion diminishes the coefficients of the other key explanatory

Table 9.1 **Summary statistics**

Variable	Min	q_1	Median	Mean	q_3	Max	Std. Dev.	IQR
Lob. presencee	0.00	1.00	3.00	5.06	6.00	72.00	6.58	5.00
In-house lob.	0.00	0.00	1.00	2.47	3.00	48.00	4.06	3.00
Outside firms	0.00	1.00	2.00	2.59	3.00	41.00	3.34	2.00
Gv't attention	0.00	9.86	14.47	15.18	18.88	38.19	7.34	9.02
Hearings (2-yr avg)	0.00	11.00	24.50	32.79	42.50	174.00	31.21	31.50
Bills (2-yr avg)	0.00	22.00	51.00	75.48	93.50	412.50	81.13	71.50
Sales	0.54	1850.97	4082.87	8585.42	9147.50	257157.00	15706.48	7296.53
RD	0.00	0.00	0.00	177.46	95.90	12183.00	607.21	95.90
Profit	–1.00	0.02	0.05	0.05	0.09	1.00	0.12	0.07
Gv't purchase dummy	0.00	0.00	0.00	0.35	1.00	1.00	0.48	1.00

Table 9.2 **Outcome variable: Marginal lobbying presence**

	2.1	2.2	2.3	2.4	2.5	2.6
Marg. lob. Presence(t–1)			0.910***	0.938***	0.949.***	0.910***
			(0.009)	(0.007)	(0.007)	(0.009)
log(Sales)	0.532***	0.523***	0.134***	0.333***		0.136***
	(0.010)	(0.010)	(0.008)	(0.025)		(0.008)
log(Sales (t–1))				–0.243***	0.071***	
				(0.025)	(0.006)	
Gv't purchase dummy	0.432***	0.432***	0.066***	0.064***	0.052**	0.064***
	(0.023)	(0.030)	(0.016)	(0.016)	(0.018)	(0.012)
Gv't attention		–0.015***	–0.001	–		
		(0.001)	(0.001)	(0.007)		
Gv't attention (t–1)				0.012	0.000	
				(0.006)	(0.001)	
log(RD)		0.003	0.000	0.008		
		(0.002)	(0.001)	(0.005)		
log(RD (t-1))				–0.009	0.000	
				(0.005)	(0.001)	
Profit		0.138	0.190***	0.046		
		(0.107)	(0.057)	(0.074)		
Profit (t–1)				0.009	0.067	
				(0.071)	(0.059)	
R^2	0.350	0.356	0.801	0.810	0.790	0.801
Adj. R^2	0.348	0.354	0.800	0.810	0.789	0.800
Num. obs.	9142	9018	9018	9011	9023	9142

*** $p < 0.001$, ** $p < 0.01$, * $p < 0.05$
Coefficients computed using OLS with fixed effects for year and clustered standard errors.

variables. Models 2.4 and 2.5 explore lagged versions of other explanatory variables, but there are no substantive changes to report. The takeaway from Table 9.2 is that lagged lobbying does indeed "dominate" the model, while government attention has virtually no impact.

Table 9.3 pushes this analysis a little further by extending the length of the lag. Again, year-to-year consistency is pretty common in politics, so a skeptic might still not be impressed. To try to convince such a skeptic, I now add lags

Table 9.3 **Outcome variable: Marginal lobbying presence**

	3.1	3.2	3.3	3.4	3.5
Marg. lob. presence (t–1)	0.783***	0.780***			
	(0.016)	(0.017)			
Marg. lob. presence (t–2)	0.116***	0.106***	0.720***	0.578***	
	(0.017)	(0.017)	(0.010)	(0.017)	
Marg. lob. presence (t–3)	0.56***	0.36**		0.175***	0.645***
	(0.013)	(0.013)		(0.016)	(0.010)
log(Sales)	0.340***	0.122***	0.184***	0.165***	0.213***
	(0.029)	(0.009)	(0.009)	(0.009)	(0.009)
log(Sales) (t–1)	−0.210***				
	(0.041)				
log(Sales) (t–2)	0.001				
	(0.037)				
log(Sales) (t–3)	−0.059*				
	(0.023)				
Gv't purchase dummy	0.067***	0.069***	0.168***	0.166***	0.226***
	(0.013)	(0.013)	(0.016)	(0.016)	(0.017)
Gv't attention	−0.017*				
	(0.007)				
Gv't attention (t–1)	0.017		−0.006***	−0.006***	−0.009***
	(0.010)		(0.001)	(0.001)	(0.001)
Gv't attention (t–2)	−0.012	−0.001			
	(0.008)	(0.001)			
Gv't attention (t–3)	0.012*				
	(0.005)				
R^2	0.816	0.806	0.706	0.719	0.655
Adj. R^2	0.816	0.806	0.705	0.718	0.654
Num. obs.	8292	8303	8698	8303	8303

*** $p < 0.001$, ** $p < 0.01$, * $p < 0.05$
Coefficients computed using OLS with fixed effects for year and clustered standard errors.

for up to three years back. I also drop the variables for R&D and profit because they were of marginal importance to the previous set of regressions, but I keep the government attention variables because of their theoretical importance. Model 3.1 includes three years of lagged lobbying in the same model, and all three are significant predictors of current-year lobbying. Most of the explanatory power is in the first-year lag, as we'd expect. But that up to three years of activity are all significant predictors holding each other constant is consistent with a high degree of stickiness to lobbying presence. Models 3.2 to 3.5 decompose the three years of lagged lobbying in different ways. The predictive capacity of lagged lobbying does decline as we go further back in time, which is not surprising. But even three years back, it is a very powerful predictor.

Models 4.1 to 4.4 in Table 9.4 push variables for lagged lobbying even farther back in time, now extending the lags up to five years (with controls for company size and government purchasing). Lobbying four years in the past

Table 9.4 **Outcome variable: Marginal lobbying presence**

	4.1	4.2	4.3	4.4
Marg. lob. presence (t–1)	0.782***			
	(0.017)			
Marg. lob. presence (t–2)	0.113***	0.568***		
	(0.017)	(0.018)		
Marg. lob. presence (t–3)	0.037*	0.144***		
	(0.016)	(0.019)		
Marg. lob. presence (t–4)	−0.006	0.055***	0.593***	
	(0.013)	(0.015)	(0.011)	
log(Sales)	0.123***	0.163***	0.248***	0.281***
	(0.009)	(0.009)	(0.010)	(0.010)
Gv't purchase dummy	0.070***	0.158***	0.252***	0.289***
	(0.013)	(0.016)	(0.019)	(0.020)
Marg. lob. Presence (t–5)				0.551***
				(0.011)
R^2	0.810	0.723	0.613	0.583
Adj. R^2	0.809	0.722	0.612	0.581
Num. obs.	8003	8003	8003	7591

*** $p < 0.001$, ** $p < 0.01$, * $p < 0.05$
Coefficients computed using OLS with fixed effects for year and clustered standard errors.

provides no additional predictive capacity when three years of lobbying are included in the model. However, it does provide predictive value when previous year's lobbying is dropped from the model. And as a solo predictor (controlling for sales and year), even lobbying presence five years in the past does a pretty good job of predicting current company lobbying levels. In other words, the stickiness of lobbying extends quite far into the future.

Models 5.1 to 5.5 in Table 9.5 decompose the measure of lobbying into its two components: in-house lobbyists and the number of outside firms (the two measures have a Pearson's correlation of 0.64). Both measures are transformed into their square roots, creating a variable that measures their marginal size. Interestingly, both offer roughly the same predictive capacity, and both measures also provide statistically significant and independent explanatory power up to three years into the past even with more recent lags included in the model. The variable for outside lobbying firms even generates a statistically significant coefficient four years into the past. This suggests that the number of in-house lobbyists and outside lobbying firms are equally important as driving factors in lobbying. Most importantly, this consistency validates the way that I've used these measures roughly interchangeably by combining them into a single measure. While there has been a general shift away from in-house lobbying and towards contract lobbying (as we saw in Chapter 7), the evidence here tells us that this shift is not particularly consequential for questions of lobbying persistence.

Tables 9.6 and 9.7 turn the independent variables in the prior model into dependent variables. These tables are primarily intended to show that the variables I consider independent variables are in fact largely independent variables in that they are not primarily determined by lagged values of lobbying (if they were, we might have reason to doubt some of the earlier models). The evidence here suggests that they are largely independent, though there are some small effects that are worth flagging.

One potentially intriguing result is that lagged lobbying predicts company revenues, even controlling for lagged company revenues (Model 6.1), suggesting that having a larger lobbying presence may help companies to grow more. However, at this point this correlation is merely suggestive. More analysis needs to be done that is beyond the scope of this book to substantiate whether this is mere correlation or actual causation, given the wide range of other possible factors that could explain changes in company size. The size of the effect is reasonable. A one-unit increase in the square root of previous year's lobbying presence—going from 4 to 9 lobbyists/outside firms, or from 9 to 16—is associated with roughly a 3 percent increase in company size. Another result worth flagging is that industries that sell a lot to the government are notably more profitable than industries that don't sell much to the government (see

Table 9.5 **Outcome variable: Marginal lobbying presence**

	5.1	5.2	5.3	5.4
Marg. in-house lob. (t–1)	0.613***	0.595***	0.482***	0.487***
	(0.007)	(0.008)	(0.019)	(0.019)
Marg. outside firms (t–1)	0.577***	0.564***	0.455***	0.454***
	(0.009)	(0.010)	(0.014)	(0.014)
Gv't attention	–0.013*			
	(0.007)			
Gv't attention (t–1)	0.011			
	(0.006)			
Gv't purchase dummy	0.063***	0.054***	0.060***	0.065***
	(0.016)	(0.013)	(0.013)	(0.013)
log(Sales)	0.336***	0.153***	0.137***	0.137***
	(0.026)	(0.008)	(0.009)	(0.009)
log(Sales) (t–1)	–0.225***			
	(0.026)			
log(RD)	0.007			
	(0.005)			
log(RD) (t–1)	–0.008			
	(0.005)			
Profit	0.067			
	(0.076)			
Profit (t–1)	0.006			
	(0.074)			
Marg. in-house lob. (t–2)			0.088***	0.091***
			(0.022)	(0.022)
Marg. in-house lob. (t–3)			0.029	0.039
			(0.016)	(0.021)
Marg. outside firms (t–2)			0.091***	0.094***
			(0.015)	(0.015)
Marg. outside firms (t–3)			0.050***	0.029*
			(0.012)	(0.014)
Marg. in-house lob. (t–4)				–0.019
				(0.017)

Table 9.5 (**Continued**)

	5.1	5.2	5.3	5.4
Marg. outside firms (t–4)				0.028*
				(0.013)
R^2	0.791	0.783	0.791	0.795
Adj. R^2	0.791	0.783	0.790	0.794
Num. obs.	9011	9142	8408	8003

*** $p < 0.001$, ** $p < 0.01$, * $p < 0.05$
Coefficients computed using OLS with fixed effects for year and clustered standard errors.

Table 9.6 **Outcome variables: Company financial measures**

	Sales	*Profit Margin*	*R & D*
Marg. lob. presence (t–1)	0.034***	−0.002	−0.051
	(0.008)	(0.002)	(0.028)
log(Sales) (t–1)	0.940***		
	(0.008)		
Attention	0.003***	0.000	−0.001
	(0.001)	(0.000)	(0.003)
log(RD)	0.002**	−0.001**	
	(0.001)	(0.000)	
Profit	0.670***		−0.169
	(0.161)		(0.204)
Profit (t–1)		0.527***	
		(0.031)	
log(Sales)		0.007**	0.080*
		(0.002)	(0.040)
log(RD) (t–1)			0.945***
			(0.005)
Gov't purchase dummy	−0.074***	0.007*	0.858***
	(0.018)	(0.003)	(0.089)
R^2	0.850	0.277	0.948
Adj. R^2	0.850	0.275	0.948
Num. obs.	9018	9016	9018

*** $p < 0.001$, ** $p < 0.01$, * $p < 0.05$
Coefficients computed using OLS with fixed effects for year and clustered standard errors.

Table 9.7 **Outcome variables: Government attention measures**

	Hearings	Bills	Government Attention
Marg. lob. presence (t–1)	−0.033*	−0.041	−0.005
	(0.015)	(0.023)	(0.006)
Marg. hearings (t–1)	0.864***		
	(0.006)		
log(Sales)	0.014	0.023	0.012*
	(0.015)	(0.026)	(0.006)
log(RD)	0.002	0.009***	−0.001
	(0.002)	(0.002)	(0.001)
Profit	0.062	0.038	0.003
	(0.112)	(0.208)	(0.046)
Marg. bills (t–1)		0.881***	
		(0.007)	
Gv't attention (t–1)			0.111***
			(0.001)
R²	0.769	0.787	0.767
Adj. R²	0.768	0.786	0.766
Num. obs.	8996	8996	8996

*** $p < 0.001$, ** $p < 0.00 1$, * $p < 0.05$
Coefficients computed using OLS with fixed effects for year and clustered standard errors.

Models 6.5 and 6.6). An explanation for why this is the case is beyond the scope of this book.

It is also worth noting that marginal lobbying presence in the previous year is correlated with decreases in both industry-relevant hearings and industry-relevant bills over the following two years (Table 9.7). However, when controls for the previous period's measures of hearings and bills are included, these effects are quite small. Still, they suggest that lobbying is more likely to take issues off the agenda than to put issues on the agenda. This is consistent with the evidence presented in Chapter 4 showing that the top reason companies lobby is to prevent government action.

Finally, Table 9.8 models companies' decisions to go from no lobbying to some lobbying. For each of these models, I selected all the observations where companies did not lobby in the previous year, and I estimated a logistic regression predicting which companies would start lobbying in the current year, again with fixed effects for year and clustered standard errors. None of these models do a particularly good job of explaining the decision, but they do suggest that size is the most likely explanation. The bigger the company, the more likely it is to start lobbying. A 10 percent increase in company size is associated with 2.3 to 3.7 percent increase in the likelihood of a company becoming politically active. Government attention, again, does not register as a significant predictor. In Model 4, I add variables for two- and three-year lobbying lags, since a few companies in this set of observations will have lobbied in the past, even if they did not lobby in the previous year. The marginal lobbying presence two years in the past is, as we might expect, substantive and significant—companies that had previously lobbied are much more likely go from no lobbying to some lobbying. Marginal lobbying presence three years back adds no additional predictive value.

The conclusion of Table 9.8 is that the most consistent explanation for why companies start lobbying is that they reach a certain size at which it makes sense for them to start lobbying, both because they can afford to do it and because they have enough at stake to justify it. However, as Chapter 4 suggested, there are likely many idiosyncratic reasons why companies start lobbying that these models are incapable of capturing.

Changing effects over time

These regressions combine more than two decades into a single model. In so doing, they ignore the possibility that some of the key coefficients may have changed over time. To investigate this possibility, I estimate separate regressions for each year, predicting current lobbying as a function of lagged lobbying, government attention, size, the government purchasing dummy variable, R&D, and profit. Figure 9.6 plots the coefficients for the three variables of most theoretical interest: government attention, lagged lobbying, and sales (the shaded areas describe the 95 percent confidence interval for the coefficients). The coefficient for lagged lobbying increases over time, while the coefficient for sales declines over time. This suggests that lobbying has become stickier over time, which would be consistent with my theory. Government attention is never statistically significant as a predictor of lobbying.

We can further investigate the increasing stickiness of lobbying by estimating separate models using lagged lobbying coefficients for one-, two-, three-, four-, and five-year lags, and then seeing how the coefficients change. The results of these changing coefficients are presented in Figure 9.7. A clear pattern emerges. Lobbying is getting stickier over time. All the coefficients increase over the course of the time series, but the increases do flatten out over time. (For simplicity, I use regression models that control only company size

Table 9.8 **Outcome variable: Probability of starting to lobby (among nonlobbying companies)**

	Model 1	Model 2	Model 3	Model 4
hline Gv't purchase dummy	−0.096	−0.095	−0.086	−0.113
	(0.104)	(0.104)	(0.103)	(0.108)
Gv't attention	−0.005	0.019		−0.005
	(0.005)	(0.025)		(0.005)
log(Sales)	0.368***	0.225*		0.349***
	(0.031)	(0.093)		(0.031)
log(RD)	0.031***	0.005		0.030***
	(0.006)	(0.026)		(0.006)
Profit	−0.079	−0.122		−0.040
	(0.371)	(0.461)		(0.366)
Gv't attention (t−1)		−0.026	−0.007	
		(0.025)	(0.005)	
log(Sales) (t−1)		0.147	0.355***	
		(0.092)	(0.030)	
log(RD) (t−1)		0.028	0.031***	
		(0.026)	(0.006)	
Profit (t−1)		0.206	0.161	
		(0.440)	(0.345)	
Marg. lob. presence (t−1)				0.542***
				(0.083)
Marg. lob. presence (t−2)				0.020
				(0.072)
AIC	5351.571	5348.084	5355.428	5246.455
BIC	5544.752	5568.831	5548.597	5453.435
Log likelihood	−2647.786	−2642.042	−2649.714	−2593.228
Deviance	5295.571	5284.084	5299.428	5186.455
Num. obs.	7327	7320	7324	7327

$^{***}p < 0.001$, $^{**}p < 0.01$, $^{*}p < 0.05$

Coefficients computed using logit regression with fixed effects for year and clustered standard errors.

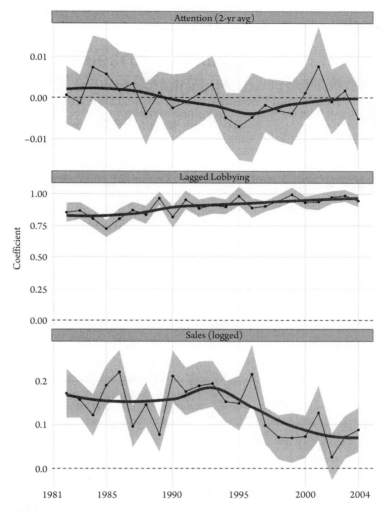

Figure 9.6 How coefficients for key variables change over time. Source: Author's calculations based on lobbyists listed in the *Washington Representatives* directory for companies in the S&P 500 sample.

and the "government purchase" dummy, since those are the most important explanatory variables across all models from my preceding analysis.)

The conclusion here is straightforward. No matter how I structure the models, lagged lobbying (even several years into the past) is by far the most substantive predictor of current-year lobbying. These effects are consistent across models, and the explanatory power of previous lobbying extends back several years. The effects are roughly similar for both in-house lobbying and outside lobbying firms. Bigger companies do lobby more, and companies in industries that sell a lot to the government lobby more.

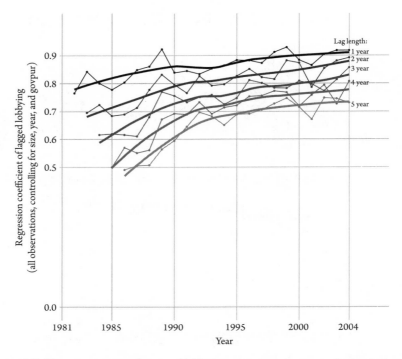

Figure 9.7 The increasing stickiness of lobbying over time. Source: Author's calculations based on lobbyists listed in the *Washington Representatives* directory for companies in the S&P 500 sample.

Government attention at the industry level, however, does not correlate with lobbying activity. This suggests that changes in industry-focused government attention do not explain changes in overall organizational commitments to lobbying.[15] Meanwhile, lobbying activity seems to exert a slight dampening effect on government activity, suggesting that as companies lobby more, they keep more issues *off* the public agenda. This is consistent with the argument I made in Chapter 2 suggesting that the growth of corporate lobbying is making the status quo harder to change.

Conclusion

This chapter has been filled with many numbers, charts, and figures. All paint the same picture in slightly different ways. They all show that once companies start lobbying, they tend to keep lobbying, and that by far the best predictor of a company's current-year lobbying is the company's previous-year lobbying. The year before that also works well as a predictor, as does the year before that.

Lobbying presence is very sticky. While bigger companies do lobby more, company lobbying activity is primarily explained by persistence factors. Big changes in presence are rare. The analysis here also suggests that companies do not seem to be particularly responsive to changes in industry-level government attention. However, bigger companies do lobby more, and company size helps to explain at least some of the variation in company lobbying presence.

Certainly, it is not unusual for a political phenomenon to exhibit a high degree of persistence and autocorrelation. In that respect, lobbying follows in a long tradition of political activities that are mostly incrementalist, with occasional punctuations.[16] However, the persistence of lobbying has important consequences. For one, it offers a new explanation for the growth of lobbying activity: Lobbying expands because lobbying begets more lobbying. But more significantly, the fact that it grows largely of its own accord has important consequences for American democracy. If lobbying merely responds to government attention, it suggests that government is the key driver of activity. Companies are merely lobbying to defend their interests when threatened, or respond when something is at stake. This suggests they will leave once that issue is resolved, and allow government to get on with the business of addressing new and different problems. But if lobbying grows of its own accord, this suggests that once companies start lobbying, they will continue to insert themselves into policymaking. Rather than allowing government to move on to new challenges, companies may prevent government from addressing some issues while demanding it address other issues.

10

The Business of America is Lobbying

> "It is grossly reckless to watch the long-term business trajectory of the U.S. to be at such risk. And we are part of the pathology that got us here. We've all had our K Street lobbyists who are part of the problem." – *Paul Stebbens, CEO, World Fuel Services (during the 2013 government shutdown)*[1]

Over the past four decades, large corporations have learned to play the Washington game. Companies now devote massive resources to politics, and their large-scale involvement increasingly re-directs and constricts the capacities of the political system. The consequence is a democracy that is increasingly unable to tackle large-scale problems, and a political economy that too often rewards lobbying over innovation.

Prior to the 1970s, few corporations had their own lobbyists, and the trade associations that did represent business demonstrated nothing close to the scope and sophistication of modern lobbying. In the 1960s and the early 1970s, when Congress passed a series of new social regulations to address a range of environmental and consumer safety concerns, the business community lacked both the political will and the political capacity to stop it. These new regulations, combined with the declining economy, awoke the sleeping political giant of American business. Hundreds of companies hired lobbyists for the first time in the mid-1970s, and corporate managers began paying attention to politics much more than they ever did before.

When corporations first became politically engaged in the 1970s, their approach to lobbying was largely reactive. They were trying to stop the continued advancement of the regulatory state. They were fighting a proposed consumer protection agency, trying to stop labor law reform, and responding to a general sense that the values of free enterprise had been forgotten and government regulation was going to destroy the economy. They also lobbied as a community. Facing a common enemy (government and labor), they hung together so they wouldn't hang separately. But as the labor movement weakened and government became much more pro-industry, companies continued to invest in politics, becoming more comfortable and more aggressive. Rather than seeing government as a threat, they started looking to government as potential source of profits and assistance. As companies devoted more resources to their own lobbying efforts, they increasing sought out their own narrow interests. As corporate lobbying investments have expanded, they have become more particularistic and more proactive. They have also become more pervasive, driven by the growing competitiveness of the process to become more aggressive.

External events may drive initial corporate investments in Washington. But once companies begin lobbying, that lobbying has its own internal momentum. Corporate managers begin to pay more attention to politics, and in so doing they see more reasons why they should be politically active. They develop a comfort and a confidence in being politically engaged. And once a company pays some fixed start-up costs, the marginal costs of additional political activity decline. Lobbyists find new issues, companies get drawn into new battles, and new coalitions and networks emerge. Managers see value in political engagement they did not see before. Lobbying is sticky.

Lobbyists drive this process. They teach companies to see the value in political activity. They also benefit from an information asymmetry that allows them to highlight information, issues, and advocacy strategies that can collectively make the strongest case for continued and expanded political engagement. Because corporate managers depend on lobbyists for both their political information and strategic advice, lobbyists are well-positioned to push companies towards increased lobbying over time.

But what effect has it all had on public policy? Social science research on political influence has found no relationship between political resources and likelihood of success.[2] However, the lack of a direct, statistically significant correlation does not mean that there is no influence. It just means that the influence is unpredictable. The policy process is neither a vending machine nor an auction. Outcomes cannot be had for reliable prices. Policy does not go to the highest bidder. Politics is far messier, and far more interesting than such simplistic models might suggest. And almost certainly, the increased competition for political outcomes has made it even more unpredictable.

Sometimes lobbying can be very influential, but its influence is contingent on so many confounding factors that it does not show up reliably in regression analysis. Yet, the study of influence is a fundamental question of politics. Rather than looking for vote buying or expecting resources to correlate predictability with policy success, we must think bigger. We must understand the ways in which increases in lobbying activity shape the policymaking environment, and how the changing environment may allow some types of interests to thrive more than others. The current political environment benefits large corporations for several reasons, which I laid in more detail in Chapter 2, but I will provide a recapitulation here.

The first reason is that the increasingly dense and competitive lobbying environment makes any major policy change very difficult. As more actors have more at stake, every attempt to change policy elicits more calls from more voices. In a political system whose many veto points already make change difficult, the proliferation of well-mobilized corporate lobbying interests, all with their own particular positions and asks, means that there are more actors with the capacity to throw more sand into the already creaky machinery of the multistage policy process. In order for any large-scale change to happen, lobbying generally must be one-sided.[3] To the extent that large corporations benefit from the status quo, a hard-to-change status quo benefits large corporations.[4]

But while the crowded political environment may make legislation harder to pass in generally, it also makes the legislation that does pass more complicated (more side bargains). Large companies are more likely to have the resources and know-how to push for technocratic tweaks at the margins, usually out of public view. This contributes to what Steven Teles calls the "complexity and incoherence of our government." Teles notes that this complexity and incoherence has a tendency to "make it difficult for us to understand just what that government is doing, and among the practices it most frequently hides from view is the growing tendency of public policy to redistribute resources upward to the wealthy and the organized at the expense of the poorer and less organized."[5] The more complicated things become, the more of an advantage it is for corporate lobbyists looking to influence the out-of-sight, hard-to-understand, but sometimes highly consequential nooks and crannies of the U.S. code.

The increasing complexity of policy also makes it more difficult for generalist and generally inexperienced government staffers to maintain an informed understanding of the rules and regulations they are in charge of writing and overseeing. They typically have neither the time to specialize nor the experience to draw on. As a result, staffers must rely more and more on the lobbyists who specialize in particular policy areas. This puts those who can afford to hire the most experienced and policy-literate lobbyists—generally large companies—at the center of the policymaking process. Increasingly, corporations are not just investing in direct lobbying, but also in think tanks and academic research and op-eds and panel discussions in order to shape the intellectual environment of Washington—to make sure that certain frames and assumptions come to mind immediately and easily when policymakers consider legislation and rules. Lobbying efforts now tend to come buffeted by footnotes; by white papers and detailed estimates of how a particular member's constituents will be impacted. It is likely that most material winds up in the "circular file" (a round trash can), and most hosted policy discussions are sparsely attended.

But collectively, they take up time and attention and mindspace. Their cease-less presence shapes the larger intellectual environment of Washington. They are also often a necessary prerequisite for being taken seriously (however aggressive or dubious the number-crunching behind them). And they take time, effort, and—most importantly—money to produce.

A growing lobbying industry also siphons more and more talent from the public sector. The lobbying firms and corporate Washington offices that cluster around K Street generally provide better hours, better working conditions, and most of all, better salaries than government, especially Capitol Hill. Congressional staffers can usually at least double their salaries by "going downtown" (shorthand for becoming a lobbyist, since K Street is downtown). An increasing share of political and policy expertise increasingly resides in the law, lobbying, and strategic advice firms of Washington, DC, where a growing number of experienced political insiders and experts are available, for a fee, to the (mostly) corporations who can afford to hire them (and by extension, their rolodexes). Few diffuse interests groups, by contrast, can afford their fees.

Of course, nothing in the current Washington policymaking environment guarantees influence for any individual corporation. If anything, these changes probably reduce the expected return on investment to lobbying by raising the costs. On many issues, companies fight other companies to a standstill for years, with only the lobbyists on both sides benefiting. But this is not a sign that pluralism is alive and well. One also needs to ask: what issues are being left off the agenda? What groups and interests can't get into the fight without attaching themselves to a cause that large corporations also care about? How much of the policy capacity of the federal government is being used up refereeing parochial industry disputes, as opposed to dealing with other issues?

Nor are these changes generally good for business as a whole. Certainly, individual market leaders may benefit from the current environment, with its strong status quo bias and its rent-seeking possibilities (at least for those who can afford the right—and right number of—lobbyists). But overall, the increasing difficulty of political change reduces the capacity of the federal government to challenge the existing status quo, even when it is anti-innovation and anti-market. The current U.S. tax code, as former representative Bill Frenzel puts it, "is a hopelessly complex mess, antithetical to growth, and is crammed with conflicting incentives."[6] Yet comprehensive tax reform has been a political impossibility for a long time. The tax code may be the most compelling example of how the increased particularism of business lobbying undermines the interests of business as a community. Most everyone in the business community realizes that the U.S. tax code is, as a whole, bad for the economy. But while there is always talk of a "grand bargain" on taxes, nobody is willing to be the first to put their tax benefits on the table. Hence, the "grand bargain" remains largely talk.

"Individual American corporations have more political power in the early twenty-first century than at any time since the 1920s," writes Mark Mizruchi. But, "unlike their predecessors in earlier decades, they are either unwilling or unable to mount any systematic approach to addressing even the problems of their own community, let alone those of the larger society."[7] Consider what happened in 2013, when partisan warfare led to a 16-day government shutdown and threatened to let the United States default on its debt. In the run-up to the government shutdown, Paul Stebbens, the CEO of World Fuel Services who had been active in the "Fix the Debt" campaign, told the *Washington Post*: "Let's start with the basic fact that business was part of the problem. In August of 2011, I was meeting with the Business Roundtable in D.C., and most business guys were running around the world being busy running their corporations and not paying a lot of attention in a general way . . . We have a higher duty of care to engage this issue. It is grossly reckless to watch the long-term business trajectory of the U.S. to be at such risk. And we are part of the pathology that got us here. We've all had our K Street lobbyists who are part of the problem."[8]

While the business community was very unhappy about the budget brinksmanship in Washington, this was not the kind of issue that companies had experience lobbying. Instead, corporate lobbying has all gone to educate congressional offices about the particular concerns of specific industries and companies. As a result, members of Congress have done impressive work on behalf of particular companies and particular industries. However, they've been misled into thinking that the sum total of all their targeted support (essentially, picking winners through public policy) is somehow good for the economy, because each policy they support is promoted individually as good for the economy or good for business.

Even if fellow business leaders did agree with Stebbens that their K Street lobbyists were indeed "part of the problem," it seems unlikely that they would tell them all to go home. Large companies are unlikely to risk ceding any political advantages to competitors. After all, if they've invested significant resources in politics, they've surely been convinced that engagement is important. Why would they change their minds now? Especially when political engagement still remains cheap relative to what is at stake.

The Missing Reform Cycle?

While it is difficult to assess the power of business, a historical perspective does provide one possible lens: the concept of the political cycle. Arthur Schlesinger Jr. famously argued that political history tends to move in 30-year cycles, with each period responding to the excesses of the previous period.[9] The laissez-faire Gilded Age led to the reformist Progressive Era, which led to the laissez-faire Roaring Twenties, which led to the reformist New Deal, which was followed by the relatively laissez-faire post-war period, which was followed by a reformist 1960s. The 1980s marked another era of laissez-faire politics. According to Schlesinger's theory, the next reform cycle should have come in the 1990s. It didn't. It still hasn't arrived. For all of the political Right's attempts to paint Barack Obama as a socialist, his landmark 2010 healthcare reform bill (the Patient Protection and Affordable Care Act) was written and passed in close consultation with the pharmaceutical and health insurance industries, and largely preserved both industries' market position. It did not enact a "public option"—an entirely publicly funded healthcare system that would have been a serious blow to the private healthcare industry. Likewise, while the landmark 2010 Wall Street reform bill (Dodd-Frank) might have been billed as the most significant financial sector reform since the series of bills that passed in the early 1930s, it did not challenge the fundamental structure of Wall Street (unlike the Glass-Steagall Act of 1933, which reshaped the organization of American finance in response to the financial collapse of 1929).

Similarly, David Vogel argues that historically, reform tends to follow corporate profitability, because the public is most willing to support reforms when corporations appear to be doing well. But when American business is struggling financially, the public is more concerned with economic growth, and business does better politically as a result.[10] Certainly one of the most effective arguments of the business resurgence in the 1970s and the early 1980s was that government regulation was preventing an economic recovery. But then the economy recovered. The "Roaring 1990s,"[11] when business was booming, would have been a likely time for the forces of reform to re-assert themselves. But they did not, and they have not since the 1960s.

Both frameworks predict a reform era that never happened. Perhaps this missing reform cycle is the consequence of the density of the business lobbying presence in Washington. Perhaps the kind of large-scale turn towards government regulation that marked previous reform cycles is no longer politically feasible given the ubiquity of corporate lobbying. Perhaps corporations simply have too many lobbyists, and too many resources devoted to influencing political outcomes, to ever allow anything like the earlier reform eras to take place.

Is the Era of Lobbying Growth over?

In 2011, reported lobbying expenditures experienced their first year-to-year decline since electronic disclosures began in 1998, falling from $3.55 billion in 2010 to $3.33 billion in 2011. The slide has continued into 2013, when reported lobbying expenditures fell to $3.21 billion. This decline has led to much speculation in Washington that lobbying hasn't really declined. Rather, there is more "shadow lobbying"—that is, there is more influence activity that doesn't meet strict Lobbying Disclosure Act definitions of lobbying, and more people who for various reasons prefer not to register as lobbyists and so structure their time and activity to avoid having to legally disclose.[12] For obvious reasons (the lack of disclosure), it is impossible to know for sure.

Still, there are good reasons why lobbying expenditures might actually have dropped 10 percent between 2010 and 2013. After all, congressional productivity has declined to record lows. The end of congressional earmarks put a damper on appropriations lobbying, and the end of two wars has made lobbying for defense procurement less lucrative. Given these factors, we might reasonably expect even more than a 10 percent decline from 2010 to 2013. Perhaps the right question is: why didn't lobbying decline even more?

One possibility is that while congressional activity declined, administrative rulemaking continued apace, even increasing in the wake of Dodd-Frank and the Affordable Care Act. A more plausible theory, based on the research presented in this book, is that large companies (which, as we have seen, account for a sizeable share of the total lobbying expenditures) have become fully convinced of the importance of political engagement, and corporate managers now view lobbying as a long-term proposition. Gridlock may have overwhelmed Washington for the moment. But that just means that now is the time to do the spadework of further issue development and relationship-building on both sides of the aisle. That way, when the gridlock breaks, the companies that put in the hard work of building widespread support for their issues will be ready to move. Moreover, in a Congress that doesn't pass much, getting *your* issue onto the agenda requires even more work. Finally, the continued chatter of tax reform, budget cuts, and other austerity measures may have launched enough vague threats that corporations see the value in making sure if there is going to be a chopping block, *somebody else* will be on it.

Additionally, in thinking about the long-term trends, it is important to note that while most of the very biggest companies have by now established major lobbying operations in Washington, the majority (close to 90 percent) of publicly traded companies still do not have their own lobbyists (preferring instead to leave representation to the trade associations). One reason may be that many corporate executives are still reflexively anti-government, and still don't think they should be participating in politics. Some quotes from lobbyists help to illustrate this point. The first two come from contract lobbyists; the third comes from an in-house lobbyist.

- "Some companies are skeptical; they think lobbyists are con artists."
- "A lot of these companies think the last thing that they would do is to get involved in DC."

- "My very first day at the company, I hopped on plane with the CEO to take a series of meetings. He has a true disdain for government. He thinks we can do it ourselves, that market forces work better."

As we've discussed, this distrust of government runs deep in American business culture.[13] Even companies that have decided to invest in government affairs frequently need to be convinced of its value, as multiple lobbyists told me. Even as recent as 2001, statements like this could be found in a how-to book on business lobbying: "Many managers, especially in highly regulated industries, view government as the enemy. You not only have to dispel that notion; you have to encourage the view that government can be influenced in ways that can advance company strategy."[14]

There are plenty of companies who have not yet been drawn into a public policy battle, and there are managers who have not yet been convinced that they need their own lobbyists in Washington. But my theory suggests that once they get drawn in, they tend to keep their lobbyists on. If Washington acts like a magnet, more and more companies will be pulled in as new policy battles arise. Consider the tech sector: one by one, the new giants of the sector—Google, Facebook, Twitter—have discovered Washington and are deepening their involvement. Google is now consistently one of the top spenders on lobbying. As new companies emerge in the economy, they will sooner or later add themselves to the ranks of major lobbying companies.

In all likelihood, the current trends are merely a temporary plateau (or a slight decline, depending on how much the reported numbers are to be believed). When partisan gridlock breaks, more companies will rush to take advantage and/or respond to others trying to take advantage. And the increased competition will only raise the costs. Of course, the system may at some point reach capacity. There may be a moment where the government becomes incapable of taking any meaningful action given the pressures it faces on all sides. Hopefully, however, the system will find a way to reform itself before that happens. And if the system needs some help in reforming itself, the following section provides a way to start that conversation.

What to Do about Lobbying

In 2006, as Democrats fought to take back the U.S. House, then–minority leader Nancy Pelosi promised that she would "drain the swamp" and on her first day as majority leader put in place new rules to "break the link between lobbyists and legislation."[15] And so, when the Democrats did come back into power, they passed a bill known as the Honest Leadership and Government Act (HLOGA).

HLOGA did a number of things to change the way lobbying worked. It put an end to meals, travel, and other gifts from lobbyists and special interests (campaign contributions, however, did not count as "gifts"). It upped lobbying disclosure filings to quarterly instead of biannually, and upped disclosure requirements for lobbyists who "bundled" multiple campaign contributions. It also slowed the revolving door—senators would have to wait two years to lobby Congress upon retirement instead of just one. It also prevented retiring top-level Senate staff (defined as those making 75 percent of a member's salary) from lobbying the entire Senate for a whole year, and prevented retiring top-level House staff from lobbying their former office or committee for an entire year.[16]

The villain in mind as the bill passed was lobbyist Jack Abramoff, who had, in January 2006, been sentenced to prison for mail fraud, conspiracy to bribe public officials, and tax evasion. Abramoff was famous for taking members of Congress on golf trips, giving them free tickets to sporting events, and letting them eat for free at his upscale Washington restaurant, Signatures.[17] Thus, the implicit theory behind the 2006 reform was that if lobbyists could no longer provide special favors to members of Congress and their staff in the form of meals, trips, and other gifts, their influence would be reduced. Government would become less corrupt.

President Obama, who had made the power of lobbyists and special interests an issue during this campaign, took another approach. On his first day in office in 2009, he signed an executive order prohibiting registered lobbyists from serving in his administration.[18] While it sent a powerful political signal, there were some practical problems. Many in the nonprofit advocacy world who had registered as lobbyists (including some who had done just to be careful, even though they probably didn't have to) were disqualified from administration positions that they had hoped to obtain. The Obama administration was also forced into a position of hypocrisy when it granted a waiver to William Lynn, the former lobbyist for defense contractor Raytheon, so that he could serve as the Deputy Secretary of Defense.[19] Moreover, the consensus in Washington was that many who might otherwise have registered as lobbyists decided not to (or simply adjusted their activities to avoid the legal definition of lobbying) for fear that such registration would prohibit them from future administration jobs.[20] Proponents of this theory have noted that the number of registered lobbyists in Washington has decreased every year since 2008 (from 14,849 in 2007 to 11,702 in 2012) after steadily increasing every year (save one) between 1998 and 2007 (*growing* from 10,408 to 14,849). However, there is also evidence to suggest that this decline may have been in response to the passage of HLOGA.[21]

Other than the optics, there is little evidence that executive branch lobbying has changed in the Obama administration (as compared to previous administrations). As James Thurber concluded: "[Obama] has limited those who can be appointed to executive positions, but it has had little impact on those who actually influence the decision-making process. Moreover, President Obama has worked closely, often in a nontransparent way, with networks of 'special interests' (lobbyists/advocates) in crafting the economic stimulus funding, health care reform, financial regulatory reforms, the federal budget deficit and debt, climate change legislation, education reform, immigration policy, and a wide array of other issues on his public policy agenda in 2009–2010."[22]

In other words, recent reforms have done very little to change the ways that lobbying actually works. That is largely because these reforms have played to popular conceptions of corruption, and in so doing have addressed the wrong problems. Contrary to popular opinion, there is not much outright quid pro quo corruption or bribery in Washington these days. Certainly, there are occasional examples; it is also certain that the best guard against corruption is an active watchdog community. However, instances of outright corruption are rare. While they make good news stories when they do occur, the media's fascination with scandal has done a disservice to political accountability.

Much public opinion on the subject of political influence suffers from a confusing and counterproductive mix of hopeless idealism and fatalistic cynicism. On the one hand, many people think that if only we could get special interests out of politics, then we would have a government run by perfectly rational Solomonic lawmakers, capable of divining the true public interest and making wise and uncorrupted judgments. On the other hand, they look at the political system and think: most politicians are at once craven and venal, ready to sell their votes for the promise of a hosted fundraiser, or even more cheaply, a few thousand dollars in PAC contributions.

The reality is, of course, more complicated, but also much more interesting. Like everyone else, politicians are motivated by a mix of both noble and not-so-noble desires. There are some good ones and some not-so-good ones, but any attempts to cut them off from the pressures of society is a betrayal of both the idea of representative democracy and the potential for collective intelligence that widespread participation on the political process allows for. The Washington lobbying community is full of many bright policy minds, and the expertise and knowledge that the business community can provide makes for a more informed policymaking process.

Any attempt to directly limit the participation of corporate lobbyists in the political process runs immediately into the practical problem that attempts to limit political influence have always encountered. If corporations (or other actors) are determined to influence the political process, they will find a way. If the history of political influence regulation has taught us anything, it should be this: that those determined to participate in the political process will find ways to do so.[23]

There are, however, three genuine problems that do need fixing, and that can be fixed in ways that work with, not against, the realities of politics.

The first problem is the balance of power. When corporate interests spend $34 for every $1 diffuse interests and unions *combined* spend on lobbying, it is not a fair fight. If we want a political system that is capable of responding to the broad societal interests, we want a political system where a broad range of societal interests are capable of presenting their most effective case. When large corporations are the dominant actors in Washington, policy attention will almost certainly reflect their priorities.

The second problem is the asymmetry of information and the related complexity. When government actors are forced to rely on outside lobbyists for policy expertise, and when that expertise is provided largely on behalf of a narrow set of actors, this is likely to distort outcomes. Additionally, policy complexity makes it easier for corporate actors with the most resources to make quiet changes with little to no scrutiny.

The third problem is particularism. Companies are increasingly oriented towards narrow, rent-seeking outcomes. Parochial intra- and inter-industry battles take up an increasing amount of Washington bandwidth, and the increasing investments in this particularism crowd out the capacity of the political system to address larger problems. What may be good for some powerful companies is almost certainly bad for the economy as a whole.

These problems are all related, and any attempt to deal with one without dealing with the others is likely to fail. Sticking with the rule of threes, I propose three types of solutions. As with the problems, the solutions are interrelated. They would be most effective as a coherent program. Piecemeal application would almost certainly be far less effective.

The treatment of these solutions is admittedly limited here. These are, at this point, roughly drawn proposals. There is still much to be worked out in their details and implementation, and certainly, they are not meant to be cure-alls. They are presented in the hopes of starting a conversation, of trying to sketch out a few ways forward based on both the lessons I've learned in researching and writing this book as well as the lessons of other recent attempts at reform.

The Madisonian Solution

I take very seriously James Madison's argument in *Federalist #10* that the problem of faction is inherent to all political systems, and that any attempt to limit the participation of factions is a cure worse than the disease. Therefore, I share Madison's faith that the best way to deal with the problem of faction is for faction to counteract faction and to "enlarge the sphere."[24] Let everyone have their say, and hope that something resembling the public interests can emerge from the dust.

Of course, this approach depends on a rough balance of power. If unions and diffuse interest groups had roughly the same resources as business interests, we might reasonably expect that the two forces would keep each other roughly in check. This, however, is not the case. As we've seen, corporate interests now spend 34 times what diffuse interest groups and unions combined spend on lobbying. Not a single corporate lobbyist I interviewed identified a diffuse interest group or a union as the primary opponent on an issue on which he or she was lobbying. Faction is not counteracting faction.

This is not likely to change on its own for two reasons. One is the simple fact that it is relatively easy for businesses to mobilize politically since they can, with just a few executive decisions, allocate some of their already-existing resources to political activity.[25] And now that a growing number of business leaders have become convinced that politics matters, there is very little to stop them from continuing to spend substantial sums. Interested citizens, by contrast, must find a way to overcome the collective action problem, pulling together resources and commitments, and then sustaining those resources and commitments over time. This is difficult to accomplish.[26] Secondly, the nature of much political conflict, in which a particular policy affects a handful of companies greatly while affecting most citizens only marginally, means that individual companies and industries have the most concentrated stakes, and therefore the biggest incentive to remain vigilant and active.[27] Businesses both have the means and the motive to spend heavily. Both their stake in political outcomes and their ability to mobilize resources are far greater than the average citizen. This is unlikely to change on its own. Fixing the participatory imbalance will require government to make an active investment. There is clearly a market failure.

Is there a public interest in fixing this imbalance? One analogy is to our legal system. Indigent criminal defendants are given court-appointed lawyers because we have decided that everybody should have the right to a lawyer when they interact with the justice system. Why does the same principle not apply to politics? Does not everybody whose interests are materially affected by the political system deserve the right to a lobbyist?

Certainly, there are difficulties in determining who has a legitimate claim for lobbying representation, and how much representation they deserve. But here's one way it could work: Groups advocating for a diffuse interest would have to demonstrate that their perspective was shared by a threshold percentage of citizens, and that the existing lobbying community was not adequately representing this viewpoint. Imagine a three-stage process. First, an under-represented perspective would have to gain threshold number of signatures (perhaps 25,000) and advocates of the perspective would need to demonstrate that they were being outspent by at least a threshold ratio (perhaps 4 to 1), and that a diffuse group of citizens were affected. Then, that perspective could be included in a regularly occurring poll that the government conducts to test for widespread support in the country. If a threshold percentage of citizens agreed with the perspective (perhaps 25 percent), a federal subsidy would be awarded so advocates of that position could hire a lobbyist. Subsidies could be awarded based on the level of support, and the ratio by which advocates for that position were being outspent by powerful interests. A more aggressive version of this proposal would require well-funded interests on the other side to fund their opposition, in order to guarantee a fair fight.

Alternately, rather than award a direct subsidy to the under-represented perspective, the federal government could create an Office of Public Lobbying, maintaining a team of public lobbyists who would then represent different public interest clients before the government. Zephy Teachout has made the case for such an institution, noting that, "Congress could hire, at a fraction of the expense paid to lobbyists, advocates to represent a range of opinions on any proposed legislation, and stage trial-like debates between them."[28] Serving as a public lobbyist might be a very appealing job for a congressional staffer whose boss lost an election or retired, or a congressional staffer just looking to do something different for a few years. Many congressional staffers may not necessarily desire to represent corporate interests, but wish to stay in Washington and remain active in public policy. Working as a public lobbyist could provide an appealing alternative to a K Street job, while giving a voice to a set of societal interests that currently lack a voice in Washington. It may also provide an alternative to working for a non-profit because it would provide more variety and job security. Additionally, an Office of Public Lobbying could actively work to identify under-represented voices, utilizing social media and other low-cost methods to tap into diffuse public concerns and give them voice.

The Genuine Public Conversation Approach

In 1946, Congress passed the Administrative Procedure Act, which created "uniform procedures for rulemaking, adjudication, and transparency on federal agencies." Now most executive branch agencies have a structured rulemaking process. Before a rule can be finalized, all interested parties have a chance to comment. Those comments are public, and agencies respond to those comments in a public way. While there is certainly additional lobbying that takes place beyond formal commenting, the comments provide a useful way to see who is participating, and whose concerns are being heard. In the age of the Internet, all agencies now post the comments online.

Lobbying Congress, by contrast, remains as haphazard as it has ever been. While organizations do have to file quarterly lobbying disclosure reports, these reports are vague. They may list specific issues, or they may not. Organizations lobbying do not have to disclose which offices they visited, nor do they have to disclose the positions for which they advocated or the draft legislation they left behind.

What if Congress passed a Congressional Lobbying Procedure Act that created a set of uniform processes for congressional lobbying? Such a system could take advantage of modern technology and require that any advocacy be posted within 48 hours on a central website. Each report would contain a short summary of the meeting, who attended, and what was advocated for.

Any white papers, draft legislation, or other leave-behinds would need to be posted in electronic form as well. The website would also serve as a repository for all arguments and advocacy. A series of clicks would take any interested member of the public to a corpus of arguments for or against particular public policies, creating a central clearinghouse.

Such a website could also could also make it much easier for citizens to offer input and register their opinions in an organized and traceable way (as opposed to the current sporadic and haphazard barrage of e-mails and phone calls, which may or may not get a response). Organizations like Project Madison[29] and Popvox[30] have done impressive work exploring how the Internet could provide a forum for wider citizen participation in the legislative process, and both offer valuable frameworks for going forward.

This hypothetical Congressional Lobbying Procedure Act would change lobbying in several ways. First, it would level the playing field between corporate interests and diffuse interests. It would make lobbying less about hiring armies of well-connected lobbyists who can spread out all over the Hill, and more about developing convincing arguments and summaries that would inform congressional offices.

It would also become easier for diffuse interests to know what corporate interests are actually arguing, which would allow them respond to those arguments in a timely matter (and vice versa). Ultimately, this website could serve as a kind of policymaking marketplace of ideas, where different interests would have the opportunity to respond to each other in real-time. It could harness the competitive nature of lobbying in service of accountability.. It would provide an instant source for all arguments on all sides, and help congressional staffers new to an issue to know where they can find more information.

Such a process could also potentially reduce particularistic lobbying efforts. By bringing real-time transparency to attempts to insert narrow provisions into legislation, this system could alert watchdogs as these attempts happen, allowing them to blow the whistle and bring public scrutiny to deals that largely depend on nobody else paying attention to them. This could make members of Congress more wary of working to advocate particularistic benefits. In turn, lobbyists would be able to anticipate the consequences of such narrow asks. They would know that the risks would be high, and the likelihood of success would be low. This would make them much less likely to make such asks in the first place. This could also have the effect of reducing lobbying, especially particularistic lobbying. This is admittedly optimistic, but it at least points in the right direction.

If lobbyists are able to put fewer particularistic policies in place, this would make it harder for them to demonstrate the bottom line benefits of lobbying to corporate bosses. It would reduce the number of purely selective benefits in corporate lobbying. As lobbying moves more towards collective benefits, companies might pay less and hope to free-ride more. An added benefit of lobbying becoming less particularistic is that legislation could become simpler. There would be less need to address the narrow concerns of every single company with a lobbyist. It would be easier to move towards more coherent policymaking.

Such a system could also alter the information asymmetry between lobbyists and corporate managers. I've argued that one of the key reasons why corporations spend more on lobbying is because managers do not get to observe what lobbyists do and how their actions do or do not move the policy needle. Lobbyists can claim that they had substantive meetings with members of Congress and overstate their influence. If corporate lobbyists had to document everything that they do to try to influence political outcomes, managers would be in a better position to evaluate their lobbyists' activities. Doing so might allow savvy corporate managers to conclude that most of what they spend on lobbying is, in fact, wasted. They might spend less on lobbying. In principal-agent literature in economics, transparency is commonly seen as a way for principals to overcome information asymmetries and thus reduce their costs.[31]

Increasing Government Policy Capacity

A third approach would give Congress more of its own policy capacity. As I have argued, one of the reasons why lobbyists have become increasingly central to the policy process is that the policy capacity of the government, and especially Congress, has declined over time while policy complexity and specialization have increased. Congressional staffers are always scrambling to play intellectual catch-up. They have to turn to lobbyists to explain increasingly complex policy for them. This gives lobbyists a tremendous advantage.

There are a number of potential ways to reduce congressional dependence on lobbyists. One is simply to improve the working conditions and salaries of congressional staff, making it a more attractive job for senior-level people. Rather than toil in anonymity at relatively low pay with long, unpredictable hours, congressional staffers should be given more acknowledgement, better pay, and more favorable working conditions. If congressional offices paid staff better, they could afford to attract and retain more top policy talent, and make it less likely that congressional staff would use their time on the Hill to plot their exit, potentially cozying up to lobbyists who might someday make them rich.

In most congressional offices, working conditions could be improved dramatically. Hours could be better, and staffers could be allowed to take more credit and ownership for the work that they produce. Instead of maintaining the fiction that it is the member of Congress who does everything, members of Congress could acknowledge that while they set the general direction and priorities for the office, voters are now electing a team of people to represent them, and that the entire team deserves some public credit.

While the private sector is likely to continue to be able to pay people more, elected officials ought to acknowledge that who they hire has an impact on how well they can serve their constituents—and be willing to invest in good people. Some of this may seem like Management 101, but Congress could use a dose of institutionalized Management 101.

Congress could also improve its independent policy capacity externally. Already, Congress has some institutions designed to help it. The Congressional Research Service (CRS) and the Government Accountability Office (GAO) are both valuable resources, and play an important role in providing independent expert advice and research. But both are limited in their capacity. [32] Perhaps, then, the most straightforward approach to improving congressional capacity is simply to significantly expand the budget for both of these organizations—allow them to hire more people, and work with congressional offices to make them as useful as possible.

Another possibility here is tapping into the knowledge and expertise that resides in American universities. House and Senate offices could officially partner with local universities, particularly public policy schools and law schools. Professors could serve as expert advisers. Universities could incentivize participation by giving formal credit to faculty who lend their expertise and lead students to help make national policy. Students could get excellent training serving as policy researchers and legislation drafters for congressional offices.

Shouldn't helping to improve the quality of public policy for the country be at least on par with publishing academic articles in small audience peer-reviewed journals? One approach in this direction comes from the Congressional Clerkship Coalition. More than 100 law school deans have urged Congress to create a "congressional clerkship" program that would be a legislative analogue to the judicial clerkship program, giving young lawyers more legislative experience and congressional offices more legal help. But while legislation to create the program has passed the House twice and enjoys widespread bipartisan support, it has not made it out of the Senate.[33]

Heather Gerken and Alex Tausanovich have suggested funding "policy research consultants" that would be available to congressional offices: "What we have in mind is the lobbyist equivalent of public-interest law firms. The aim would be to allow legislators to hire 'research consultants' who can provide information during the major stages of decision-making as well as during the period in which the bill is amended. These independent consultants would have a semi-permanent status, and thus able to offer the "long-term commitment" that bears fruit in the lobbying world. They would be able to assist members with thinking through issues before they even get on the agenda of a particular committee, and they would be able to put their time and effort into developing good policies over the long-term."[34] Congressional offices would be able to choose whomever they want as their consultants. They could choose lobbyists from the oil industry, but as Gerken and Tausanovich argue, they would have no reason to do so, since they already get plenty of policy support from the industry, which happily provides it for free. Rather, these research consultants will allow them to get the legislative subsidies that they can't get elsewhere.

Though executive branch agencies tend to have better salaries and working conditions, and to also attract more policy expertise, even they are increasingly having a hard time maintaining the levels of internal expertise necessary to make policy in complex environments. They also suffer similar pay gaps and could benefit from more policy resources.

The basic thread of all these capacity-building reforms, however, is the same. In order to make the best policy, government needs the best people, and many of them. If key policymakers don't have the resources to adequately evaluate policy and have confidence in their observations, they will be forced to rely excessively on those interests who have the most at stake.

How These Reforms would Work Together

Perhaps the best way to understand how these reforms work together is to see how they solve the possible objections that could arise from applying the reforms piecemeal. The most obvious objection to the Madisonian approach of enlarging the sphere is that Washington lobbying is already exceedingly competitive, and this competition is a source of gridlock. Wouldn't more competitive lobbying mean even more gridlock? This is a legitimate concern, especially if it means that congressional offices become even more overwhelmed by an onslaught of lobbying. But moving lobbying into an online public conversation and giving offices more of their own policy capacity would both help to better channel all the lobbying activity. Rather than being overwhelmed by all the arguments and advocacy, congressional offices would have the expertise and knowledge to sort through the information and pressures more productively. Moreover, the capacity of an online platform to organize the information would help staffers who often lack the time to stay organized. It would remind them of the bigger picture, rather than being susceptible to whomever they met with last.

The limitation of real-time online lobbying is that the corporate interests with the most resources can simply overwhelm this process, like they overwhelm every other process. They can invest more resources in shaping the intellectual environment and more resources in responding to the opposing concerns. While the platform has some leveling effects, they are not nearly enough. In the absence of other reforms, this will almost certainly be the case. But if the government can take active steps to level the playing field by subsidizing diffuse interests, this is less of a problem. If lawmakers have more capacity to evaluate the information without the help of lobbyists, this is also less of a problem.

Even with expanded government policy capacity, government actors will still need the help of outside interests. They may need less help, but they will still require some assistance to develop, vet, and especially build external support for policy initiatives. After all, the "legislative subsidy" that lobbyists provide isn't only about policy expertise. It also covers the entire policy process. Without making some attempts to level the imbalance of lobbying resources, it will still be difficult for congressional offices to advance causes that lack organized lobbying resources. Government intervention to balance the playing field can help. Moving lobbying online and creating a repository of policy arguments can also help, because it will give congressional offices more resources on which to draw.

Another critique of this build-more-capacity approach is that expertise is never neutral, and just because members of Congress have access to more policy capacity doesn't necessarily mean that they won't simply use it in service of whatever narrow ends they might already be working towards, and to pick and choose studies that support their existing beliefs.[35] This is certainly a fair critique. Dreams of a perfectly rational, scientifically minded technocracy never end well, but all else equal, more expertise and more policy capacity are almost certainly better than less. Certainly, there will be members of Congress who will be unaffected, but ideally this approach would push policymaking in a smarter direction. It would provide policymakers with the resources to stand up to industry "experts" whom they might have reason to doubt but lack the topic knowledge to confront.

In short, this package of reform works best as a coherent program. One strength of this program, as compared to many other reform programs, is that it embraces politics, rather than attempting to sublimate it. It is built on the premise that more lobbying and more political engagement is better, and more money and more resources (rather than fewer) ought to go into shaping public policy, and argues it is possible to channel political competition in a constructive way. It also does not treat members of Congress as venal, corrupt individuals who are incapable of standing up to moneyed interests. It acknowledges that they would like to serve a broader public interest, and could do so more effectively if they had some additional help.

Campaign Finance

This book has not devoted much attention to campaign finance, other than to acknowledge that contributing to campaigns is one of many strategies companies use to try to influence public policy. Again, companies spend roughly 13 times more on lobbying than they do on PAC contributions. This is not to say that money is not important. It undoubtedly improves access, and plays an important gatekeeping role in who can run for office and puts limits on what policies they can publicly support.

Members of Congress spend far too much time fundraising. As the costs of campaigns continue to rise, members of Congress spend more and more hours a day in "call time."[36] Increasingly, the main qualification for the job is having a unique personality trait that allows one to withstand several hours a day of begging rich people for money. In 2012, 28 percent of the nearly $6 billion in contributions from identifiable sources in the last campaign cycle came from just 31,385 individuals, a number equal to 1 percent of 1 percent of the U.S. population.[37] Those who can appeal to these kinds of donors can run for office. Those who can't appeal to these donors usually can't.

Appealing to wealthy donors involves both taking on policy positions that are comfortable for these donors and not wasting time with issues that do not concern them. It also involves listening to the donors' concerns, and at least acknowledging their arguments. As Senator Chris Murphy (D-CT) once described his campaign donors: "They have fundamentally different problems than other people. And in Connecticut especially, you spend a lot of time on the phone with people who work in the financial markets. And so you're hearing a lot about problems that bankers have and not a lot of problems that people who work at the mill in Thomaston, Conn., have. You certainly have to stop and check yourself."[38] Over time, this can lead to a kind of self-interested worldview osmosis, where candidates take on donors' perspectives as part of a need to appeal to them. If you hear an argument enough times, and you repeat it enough times to raise money, eventually you may even start to believe it. Or at the very least, whatever zeal you may have had on the other side of the issue is gradually replaced by doubt.

Certainly, proposals to create a small-donor matching system or to establish fully publicly funded elections (as is the norm in almost all other industrialized democracies) would level an unequal playing field, and almost certainly change the types of people who run for Congress in the first place. Politicians would spend less time nodding to the concerns of wealthy donors. They would be able to worry less about how various policy stances would affect their future fundraising.

However, even if elections were partially or fully publicly funded, this would not solve the expertise and experience problems we've discussed. It would not solve the complexity problem we've discussed. It would not change the revolving door. Corporations would continue to overwhelm the intellectual environment of Washington. There would continue to be an imbalance in the intensity of preference and attention on a wide range of highly technical issues. Taking high-dollar contributions out of campaigns would almost certainly push corporations to redouble their efforts in other areas of influence. Some public funding of election mechanisms should be included in any larger reform package, but focusing only on the electoral aspects of influence is limited.

American Business and American Democracy

Scholars have long argued over whether or not corporate participation in politics distorts American democracy. To the extent that corporations have an operating principle, it is to maximize profits while minimizing and externalizing costs. To the extent that democracy has an operating principle, it is to allow people to rule themselves. These two principles run into potential conflict when the corporate goal of maximizing profits spills over into the mechanisms designed to allow the people to govern themselves, which was Charles Lindblom's fundamental concern in *Politics and Markets* when he concluded that "the large private corporation fits oddly into democratic theory and vision. Indeed, it does not fit."[39] If, instead of attending to the concerns of dispersed citizens, the mechanisms of democracy are primarily taken up with responding to the concerns and interests of the small number of citizens who either lead corporations or own significant amounts of their stock, this would appear to be a distortion of democracy.

Of course, business lobbyists will argue that they are advocating on behalf of policies that benefit the economy, and thus all citizens. In their advocacy, they tell a convincing story about the jobs they will create or save, the ways in which consumers will benefit from their products and services, and why what they advocate is good public policy. In a competitive lobbying environment, they have to.[40] Companies work hard to polish their image and to show why want they want is good for all of America. Corporate lobbyists will also argue that they are not as powerful as they are often made out to be, and quite often they don't get what they want.

Such an argument can go back and forth indefinitely. Arguably, it has already been raging for many years. But what such a back-and-forth misses is that the process of widespread business political mobilization has changed the contours of policymaking. Corporate lobbying has become more proactive, particularistic, and pervasive. The size and scope of the modern corporate lobbying operations are unprecedented in American history. And the environment it has produced is one that is very hospitable to corporate lobbyists.

These changes, however, do not mean that corporations automatically get what they want if they spend large sums of money. There is no evidence to support this. However, these changes do make it more likely that large corporations that can spend large sums of money on lobbying will be more successful than the diffuse interests or groups that don't have the same resources to get their issues on the agenda. While individual policy outcomes are unpredictable, in the aggregate, policy outcomes lean towards the preferences of corporate interests and wealthy donors.[41]

Over the last four decades, American corporations have learned how to play politics, and more and more corporate executives have come to view political engagement as an important part of their business. They have hired lobbyists who have told them to see politics as important. The large-scale result has not only been distortion of democratic priorities. It is also increasingly an immobilization of democracy. If the trends described in this book continue, American democracy will continue to decline. And it will not be because corporations necessarily get the policy outcomes they want. It will undermine the functioning of American democracy because it will diminish the problem-solving capacity of government, which will mean that hardly anybody will get anything that they want. To quote an old Kenyan proverb, "When the elephants fight, it is the grass that suffers." Increasingly, that grass is the functioning of the democratic process.

There may be those who argue it is too late to change things. They may look at the current corporate investments in Washington, and the ways in which these investments have come to overwhelm the key government decision-making processes, and see no hope. Certainly, the narrative arc of the story told in the proceeding pages does not point in an optimistic direction.

But it is important to understand that reform is in everybody's long-term interests. Business as a whole does not benefit from the current system, which is widely criticized as being market-distorting and anti-growth. Business leaders frequently express frustrations with the inability of Congress to do anything. The only winners in the current system seem to be the lobbyists—but even they should have a long-term incentive for change. If the political system becomes incapable of accomplishing anything, companies will begin to question why they are investing in Washington and lobbying revenue will dry up. Arguably, this drying up has already begun.

Despite the general pessimism, I wish to close on a note of optimism. It is my sincere hope that this book will contribute to our collective understanding of how lobbying works, what motivates corporations to spend large sums of money on politics, and how these increasing sums have changed the ways in which the policy process operates. It is also my sincere hope that this knowledge can help to inform political reforms that will continue to strengthen the quality of American democracy and move us just a little closer to that more perfect union that always lingers just over the horizon.

NOTES

Prelims

1. Kay Lehman Schlozman, Sidney Verba, and Henry E. Brady, *The Unheavenly Chorus: Unequal Political Voice and the Broken Promise of American Democracy* (Princeton University Press, 2012), 622.

Chapter 1

1. Charles Edward Lindblom, *Politics and Markets: The World's Political Economic Systems* (New York: Basic Books, 1977).
2. See, e.g., Russell Pittman, "Market Structure and Campaign Contributions," *Public Choice* 31, no. 1 (September 1, 1977): 37–52; Daniel C. Esty and Richard E. Caves, "Market Structure and Political Influence: New Data on Political Expenditures, Activity, and Success," *Economic Inquiry* 21, no. 1 (1983): 24–38; Asghar Zardkoohi, "On the Political Participation of the Firm in the Electoral Process," *Southern Economic Journal* 51, no. 3 (January 1985): 804; Gary J. Andres, "Business Involvement in Campaign Finance: Factors Influencing the Decision to Form a Corporate PAC," *PS* 18, no. 2 (Spring 1985): 213–20; John L. Boies, "Money, Business, and the State: Material Interests, Fortune 500 Corporations, and the Size of Political Action Committees," *American Sociological Review* 54, no. 5 (October 1, 1989): 821–33; Graham K. Wilson, "Corporate Political Strategies," *British Journal of Political Science* 20, no. 2 (April 1990): 281–88; Kevin B. Grier, Michael C. Munger, and Brian E. Roberts, "The Industrial Organization of Corporate Political Participation," *Southern Economic Journal* 57, no. 3 (January 1, 1991): 727–38, Kevin B. Grier, Michael C. Munger, and Brian E. Roberts, "The Determinants of Industry Political Activity, 1978–1986," *The American Political Science Review* 88, no. 4 (December 1, 1994): 911–26; Neil J. Mitchell, *The Conspicuous Corporation: Business, Public Policy, and Representative Democracy* (Ann Arbor: University of Michigan Press, 1997); Kathleen A. Rehbein, "Foreign-Owned Firms' Campaign Contributions in the United States: An Exploratory Study," *Policy Studies Journal* 23, no. 1 (1995): 41–61; Davis F. Taylor, "The Relationship between Firm Investments in Technological Innovation and Political Action," *Southern Economic Journal* 63, no. 4 (April 1, 1997): 888–903; Wendy L. Hansen and Neil J. Mitchell, "Disaggregating and Explaining Corporate Political Activity: Domestic and Foreign Corporations in National Politics," *The American Political Science Review* 94, no. 4 (December 2000): 891–903; Wendy L. Hansen, Neil J. Mitchell, and Jeffrey M. Drope, "The Logic of Private and Collective Action," *American Journal of Political Science* 49, no. 1 (January 1, 2005): 150–67; Wendy L. Hansen, Neil J. Mitchell, and Jeffrey M. Drope, "Collective Action, Pluralism, and the Legitimacy Tariff: Corporate Activity or Inactivity in Politics," *Political Research Quarterly* 57, no. 3 (September 2004): 421–29; Jeffrey M. Drope and Wendy L. Hansen, "Does Firm Size Matter? Analyzing Business Lobbying in

the United States," *Business and Politics* 8, no. 2 (2006): 1160; Henry E. Brady et al., "Corporate Lobbying Activity in American Politics," in paper given at the American Political Science Association Annual Meeting (Chicago, IL, 2007).

3. Hansen and Mitchell, "Disaggregating and Explaining Corporate Political Activity: Domestic and Foreign Corporations in National Politics." p. 892

4. Arthur L. Stinchcombe, *Information and Organizations* (Berkeley: University of California Press, 1990).

5. Ibid. p. 2

6. Eric M. Patashnik, *Reforms at Risk: What Happens After Major Policy Changes Are Enacted* (Princeton, NJ: Princeton University Press, 2008).

7. Gene M. Grossman and Elhanan Helpman, "Protection for Sale," *The American Economic Review* 84, no. 4 (September 1, 1994): 833–50; Gene M. Grossman and Elhanan Helpman, *Special Interest Politics* (Cambridge, MA: MIT, 2001); David P. Baron, "Service-Induced Campaign Contributions and the Electoral Equilibrium," *The Quarterly Journal of Economics* 104, no. 1 (February 1989): 45–72.

8 David Vogel, "Why Businessmen Distrust Their State: The Political Consciousness of American Corporate Executives," *British Journal of Political Science* 8, no. 1 (January 1, 1978): 45–78.

9. David Bicknell Truman, *The Governmental Process; Political Interests and Public Opinion* (New York: Knopf, 1951).

10. Truman, *The Governmental Process*; Virginia Gray and David Lowery, "Interest Representation and Democratic Gridlock," *Legislative Studies Quarterly* 20, no. 4 (November 1, 1995): 531–52; Beth L. Leech et al., "Drawing Lobbyists to Washington: Government Activity and the Demand for Advocacy," *Political Research Quarterly* 58, no. 1 (March 2005): 19–30; Frank R. Baumgartner et al., "Congressional and Presidential Effects on the Demand for Lobbying," *Political Research Quarterly* 64, no. 1 (March 1, 2011): 3–16.

11. John Mark Hansen, "The Political Economy of Group Membership," *The American Political Science Review* 79, no. 1 (March 1, 1985): 79–96; Jack L. Walker, *Mobilizing Interest Groups in America: Patrons, Professions, and Social Movements* (Ann Arbor: University of Michigan Press, 1991).

12. James M. Buchanan and Gordon Tullock, *The Calculus of Consent: Logical Foundations of Constitutional Democracy* (Ann Arbor, MI: University of Michigan Press, 1967); George J. Stigler, "The Theory of Economic Regulation," *The Bell Journal of Economics and Management Science* 2, no. 1 (April 1, 1971): 3–21; Anne O. Krueger, "The Political Economy of the Rent-Seeking Society," *The American Economic Review* 64, no. 3 (June 1, 1974): 291–303.

13. David Austen-Smith and John R. Wright, "Counteractive Lobbying," *American Journal of Political Science* 38, no. 1 (February 1994): 25–44.

14. Robert Reich, *Supercapitalism* (New York: Knopf, 2007), p. 134.

15. Timothy M. LaPira, "How Much Lobbying Is There in Washington? It's DOUBLE What You Think," *Sunlight Foundation*, November 25, 2013, http://sunlightfoundation.com/blog/2013/11/25/how-much-lobbying-is-there-in-washington-its-double-what-you-think/.

16. Frank R. Baumgartner and Beth L. Leech, *Basic Interests: The Importance of Groups in Politics and in Political Science* (Princeton, NJ: Princeton University Press, 1998), pp. 95–101.

17. Elmer E. Schattschneider, *The Semi-Sovereign People: A Realist's View of Democracy in America* (Hinsdale, IL: The Dryden Press, 1975).The "pluralist heaven" referred to a claim, made by some at the time of the book's initial publication (1960), that the ideal of democratic pluralism in which faction regularly counteracted faction was alive and well, and that American democracy was accordingly thriving (or at least performing as well as could be expected). Schattschneider dissented, noticing that most of the participants in politics represented the very well-off.

18. Baumgartner and Leech, *Basic Interests: The Importance of Groups in Politics and in Political Science*; Kay Lehman Schlozman, Sidney Verba, and Henry E. Brady, *The Unheavenly Chorus: Unequal Political Voice and the Broken Promise of American Democracy* (Princeton, NJ: Princeton University Press, 2012).

19. This quote, and all other anonymous quotes from lobbyists, come from author interviews. For more details on these interviews, see Notes on Sources.

20. Lewis Powell, "Confidential Memorandum: Attack on the Free Enterprise System," August 23, 1971.
21. I use the term "diffuse interest" to refer to organizations that speak for a diffuse constituency, such as consumers, the environment, good government, or conservative principles. Sometimes these groups are considered "citizens groups" or "public interests." I take the term "diffuse" from James Q. Wilson (1980). Wilson posited diffuse interests as the opposite of concentrated interests. Diffuse interests are spread out. Concentrated interests are, well, concentrated. Corporations and industries are concentrated interests. Diffuse interest groups are most likely to directly oppose the narrow interests of corporations because these groups purport to advocate on behalf of a general interest. In this definition, I make no distinction between conservative groups and liberal groups (this category includes conservative groups like FreedomWorks and Heritage Action for America alongside the Consumer Federation of America and Public Citizen). I only ask whether the group is motivated by what it believes is a public good that extends beyond its members. For this reason, I do not include groups like AARP or any religious or ethnic identity groups, which advocate on behalf of a specific membership constituency. This definition includes the National Rifle Association, but does not include AIPAC (The American Israel Public Affairs Committee).
22. Lester W. Milbrath, "Lobbying as a Communication Process," *Public Opinion Quarterly* 24, no. 1 (March 20, 1960): 32–53.
23. Steven M. Teles, *The Rise of the Conservative Legal Movement: The Battle for Control of the Law* (Princeton, NJ: Princeton University Press, 2012), p. 20.
24. John P. Heinz et al., *The Hollow Core: Private Interests in National Policy Making* (Cambridge, MA: Harvard University Press, 1993), p. 348.
25. I thank Kay Lehman Schlozman for her help in diagnosing this discontinuity.
26. Expenditures are a better measure because they reflect the actual effort spent on lobbying. Merely being registered as a lobbyist reveals no information about the amount of time spent lobbying. In 2007, the two measures (expenditures and lobbying presence) had a 0.85 correlation across all active companies.
27. All dollar figures in this chapter are in constant 2012 dollars
28. Thomas B. Edsall, "The Unlobbyists," *New York Times*, December 31, 2013, http://www.nytimes.com/2014/01/01/opinion/edsall-the-unlobbyists.html; Thomas Edsall, "The Shadow Lobbyist," *New York Times*, 2013, http://opinionator.blogs.nytimes.com/2013/04/25/the-shadow-lobbyist/.
29. Marie Hojnacki et al., "Studying Organizational Advocacy and Influence: Reexamining Interest Group Research," *Annual Review of Political Science* 15, no. 1 (2012): 379–99.
30. Graham K. Wilson, "Thirty Years of Business and Politics," in *Business and Government: Methods and Practice* (Farmington Hills, MI: Barbara Budrich, 2006), 33–50.
31. David M. Hart, "'Business' Is Not an Interest Group: On the Study of Companies in American National Politics," *Annual Review of Political Science* 7, no. 1 (2004): 47–69.
32. Robert A. Dahl, "Business and Politics: A Critical Appraisal of Political Science," *The American Political Science Review* 53, no. 1 (March 1, 1959): 1–34, p. 3.
33. Lobbying and Disclosure Act of 1995 (2 U.S.C. §1601)
34. Lester W. Milbrath, *The Washington Lobbyists* (Chicago: Rand McNally, 1963).
35. American League of Lobbyists, *Recommendations for Improving the Regulation of Federal Lobbyists*, 2012; available at: http://grprofessionals.org/wp-content/uploads/2013/07/lda_wg_report_04-09-12.pdf.
36. League president Monte Ward said: "In a recent survey of our board and membership, and after three recent focus groups, we discovered that a majority of our membership no longer identified themselves as 'only lobbyists.' In fact, most of those surveyed stated that their responsibilities as a lobbyist encompassed just a fraction of their duties. While our organization was founded in 1979 to support the lobbying community, this industry has evolved dramatically over the years and now includes a variety of disciplines involved in government affairs, lobbying and public policy arena."
37. Lee Drutman and Daniel J. Hopkins, "The Inside View: Using the Enron E-Mail Archive to Understand Corporate Political Attention," *Legislative Studies Quarterly* 38, no. 1 (2013): 5–30.

38. Stephen Ansolabehere, John M. de Figueiredo, and James M. Snyder Jr., "Why Is There so Little Money in U.S. Politics?," *The Journal of Economic Perspectives* 17, no. 1 (January 1, 2003): 105–30.

39. Laura I. Langbein, "Money and Access: Some Empirical Evidence," *The Journal of Politics* 48, no. 04 (1986): 1052–62; Richard L. Hall and Frank W. Wayman, "Buying Time: Moneyed Interests and the Mobilization of Bias in Congressional Committees," *The American Political Science Review* 84, no. 3 (September 1990): 797–820.

Chapter 2

1. Consider, for example, that a January 2006 Pew poll found that 81 percent of respondents thought it was common for lobbyists to bribe members of Congress. In addition, an April 2011 Gallup poll found that the two institutions most respondents thought had too much power were lobbyists (71 percent) and "major corporations" (67 percent). A September 2008 Zogby poll found that 82 percent of respondents thought that "political parties, presidential candidates and candidates for the U.S. Congress should be banned from receiving financial contributions from lobbyists or other representatives from those industries that are vital to the financial and national security of the country."

2. Evan Thomas and Jamie Reno, "Top Gun's Tailspin; Randy Cunningham was a high-flying aviator whose taste for the lavish perks of politics brought him low," *Newsweek*, December 12, 2005.

3. Allan Lengel, "FBI Says Jefferson Was Filmed Taking Cash," *Washington Post*, May 22, 2006.

4. See Ken Silverstein, *Washington on $10 Million a Day* (Boston: Common Courage Press, 1998); Micah Sifry and Nancy Walzman, *Is That a Politician in Your Pocket: Washington on $2 Million a Day* (New York: John Wiley & Sons, 2004); Charles Lewis, *The Buying of the President, 2004: Who's Really Bankrolling Bush and His Democratic Challengers—and what They Expect in Return* (New York, HarperCollins, 2004); a more balanced view can be found in Jeffrey H. Birnbaum, *The Lobbyists* (New York: Times Books, 1991); and Jeffrey H. Birnbaum and Alan S. Murray, *Showdown at Gucci Gulch* (New York: Vintage Press, 1987).

5. Robert Alan Dahl, "The Concept of Power," *Behavioral Science* 2 (1957): 202–3.

6. Max Weber, *Economy and Society: An Outline of Interpretive Sociology* (Oakland, CA: University of California Press, 1978).

7. Talcott Parsons, "The Distribution of Power in American Society," *World Politics* 10, no. 01 (1957): 123–43, doi:10.2307/2009229.

8. Frank R. Baumgartner and Beth L. Leech, *Basic Interests: The Importance of Groups in Politics and in Political Science* (Princeton, NJ: Princeton University Press, 1998), p. 13.

9. Richard A. Smith, "Interest Group Influence in the U.S. Congress," *Legislative Studies Quarterly* 20, no. 1 (February 1, 1995): 89–139, doi:10.2307/440151.

10. Frank R. Baumgartner et al., *Lobbying and Policy Change: Who Wins, Who Loses, and Why* (University of Chicago Press, 2009).

11. Kay Lehman Schlozman, Sidney Verba, and Henry E. Brady, *The Unheavenly Chorus: Unequal Political Voice and the Broken Promise of American Democracy* (Princeton, NJ: Princeton University Press, 2012).

12. Daniel Schuman, "Keeping Congress Competent: The Senate's Brain Drain," *Sunlight Foundation*, 2012, http://sunlightfoundation.com/; Lorelei Kelly, *Congress' Wicked Problem: Seeking Knowledge Inside the Information Tsunami* (New America Foundation, 2012).

13. Lester W. Milbrath, "Lobbying as a Communication Process," *Public Opinion Quarterly* 24, no. 1 (March 20, 1960): 32–53, doi:10.1086/266928.

14 Robert H. Salisbury, "The Paradox of Interest Groups in Washington DC: More Groups and Less Clout," in *The New American Political System* (Washington, DC: American Enterprise Institute, 1990).

15. George Tsebelis, "Decision Making in Political Systems: Veto Players in Presidentialism, Parliamentarism, Multicameralism and Multipartyism," *British Journal of Political Science* 25, no. 03 (1995): 289–325, doi:10.1017/S0007123400007225.

16. Baumgartner et al., *Lobbying and Policy Change*; see also Amy McKay, "Negative Lobbying and Policy Outcomes," *American Politics Research* 40, no. 1 (January 1, 2012): 116–46, doi:10.1177/1532673X11413435.

17. Daniel Kahneman, *Thinking, Fast and Slow,* reprint edition (New York: Farrar, Straus and Giroux, 2013).

18. Jonathan Rauch, *Government's End: Why Washington Stopped Working,* revised vol. (New York: PublicAffairs, 1999); Mancur Olson, *The Rise and Decline of Nations: Economic Growth, Stagflation, and Social Rigidities,* (New Haven, CT: Yale University Press, 1982); Jack L. Walker, *Mobilizing Interest Groups in America: Patrons, Professions, and Social Movements* (Ann Arbor, MI: University of Michigan Press, 1991); Andrea Louise Campbell, *How Policies Make Citizens: Senior Political Activism and the American Welfare State* (Princeton, NJ: Princeton University Press, 2003).

19. R. Douglas Arnold, "The Logic of Congressional Action" (New Haven, CT: Yale University Press, 1990).

20. James Q. Wilson, *The Politics of Regulation* (New York: Basic Books, 1980).

21. Virginia Gray and David Lowery, "Interest Representation and Democratic Gridlock," *Legislative Studies Quarterly* 20, no. 4 (November 1, 1995): 547, doi:10.2307/440192.

22. The President's Advisory Panel on Tax Reform, November 2005, "Simple, Fair and Pro-Growth: Proposal's to Fix America's Tax System" p. 16; available at http://www.taxfoundation.org/blog/show/1156.html

23. Eamon Javers, "The 'Mother of All Tax Bills'," *BusinessWeek,* October 25, 2007, http://www.businessweek.com/stories/2007-10-25/the-mother-of-all-tax-billsbusinessweek-business-news-stock-market-and-financial-advice.

24. Author calculation, based on a search of lobbying records for keywords and key bill numbers.

25. Author calculation, based on a search of lobbying records for keywords and key bill numbers.

26. Vital Statistics on Congress, Table 6-4.

27. James B. Stewart, "Volcker Rule Grows From Simple to Complex," *New York Times,* October 21, 2011, sec. Business Day, http://www.nytimes.com/2011/10/22/business/volcker-rule-grows-from-simple-to-complex.html.

28. Ryan Tracy, James Sterngold, and Stephanie Armour, "Banks, Agencies Draw Battle Lines Over 'Volcker Rule,'" *Wall Street Journal,* December 12, 2013, sec. Markets, http://online.wsj.com/news/articles/SB10001424052702304202204579252592600657058.

29. Ryan Tracy And Stephanie Armour, "Enforcing Volcker Rule May Require Maze of Regulators," *Wall Street Journal,* December 10, 2013, sec. Markets, http://online.wsj.com/news/articles/SB10001424052702303560204579250303422620332.

30. Robert Lenzner, "The Six Gaping Loopholes in the Controversial Volcker Rule," *Forbes,* December 12, 2013, http://www.forbes.com/sites/robertlenzner/2013/12/12/the-six-gaping-loopholes-exemptions-to-the-controversial-volcker-rule/.

31. Steven M. Teles, "Kludgeocracy in America," *National Affairs,* 2013.

32. Pepper D. Culpepper, *Quiet Politics and Business Power: Corporate Control in Europe and Japan* (Cambridge University Press, 2010), p. 177.

33. Mark A. Smith, *American Business and Political Power: Public Opinion, Elections, and Democracy,* 1st ed. (University Of Chicago Press, 2000).

34. Theodore J. Lowi, *The End of Liberalism: The Second Republic of the United States,* vol. 2 (New York: Norton, 1979).

35. The President's Advisory Panel on Tax Reform, November 2005, "Simple, Fair and Pro-Growth: Proposal's to Fix America's Tax System" p. 16; available at http://www.tax-foundation.org/blog/show/1156.html

36. The President's Advisory Panel on Tax Reform, p. 16.

37. David Kocieniewski, "I.R.S. Watchdog Calls for Tax Code Overhaul," *New York Times,* January 5, 2011, sec. Business Day/Economy, http://www.nytimes.com/2011/01/06/business/economy/06tax.html.

38 Lee Drutman and Alexander Furnas, "K Street Pays Top Dollar for Revolving Door Talent," *Sunlight Foundation,* January 21, 2014, http://sunlightfoundation.com/blog/2014/01/21/revolving-door-lobbyists-government-experience/.

39. Timothy M. LaPira and Herschel F. Thomas, *Just How Many Newt Gingrich's Are There on K Street? Estimating the True Size and Shape of Washington's Revolving Door,* SSRN

Scholarly Paper (Rochester, NY: Social Science Research Network, April 2, 2013), http://papers.ssrn.com/abstract=2241671.

40. Congressional Management Foundation, *Working in Congress: The Staff Perspective* (Congressional Management Foundation, December 16, 1994).

41. Robert H. Salisbury and Kenneth A. Shepsle, "Congressional Staff Turnover and the Ties-That-Bind," *The American Political Science Review* 75, no. 2 (June 1, 1981): 381–96, doi:10.2307/1961372.

42. Barbara S. Romzek, "Accountability of Congressional Staff," *Journal of Public Administration Research and Theory* 10, no. 2 (April 1, 2000): 413–46.

43. Baumgartner et al., *Lobbying and Policy Change*.

44. Lawrence Lessig, *Republic, Lost: How Money Corrupts Congress—and a Plan to Stop It*, 1st ed. (New York, NY: Twelve, 2011), p. 123.

45. Congressional Management Foundation, *2009 House of Representatives Compensation Study*, 2009, http://www.scribd.com/doc/24769228/2009-House-of-Representatives-Compensation-Study.

46. I saw this firsthand during my time in the Senate.

47. Daniel Schuman, "Keeping Congress Competent: Staff Pay, Turnover, And What It Means for Democracy," Sunlight Foundation blog, December 21, 2010, http://sunlight-foundation.com/blog/2010/12/21/keeping-congress-competent-staff-pay-turnover-and-what-it-means-for-democracy/

48. Daniel Schuman and Alisha Green, "When It Comes to Pay, All Feds Aren't Created Equal," *Sunlight Foundation*, December 6, 2012.

49. Daniel Schuman, "Keeping Congress Competent: Staff Pay, Turnover, and What It Means for Democracy," *Sunlight Foundation*, December 21, 2010.

50. Bruce Allen Bimber, *The Politics of Expertise in Congress: The Rise and Fall of the Office of Technology Assessment* (Albany, NY: SUNY Press, 1996).

51. Kelly, *Congress' Wicked Problem: Seeking Knowledge Inside the Information Tsunami*.

52. David Whiteman, *Communication in Congress* (Lawrence, KS: University Press of Kansas, 1995).

53. Bryan D. Jones and Frank R. Baumgartner, *The Politics of Attention: How Government Prioritizes Problems* (Chicago: University of Chicago Press, 2005), p. 9.

54. Richard L. Hall, *Participation in Congress* (London: Yale University Press, 1996), p. 90.

55. Herbert A. Simon, *Models of Man: Social and Rational; Mathematical Essays on Rational Human Behavior in Society Setting* (Wiley, 1957), p. 198.

56. George A. Miller, "The Magical Number Seven, Plus or Minus Two: Some Limits on Our Capacity for Processing Information," *Psychological Review* 63, no. 2 (1956): 81–97, doi:10.1037/h0043158.

57. Herbert A. Simon, "Invariants of Human Behavior," *Annual Review of Psychology* 41, no. 1 (1990): 1–20, doi:10.1146/annurev.ps.41.020190.000245.

58. Jones and Baumgartner, *The Politics of Attention: How Government Prioritizes Problems*.

59. Deborah A. Stone, *Policy Paradox: The Art of Political Decision Making* (New York, NY: W. W. Norton & Company, 1997); John W Kingdon, *Agendas, Alternatives, and Public Policies* (New York: Harper Collins, 1990).

60. Andrew Rich and R. Kent Weaver, "Think Tanks in the U.S. Media," *The Harvard International Journal of Press/Politics* 5, no. 4 (2000): 81–103.

61. Thomas Medvetz, *Think Tanks in America* (Chicago, IL: University of Chicago Press, 2012).

62. Lydia DePillis. "At the Bipartisan Policy Center, Is Cash the Real Divide?" *The Washington Post*, August 15, 2013. http://www.washingtonpost.com/blogs/wonkblog/wp/2013/08/15/at-the-bipartisan-policy-center-is-cash-the-real-divide/.

63. Center for American Progress one-pager, http://www.thenation.com/sites/default/files/user/20/American_Progressive_Business_large2.png

64. Ken Silverstein, "The Secret Donors Behind the Center for American Progress and Other Think Tanks [Updated on 5/24]," *The Nation*, May 21, 2013, http://www.thenation.com/article/174437/secret-donors-behind-center-american-progress-and-other-think-tanks?page=full.

65. Tom Hamburger and Matea Gold, "Google, Once Disdainful of Lobbying, Now a Master of Washington Influence," *The Washington Post*, April 15, 2014, sec. Politics, http://www.washingtonpost.com/politics/how-google-is-transforming-power-and-politicsgoogle-once-disdainful-of-lobbying-now-a-master-of-washington-influence/2014/04/12/51648b92-b4d3-11e3-8cb6-284052554d74_story.html?tid=pm_pop.

66. Andrew Rich, *Think Tanks, Public Policy, and the Politics of Expertise* (New York, NY: Cambridge University Press, 2005), p. 28.

67. Kingdon, *Agendas, Alternatives, and Public Policies*; David L. Weimer, "Theories of and in the Policy Process," *Policy Studies Journal* 36, no. 4 (November 1, 2008): 489–95, doi:10.1111/j.1541–0072.2008.00280.x.

68. Eric Lipton, "Fight Over Minimum Wage Illustrates Web of Industry Ties," *New York Times*, February 9, 2014, http://www.nytimes.com/2014/02/10/us/politics/fight-over-minimum-wage-illustrates-web-of-industry-ties.html.

69. Cass R. Sunstein, *Simpler: The Future of Government* (New York, NY: Simon and Schuster, 2013), p. 150.

70. Sunstein, p. 175

71. Kevin M. Esterling, *The Political Economy of Expertise: Information and Efficiency in American National Politics* (Ann Arbor, MI: University of Michigan Press, 2004), p. 9.

72. See also: John R. Wright, *Interest Groups and Congress: Lobbying, Contributions, and Influence* (Boston: Allyn and Bacon, 1996).

73. Nicholas W. Allard, "Lobbying Is an Honorable Profession: The Right to Petition and the Competition to Be Right," *Stanford Law and Policy Review* 19, no. 1 (2008). p. 44.

74. "The House bill scheduled for a vote Wednesday would significantly curb the requirement that banks separate their derivatives trading operations, a plan that was created as a compromise by Citigroup lobbyists . . . As it now reads, Citigroup's recommendations are reflected in more than 70 of the 85 lines of the House bill." Eric Lipton and Ben Protess, "House, Set to Vote on 2 Bills, Is Seen as an Ally of Wall St." *New York Times*, November 1, 2013.

75. Lee Drutman and Daniel J. Hopkins, "The Inside View: Using the Enron E-Mail Archive to Understand Corporate Political Attention," *Legislative Studies Quarterly* 38, no. 1 (2013): 5–30, doi:10.1111/lsq.12001.

76. Richard L. Hall and Alan V. Deardorff, "Lobbying as Legislative Subsidy," *American Political Science Review* 100, no. 1 (2006): 69–84.

77. Marianne Bertrand, Matilde Bombardini, and Francesco Trebbi, *Is It Whom You Know or What You Know? An Empirical Assessment of the Lobbying Process*, Working Paper (National Bureau of Economic Research, February 2011), http://www.nber.org/papers/w16765; Jordi Blanes i Vidal, Mirko Draca, and Christian Fons-Rosen, "Revolving Door Lobbyists," *American Economic Review* 102, no. 7 (December 2012): 3731–48, doi:10.1257/aer.102.7.3731.

78. Allard, "Lobbying Is an Honorable Profession: The Right to Petition and the Competition to Be Right."

79. Marissa Martino Golden, "Interest Groups in the Rule-Making Process: Who Participates? Whose Voices Get Heard?," *Journal of Public Administration Research and Theory* 8, no. 2 (April 1, 1998): 245–70; Scott R. Furlong, "Interest Group Influence on Rule Making," *Administration & Society* 29, no. 3 (July 1, 1997): 325–47, doi:10.1177/009539979702900304; Scott R. Furlong and Cornelius M. Kerwin, "Interest Group Participation in Rule Making: A Decade of Change," *Journal of Public Administration Research and Theory* 15, no. 3 (July 2005): 353–70, doi:10.1093/jopart/mui022; Jason Webb Yackee and Susan Webb Yackee, "A Bias Towards Business? Assessing Interest Group Influence on the U.S. Bureaucracy," *The Journal of Politics* 68, no. 1 (February 2006): 128–39; Amy McKay and Susan Webb Yackee, "Interest Group Competition on Federal Agency Rules," *American Politics Research* 35, no. 3 (May 1, 2007): 336–57, doi:10.1177/1532673X06296571.

80. McKay and Yackee, "Interest Group Competition on Federal Agency Rules.," p. 350.

81. Nolan McCarty, "Complexity, Capacity, and Capture," in *Preventing Regulatory Capture: Special Interest Influence and How to Limit It*, ed. Daniel P. Carpenter and David A. Moss (New York, NY: Cambridge University Press, 2014), 102–3.

82. James Kwak, "Cultural Capture and the Financial Crisis," in *Preventing Regulatory Capture: Special Interest Influence and How to Limit It*, ed. Daniel P. Carpenter and David A. Moss (New York, NY: Cambridge University Press, 2014).

83. Jacob S. Hacker and Paul Pierson, *Winner-Take-All Politics: How Washington Made the Rich Richer—and Turned Its Back on the Middle Class* (New York, NY: Simon and Schuster, 2010); see also Baumgartner et al., *Lobbying and Policy Change*.

84. Rauch, *Government's End: Why Washington Stopped Working*.

85. David Kocieniewski, "G.E.'s Strategies Let It Avoid Taxes Altogether," *New York Times*, March 24, 2011, sec. Business Day/Economy, http://www.nytimes.com/2011/03/25/business/economy/25tax.html.

86. Alex Tabarrok, "The 57,000 Page Tax Return," *Marginal Revolution*, November 21, 2011.

87. Tabarrok, "The 57,000 Page Tax Return".

88. Jeff Gerth, "5 Ways GE Plays the Tax Game," ProPublica, April 4, 2011

89. Taxpayer Advocate Service, "2010 Annual Report to Congress," IRS http://www.irs.gov/pub/irs-utl/2010arcmsp1_taxreform.pdf

90. Jeffrey M. Berry, *The New Liberalism: The Rising Power of Citizen Groups*, 1st ed. (Washington, DC: Brookings Institution Press, 1999).

91. Baumgartner et al., *Lobbying and Policy Change*.

92. Mancur Olson, *The Rise and Decline of Nations: Economic Growth, Stagflation, and Social Rigidities*, (New Haven, CT: Yale University Press, 1982); Jonathan Rauch, *Government's End: Why Washington Stopped Working*, revised vol. (New York: PublicAffairs, 1999).

93. Joshua Kopstein, "Dear Congress, It's No Longer OK to not Know How the Internet Works," *Motherboard*, December 16, 2011, http://motherboard.vice.com/blog/dear-congress-it-s-no-longer-ok-to-not-know-how-the-internet-works.

94 Lee Drutman, "Google Gets a DC Insider to Run Its Washington Office," *Sunlight Foundation*, February 23, 2012, http://sunlightfoundation.com/blog/2012/02/23/google-gets-a-dc-insider-to-run-its-washington-office/.

95 Henry Farrell, "Five Key Questions – and Answers – about the Leaked TPP Text," *Washington Post*, December 15, 2013, http://www.washingtonpost.com/blogs/monkey-cage/wp/2013/11/15/five-key-questions-and-answers-about-the-leaked-tpp-text/.

96. John P. Heinz et al., *The Hollow Core: Private Interests in National Policy Making* (Cambridge, MA: Harvard University Press, 1993), p. 5.

Chapter 3

1. "Space Yes; Space Station No," *New York Times* editorial, June 6, 1991.

2. Clifford Krauss, "House Approves $1.73 Billion for Space Station," *New York Times*, July 30 1992 (the quote is from Rep. Marcy Kaptur [D-Ohio]).

3. "Boeing and China to Compete and Cooperate" *China Daily*, June 26, 2008.

4. Lawrence Lessig, *Republic, Lost: How Money Corrupts Congress—and a Plan to Stop It*, 1st ed. (New York, NY: Twelve, 2011).

5. Robert C. Byrd and Wendy Wolff, *The Senate, 1789–1989: Addresses on the History of the United States Senate* (Government Printing Office, 1988).

6. Daniel J. Tichenor and Richard A. Harris, "Organized Interests and American Political Development," *Political Science Quarterly* 117, no. 4 (2002): 587–612, p. 609; Edward Pendleton Herring, *Group Representation Before Congress* (Washington, DC: Brookings Institution Press, 1929).

7. Marc Allen Eisner, *Regulatory Politics in Transition* (Baltimore: Johns Hopkins University Press, 1993), pp. 83–4.

8. Kim McQuaid, *Uneasy Partners: Big Business in American Politics, 1945–1990* (Baltimore: Johns Hopkins University Press, 1994).

9. Richard Hofstadter, *The Paranoid Style in American Politics, and Other Essays* (Random House, 1964), p. 141.

10. David Vogel, *Fluctuating Fortunes: The Political Power of Business in America* (New York: Basic Books, 1989), p. 33.

11. Graham K. Wilson, *Interest Groups in the United States* (New York: Oxford University Press, 1981), p. 72.

12. John Kenneth Galbraith, *The New Industrial State* (Boston: Houghton Mifflin, 1967).

13. Vogel, *Fluctuating Fortunes: The Political Power of Business in America*.

14. Raymond Augustine Bauer, Ithiel de Sola Pool, and Lewis Anthony Dexter, *American Business & Public Policy; the Politics of Foreign Trade* (Chicago: Aldine, 1972), p. 324.

15. Lester W. Milbrath, *The Washington Lobbyists* (Chicago: Rand McNally, 1963), p. 354.

16. Marver H. Bernstein, *Regulating Business by Independent Commission* (Princeton, N.J.: Princeton University Press, 1955); Douglass Cater, *Power in Washington: A Critical Look at Today's Struggle to Govern in the Nation's Capital* (New York: Random House, 1964); Grant McConnell, *Private Power & American Democracy* (New York: Knopf, 1966); Theodore J. Lowi, *The End of Liberalism: The Second Republic of the United States*, vol. 2 (New York: Norton, 1979); George J. Stigler, "The Theory of Economic Regulation," *The Bell Journal of Economics and Management Science* 2, no. 1 (April 1, 1971): 3–21, doi:10.2307/3003160.

17. C. Wright Mills, *The Power Elite* (New York: Oxford University Press, 1956); G. William Domhoff, *Who Rules America?* (Englewood Cliffs, NJ: Prentice-Hall, 1967).

18. Peter Bachrach and Morton S. Baratz, "Two Faces of Power," *American Political Science Review* 56, no. 4 (December 1, 1962): 947–52, doi:10.2307/1952796.

19. Milbrath, *The Washington Lobbyists*, p. 156.

20. Data from Schlozman, Verba, Brady.

21. Milbrath, *The Washington Lobbyists*, p. 156.

22. Milbrath, p. 155.

23. Paul W. Cherington and Ralph L. Gillen, *The Business Representative in Washington: A Report on the Round-Table Discussions of Nineteen Washington Representatives on Their Job as They See It* (Brookings Institution, 1962). Marketing, according to the study, "includes not only the sale of the company's products, directly or indirectly, but also a great deal of what in commercial practice is usually referred to as missionary and intelligence work, not only for established products but for research and development contracts." The study was based on a roundtable with only 19 representatives, however, so the conclusions we can draw are somewhat limited.

24. Cherington and Gillen, p. 70.

25. Phyllis S. McGrath, *Redefining Corporate-Federal Relations: A Research Report from the Conference Board's Division of Management Research* (New York: The Conference Board, 1979).

26. Marianne M. Jennings and Frank M. Shipper, *Business Strategy for the Political Arena*. (Westport, CT: Praeger, 1984), p. 50.

27. David Vogel, "Why Businessmen Distrust Their State: The Political Consciousness of American Corporate Executives," *British Journal of Political Science* 8, no. 1 (January 1, 1978): 45–78.

28. Vogel, "Why Businessmen Distrust Their State: The Political Consciousness of American Corporate Executives," p. 45.

29. John Kenneth Galbraith, *The Affluent Society* (London: Houghton Mifflin, 1958), p. 148.

30. Marver H. Bernstein, "Political Ideas of Selected American Business Journals," *Public Opinion Quarterly* 17, no. 2 (June 20, 1953): 258–67, p. 262

31. Francis X. Sutton, Seymour Harris, Carl Naysen, and James Tobin, *The American Business Creed* (New York: Schocken Books 1956).

32. Francis X. Sutton, *The American Business Creed* (Cambridge, MA: Harvard University Press, 1956), p. 185.

33. Elmer E. Schattschneider, *The Semi-Sovereign People: A Realist's View of Democracy in America*, (Hinsdale, IL: The Dryden Press, 1975), p. 41.

34. Thomas J. Watson, *A Business and Its Beliefs: The Ideas That Helped Build IBM*, 1st ed. (New York: McGraw-Hill, 1963), p. 88–9.

35. Mark S Mizruchi, *The Fracturing of the American Corporate Elite* (Cambridge, MA: Harvard University Press, 2013)

36. Lewis Anthony Dexter, *How Organizations Are Represented in Washington* (Indianapolis: Bobbs-Merrill, 1969).

37. Justin Martin, *Nader: Crusader, Spoiler, Icon* (New York; Oxford: Basic; Oxford Publicity Partnership, 2003).

38. Richard A. Harris, "Politicized Management: The Changing Face of Business in American Politics," in *The Changing Face of Business in American Politics.* (San Francisco: Wetsview Press, 1989), 261–85.

39. Vogel, *Fluctuating Fortunes: The Political Power of Business in America*, p. 194.

40. Martin, *Nader*.

41. Vogel, *Fluctuating Fortunes: The Political Power of Business in America*, p. 74.

42. David B. Yoffie, "Corporate Strategies for Political Action: A Rational Model," in *Business Strategy and Public Policy: Perspectives From Industry and Academia*, ed. Alfred A. Marcus, Allen M. Kauffman, and David R. Beam (New York: Quorum Books, 1987), 43–60, p. 45.

43. Benjamin C. Waterhouse, *Lobbying America: The Politics of Business from Nixon to NAFTA* (Princeton, NJ: Princeton University Press, 2013), p. 14.

44. Lewis Powell, "Confidential Memorandum: Attack on the Free Enterprise System," August 23, 1971. While there is considerable debate over whether Powell's memo was the strategic blueprint of a modern business conservative movement or merely one of many *cri de cœurs* floating around the business community at the time, it was a powerful distillation of the building anxiety that many in the business community felt.

45. Vogel, *Fluctuating Fortunes: The Political Power of Business in America*.

46. Waterhouse, *Lobbying America*, p. 90.

47. Sar A. Levitan and Martha R. Cooper, *Business Lobbies: The Public Good & the Bottom Line* (Baltimore: Johns Hopkins University Press, 1984).

48. Vogel, *Fluctuating Fortunes: The Political Power of Business in America*, p. 197.

49. Vogel, pp. 195–204

50. Waterhouse, Lobbying America, p. 171.

51. Waterhouse, p. 187.

52. McGrath, *Redefining Corporate-Federal Relations*, p. 2.

53. McGrath, p.4

54. McGrath, p. 5.

55. McGrath, p. 56.

56. Waterhouse, *Lobbying America*, p. 195.

57. Vogel, *Fluctuating Fortunes: The Political Power of Business in America*.

58. Jonathan B. Baker and Carl Shapiro, "Reinvorgorating Horizontal Merger Enforcement," in *How the Chicago School Overshot the Mark: The Effect of Conservative Economic Analysis on U.S. Antitrust*, ed. Robert Pitofsky (Oxford; New York: Oxford University Press, 2008).

59. Levitan and Cooper, *Business Lobbies*, p. 55.

60. "How business is getting through to Washington," *BusinessWeek*, October 4, 1982

61. Mizruchi, *The Fracturing of the American Corporate Elite*, p. 19.

62. Mark Mizruchi also argues that the decline of commercial banks—"whose boards of directors had served as meeting places for the heads of the leading nonfinancial corporations" (7)—meant that corporate elites began to split apart into their own communities, where they thought more and more in terms of their own narrow interests.

63. Waterhouse, *Lobbying America*, pp. 217–8.

64. Waterhouse, *Lobbying America*, pp. 217–1=8.

65. Jeffrey H. Birnbaum, *Showdown at Gucci Gulch: Lawmakers, Lobbyists, and the Unlikely Triumph of Tax Reform*, 1st ed. (New York: Random House, 1987), https://catalyst.library.jhu.edu/catalog/bib_661524.

66. Waterhouse, *Lobbying America*, p. 232.

67. Gary Mucciaroni, *Reversals of Fortune: Public Policy and Private Interests* (Washington, DC: Brookings Institution, 1995), pp. 69–77.

68 Lynn Stout, *The Shareholder Value Myth: How Putting Shareholders First Harms Investors, Corporations, and the Public*, 1st ed. (San Francisco: Berrett-Koehler Publishers, 2012).

69. Mizruchi, *The Fracturing of the American Corporate Elite*, p. 217.

70. Martha Derthick and Paul J. Quirk, *The Politics of Deregulation* (Washington, DC: Brookings Institution Press, 1985).

71. Robert B. Reich, *Supercapitalism: The Transformation of Business, Democracy, and Everyday Life* (New York: Alfred A. Knopf, 2007), http://www.loc.gov/catdir/toc/ecip079/2007002471.html.

72. Paul Pierson, "Increasing Returns, Path Dependence, and the Study of Politics," *The American Political Science Review* 94, no. 2 (June 1, 2000): 251–67, doi:10.2307/2586011.

73. Edward A. Grefe and Martin Linsky, *The New Corporate Activism: Harnessing the Power of Grassroots Tactics for Your Organization* (New York: Mcgraw-Hill, 1995), p. 2.

74. Levitan and Cooper, *Business Lobbies*, p. 137.

75. Timothy M. LaPira, "The Allure of Reform: The Increasing Demand for Health Care Lobbying From Clinton's Task Force to Obama's Big [Expletive] Deal," in *Interest Group Politics*, 8th ed., ed. Allan Cigler and Burdett Loomis (Washington, DC: CQ Press, 2012).

76. Nicholas Confessore, "Welcome to the Machine: How the GOP Disciplined K Street and Made Bush Supreme," *The Washington Monthly*, 2003.

77. Elizabeth Drew, *Showdown: The Struggle Between the Gingrich Congress and the Clinton White House*, 1st ed. (New York: Touchstone, 1997), p. 116. Drew goes onto note that "Putting policy directives in appropriations bills—especially regulatory policy—became a specialty of the House Republicans later in the year."

78. David Maraniss and Michael Weisskopf, *Tell Newt to Shut Up!* (New York: Simon & Schuster, 1996), p. 11.

79. Confessore, "Welcome to the Machine: How the GOP Disciplined K Street and Made Bush Supreme."

80. John Friedman, "The Incidence of the Medicare Prescription Drug Benefit: Using Asset Prices to Assess Its Impact on Drug Makers," *Working Paper*, 2009.

Chapter 4

1. Nicholas W. Allard, "Lobbying Is an Honorable Profession: The Right to Petition and the Competition to Be Right," *Stanford Law and Policy Review* 19, no. 1 (2008). P. 46.

2. Mancur Olson, *The Logic of Collective Action; Public Goods and the Theory of Groups*, (Cambridge, MA: Harvard University Press, 1965); Robert H. Salisbury, "An Exchange Theory of Interest Groups," *Midwest Journal of Political Science* 13, no. 1 (February 1, 1969): 1–32, doi:10.2307/2110212; Terry M. Moe, "Toward a Broader View of Interest Groups," *The Journal of Politics* 43, no. 2 (May 1, 1981): 531–43, doi:10.2307/2130382; Jack L. Walker, "The Origins and Maintenance of Interest Groups in America," *The American Political Science Review* 77, no. 2 (June 1, 1983): 390–406, doi:10.2307/1958924; John Mark Hansen, "The Political Economy of Group Membership," *The American Political Science Review* 79, no. 1 (March 1, 1985): 79–96, doi:10.2307/1956120; Jack L. Walker, *Mobilizing Interest Groups in America: Patrons, Professions, and Social Movements* (Ann Arbor: University of Michigan Press, 1991).

3. Wendy L. Hansen, Neil J. Mitchell, and Jeffrey M. Drope, "The Logic of Private and Collective Action," *American Journal of Political Science* 49, no. 1 (January 1, 2005): 150–67, doi:10.1111/ajps.2005.49.issue-1; Henry E. Brady et al., "Corporate Lobbying Activity in American Politics," in paper given at the American Political Science Association Annual Meeting (Chicago, IL, 2007).

4. R. Kenneth Godwin, Scott Ainsworth, and Erik K. Godwin, *Lobbying and Policymaking* (Thousand Oaks, CA: CQ Press, 2012); R. Kenneth Godwin, Edward J. Lopez, and Barry J. Seldon, "Allocating Lobbying Resources between Collective and Private Rents," *Political Research Quarterly*, February 29, 2008, doi:10.1177/1065912907307290; Erik K. Godwin, R. Kenneth Godwin, and Scott Ainsworth, "Is Corporate Lobbying Rational or Just a Waste of Money?" in *Interest Group Politics*, vol. 7, 2007, pp. 256–78.

5. Hansen, Mitchell, and Drope, "The Logic of Private and Collective Action."

6. Douglass Cater, *Power in Washington: A Critical Look at Today's Struggle to Govern in the Nation's Capital* (New York: Random House, 1964); Grant McConnell, *Private Power & American Democracy* (New York: Knopf, 1966); Theodore J. Lowi, *The End of Liberalism:*

The Second Republic of the United States, vol. 2 (New York: Norton, 1979); James Q. Wilson, *The Politics of Regulation* (New York: Basic Books, 1980); Mark A. Smith, *American Business and Political Power: Public Opinion, Elections, and Democracy*, 1st ed. (Chicago: University Of Chicago Press, 2000).

7. Peter Bachrach and Morton S. Baratz, "Two Faces of Power," *The American Political Science Review* 56, no. 4 (December 1, 1962): 947–52, doi:10.2307/1952796.

8. It might be noted that this finding is somewhat contrary to Baumgartner and colleagues' conclusion that on 26 percent of the issues they studied, "citizen groups" were considered major players. See: Frank R. Baumgartner et al., *Lobbying and Policy Change: Who Wins, Who Loses, and Why* (University of Chicago Press, 2009). There are a few possible reasons for this discrepancy. The first is that Baumgartner et al. built their sample by overweighting the most actively lobbied issues, whereas I started with companies. Citizen groups may be more likely to be major players on active issues since they gravitate towards live political battles, whereas companies may be more involved in narrow issues in which the primary goal is getting attention (and those issues on which citizen groups would be less likely to show up as major players). A second possible reason is that lobbyists are not likely to identify diffuse interest groups as opponents because they don't want to be seen as lobbying against the public interest, but might volunteer them as major players because they want to lend legitimacy to their side. A third possible reason may be that Baumgartner et al. identified their issues during 1999–2002, where as I conducted interviews in 2007–2008. As I described in Chapter 1, the countervailing power index hit a low of about 22 to 1 in 2001, but has since been rising. While none of these explanations can explain the discrepancy by itself, collectively they make the discrepancy less glaring.

9. Anthony Nownes, *Total Lobbying: What Lobbyists Want (And How They Try to Get It)* (New York, NY: Cambridge University Press, 2006), p. 3.

10. Frank R. Baumgartner and Beth L. Leech, *Basic Interests: The Importance of Groups in Politics and in Political Science* (Princeton, NJ: Princeton University Press, 1998), p. 148.

11. Lee Drutman and Daniel J. Hopkins, "The Inside View: Using the Enron E-Mail Archive to Understand Corporate Political Attention," *Legislative Studies Quarterly* 38, no. 1 (2013): 5–30, doi:10.1111/lsq.12001.

12. Kay Lehman Schlozman and John T. Tierney, *Organized Interests and American Democracy* (New York: Harper & Row, 1986); John P. Heinz et al., *The Hollow Core: Private Interests in National Policy Making* (Cambridge, MA: Harvard University Press, 1993); Jeffrey M. Berry and Clyde Wilcox, *The Interest Group Society*, 5th ed. (New York: Pearson, 2008).

13. John W Kingdon, *Agendas, Alternatives, and Public Policies* (New York: Harper Collins, 1990); Frank R. Baumgartner and Bryan D. Jones, *Agendas and Instability in American Politics* (Chicago: University of Chicago Press, 1993).

14. Admittedly, these categories are somewhat arbitrary. I selected nice round numbers to give us a conceptual understanding of how many companies are at different levels of lobbying. They are not quartiles.

15. Under the Lobbing Disclosure Act, lobbying disclosure reports include both a general issue and specific issue field. Using the general issue field, we can see where companies are putting their lobbying efforts. While the specific issue field offers more granularity (specific bills and issues), the quality of disclosure is inconsistent. The general issue field offers much less granularity, but enough consistency to make some broad observations.

16. Some might note that 2008 is the election year, so it might be misleading to use 2007. However, I would argue that it is more appropriate to use 2007, since PAC contributions made in 2007 are most likely to be oriented towards access and policy influence, whereas contributions in 2008 might be electorally oriented. As it turns out, the totals are very similar, and it makes little difference whether we use 2008 or 2007.

17. Richard L. Hall and Frank W. Wayman, "Buying Time: Moneyed Interests and the Mobilization of Bias in Congressional Committees," *The American Political Science Review* 84, no. 3 (September 1990): 797–820; Laura I. Langbein, "Money and Access: Some Empirical Evidence," *The Journal of Politics* 48, no. 4 (1986): 1052–62; Broockman, David E., and Joshua L. Kalla. *Congressional Officials Grant Access Due To Campaign Contributions: A Randomized Field Experiment*. Working Paper, 2014. For an alternate view, see Marie

Hojnacki and David C. Kimball, "PAC Contributions and Lobbying Contacts in Congressional Committees," *Political Research Quarterly* 54, no. 1 (March 2001): 161, doi:10.2307/449213.

18. Stephen Ansolabehere, John M. de Figueiredo, and James M. Snyder Jr., "Why Is There so Little Money in U.S. Politics?" *The Journal of Economic Perspectives* 17, no. 1 (January 1, 2003): 105–30; Thomas Stratmann, "Some Talk: Money in Politics. A (Partial) Review of the Literature," *Public Choice* 124, no. 1/2 (July 1, 2005): 135–56.

Chapter 5

1. Mancur Olson, *The Logic of Collective Action; Public Goods and the Theory of Groups*, vol. 124 (Cambridge, MA: Harvard University Press, 1965).
2. R. Kenneth Godwin, Edward J. Lopez, and Barry J. Seldon, "Allocating Lobbying Resources between Collective and Private Rents," *Political Research Quarterly*, February 29, 2008, doi:10.1177/1065912907307290., p. 357
3. Graham K. Wilson, "Corporate Political Strategies," *British Journal of Political Science* 20, no. 2 (April 1990): 281–8.
4. http://politicalaccountability.net/index.php?ht=a/GetDocumentAction/i/7260)
5. http://www.prudential.com/documents/public/PAC_Annual_Report_11-Final.pdf
6. Individual disclosures of corporate political spending on associations have been collected by the Center for Corporate Accountability: http://www.politicalaccountability.net/
7. Marie Hojnacki, "Interest Groups' Decisions to Join Alliances or Work Alone," *American Journal of Political Science* 41, no. 1 (January 1, 1997): 61–87, doi:10.2307/2111709.
8. Olson, *The Logic of Collective Action; Public Goods and the Theory of Groups.*
9. Godwin, Lopez, and Seldon, "Allocating Lobbying Resources between Collective and Private Rents."
10. David M. Hart, "New Economy, Old Politics: The Evolving Role of the High-Technology Industry in Washington, D.C.," n.d.
11. Wilson, "Corporate Political Strategies"; Wendy L. Hansen, Neil J. Mitchell, and Jeffrey M. Drope, "Collective Action, Pluralism, and the Legitimacy Tariff: Corporate Activity or Inactivity in Politics," *Political Research Quarterly* 57, no. 3 (September 2004): 421–29.; Hansen and colleagues conclude: "in general, firm and organizational activities are complements rather than substitutes in a firm's efforts to influence policymakers."
12. A simple bivariate OLS regression in which the natural log of company spending at the industry level is used to predict the natural log of trade association spending at the industry level can explain 54 percent of the variation across industries. If the variables are not logged, the percentage of explained variation increases to 59 percent. However, because the distribution of spending by industry follows a power-law distribution, it makes sense to log the value.
13. In this case, total industry spending (logged) explains 34 percent of the variation in the share of lobbying done by companies in a simple OLS regression.
14. There is, however, a fair amount of variability in these changes. In the bivariate OLS regression, the change in trade association spending predicts 19.2 percent of the change in corporate level spending, indicating that there are other unobserved factors that explain the changing balance.
15. Foundation for Public Affairs, *2011–2012 State of Public Affairs Report*, 2012.

Chapter 6

1. Isaac Balbus, "The Concept of Interest in Pluralist and Marxian Analysis," *Politics and Society* 1, no. 2 (1971): 151–77; Connolly, William E., "On 'Interests' in Politics," *Politics and Society* 2, no. 4 (1972): 459–77; Kay Lehman Schlozman and John T Tierney, *Organized Interests and American Democracy* (New York: Harper & Row, 1986).
2. John P. Heinz et al., *The Hollow Core: Private Interests in National Policy Making* (Cambridge, MA: Harvard University Press, 1993), p. 24.
3. Heinz et al., p. 360.

4. Michael Watkins, Mickey Edwards, and Usha Thakrar, *Winning the Influence Game: What Every Business Leader Should Know about Government* (New York: Wiley and Sons, 2001), p. 27.
5. Watkins, Edwards, and Thakar, p. 28.
6. Watkins, Edwards, and Thakar, p. 29.
7. Cornelia Woll, *Firm Interests: How Governments Shape Business Lobbying on Global Trade* (Cornell, NY: Cornell University Press, 2008), p. 38.
8. Peter Hall, "Preference Formation as a Political Process: The Case of Monetary Union in Europe," in *Preferences and Situations*, ed. Ira Katznelson and Barry R. Weingast, 2005, 129–60, p. 134.
9. Cathie J. Martin, *Stuck in Neutral: Business and the Politics of Human Capital Investment Policy* (Princeton, NJ: Princeton University Press, 2000), 126.
10. Martin, p. 35.
11. Kathleen A. Rehbein and Douglas A. Schuler, "Testing the Firm as a Filter of Corporate Political Action," *Business & Society* 38, no. 2 (June 1, 1999): 144–66, p. 145; Douglas A. Schuler and Kathleen Rehbein, "The Filtering Role of the Firm in Corporate Political Involvement," *Business & Society* 36, no. 2 (June 1, 1997): 116–39, doi:10.1177/000765039703600202.
12. Raymond Augustine Bauer, Ithiel de Sola Pool, and Lewis Anthony Dexter, *American Business & Public Policy; the Politics of Foreign Trade* (Chicago: Aldine, 1972).
13. James G. March and Johan P. Olsen, "The Uncertainty of the Past: Organizational Learning Under Ambiguity," *European Journal of Political Research* 3, no. 2 (June 1, 1975): 147–71, doi:10.1111/j.1475–6765.1975.tb00521.x.
14. William H. Starbuck and Frances J. Milliken, "Executives Perceptual Filters: What They Notice and How They Make Sense," in *The Executive Effect: Concepts and Methods for Studying Top Managers* (Greenwich. CT: JAI Press, 1988), 35–65.
15. Jeffrey Pfeffer and Gerald R. Salancik, *The External Control of Organizations : A Resource Dependence Perspective* (New York: Harper & Row, 1978), p. 74.
16. Starbuck and Milliken, "Executives Perceptual Filters: What They Notice and How They Make Sense."
17. William R. Dill, "Environment as an Influence on Managerial Autonomy," *Administrative Science Quarterly* 2, no. 4 (March 1, 1958): 409–43, doi:10.2307/2390794; Paul R. Lawrence and Jay William Lorsch, *Organization and Environment: Managing Differentiation and Integration* (Division of Research, Graduate School of Business Administration, Harvard University, 1967).
18. Robert B. Duncan, "Characteristics of Organizational Environments and Perceived Environmental Uncertainty," *Administrative Science Quarterly* 17, no. 3 (September 1972): 313–27.
19. Donald C. Hambrick and Phyllis A. Mason, "Upper Echelons: The Organization as a Reflection of Its Top Managers," *The Academy of Management Review* 9, no. 2 (April 1984): 193–206; Starbuck and Milliken, "Executives Perceptual Filters: What They Notice and How They Make Sense."
20. Richard L. Daft and Karl E. Weick, "Toward a Model of Organizations as Interpretation Systems," *Academy of Management Review* 9, no. 2 (1984): 284–95, p. 285.
21. Daft and Weick, p. 286.
22. Karl E. Weick, *Social Psychology of Organizing*, 2nd ed. (New York, NY: McGraw Hill, 1979), p. 40.
23. Francis Joseph Aguilar, *Scanning the Business Environment* (New York: Macmillan, 1967).
24. Jay Galbraith, *Organization Design* (Reading, MA: Addison Wesley Publishing Company, 1977), p. 36.
25. W. Richard Scott, *Organizations: Rational, Natural, and Open Systems*, 4th ed. (Upper Saddle River, NJ: Prentice Hall College Div, 1997), p. 142.
26. James D. Thompson, *Organizations in Action; Social Science Bases of Administrative Theory* (New York: McGraw-Hill, 1967).
27. Howard Aldrich, *Organizations and Environments* (Englewood Cliffs, NJ: Prentice-Hall, 1979); Richard L. Daft and Robert H. Lengel, "Organizational Information Requirements,

Media Richness and Structural Design," *Management Science* 32, no. 5, (May 1986): 554–71; James B. Thomas, Shawn M. Clark, and Dennis A. Gioia, "Strategic Sensemaking and Organizational Performance: Linkages Among Scanning, Interpretation, Action, and Outcomes," *Academy of Management Journal* 36, no. 2 (April 1, 1993): 239–70, doi: 10.2307/256522.

28. James A. Thomas and Jr., Reuben R. McDaniel, "Interpreting Strategic Issues: Effects of Strategy and the Information-Processing Structure of Top Management Teams," *Academy of Management Journal* 33, no. 2 (June 1990): 286–306, doi:10.2307/256326.

29. Frank R. Baumgartner et al., *Lobbying and Policy Change: Who Wins, Who Loses, and Why* (Chicago: University of Chicago Press, 2009); Stephen Ansolabehere, John M. de Figueiredo, and James M. Snyder Jr., "Why Is There so Little Money in U.S. Politics?" *The Journal of Economic Perspectives* 17, no. 1 (January 1, 2003): 105–30; Frank R. Baumgartner and Beth L. Leech, *Basic Interests: The Importance of Groups in Politics and in Political Science* (Princeton, NJ: Princeton University Press, 1998).

30. Baumgartner et al., *Lobbying and Policy Change.*

31. Baumgartner et al., p. 244.

32. Baumgartner et al. pp. 244–5.

33. Heinz et al., *The Hollow Core: Private Interests in National Policy Making*, p. 5.

34. "Lobbyists' Delight," *The Economist*, October 14, 2004, http://www.economist.com/node/3291288.

35. David Lowery and Kathleen Marchetti, "You Don't Know Jack: Principals, Agents and Lobbying," *Interest Groups & Advocacy* 1, no. 2 (October 2012): 139–70, doi:10.1057/iga.2012.15.

36. Matilde Bombardini, "Firm Heterogeneity and Lobby Participation," *Journal of International Economics* 75, no. 2 (July 2008): 329–48, doi:10.1016/j.jinteco.2008.03.003.

37. William R. Kerr, William F. Lincoln, and Prachi Mishra, *The Dynamics of Firm Lobbying*, Working Paper (National Bureau of Economic Research, November 2011), http://www.nber.org/papers/w17577.

38. Timothy M. LaPira, "Lobbying after 9/11: Policy Regime Emergence and Interest Group Mobilization," *Policy Studies Journal* 42, no. 2 (2014): 226–48.

39. David J Teece, "Economic Analysis and Strategic Management," *California Management Review* 26, no. 3 (1984): 87–110; Birger Wernerfelt, "A Resource-Based View of the Firm," *Strategic Management Journal* 5, no. 2 (June 1984): 171–80; Jay B. Barney, "Strategic Factor Markets: Expectations, Luck, and Business Strategy," *Management Science* 32 (1986): 1231–41; Richard R. Nelson, "Why Do Firms Differ, and How Does It Matter?" *Strategic Management Journal* 12, no. S2 (1991): 61–74, doi:10.1002/smj.4250121006; Alfred D. Chandler, "Organizational Capabilities and the Economic History of the Industrial Enterprise," *The Journal of Economic Perspectives* 6, no. 3 (Summer 1992): 79–100; David J. Teece, Gary Pisano, and Amy Shuen, "Dynamic Capabilities and Strategic Management," *Strategic Management Journal* 18, no. 7 (August 1997): 509–33.

40. Barney, "Strategic Factor Markets: Expectations, Luck, and Business Strategy," p. 1231.

41. Nelson, "Why Do Firms Differ, and How Does It Matter?" p. 65.

42. Teece, Pisano, and Shuen, "Dynamic Capabilities and Strategic Management," p. 514.

43. Herbert A. Simon, *Administrative Behavior: A Study of Decision-Making Processes in Administrative Organization* (New York: Macmillan, 1947).

44. Richard Michael Cyert and James G. March, *A Behavioral Theory of the Firm* (Englewood Cliffs, NJ: Prentice Hall, 1963).

45. Sidney Verba, Kay Lehman Schlozman, and Henry E. Brady, *Voice and Equality: Civic Voluntarism in American Politics* (Cambridge, MA: Harvard University Press, 1995).

Chapter 7

1. Rogan Kersh, "State Autonomy & Civil Society: The Lobbyist Connection," *Critical Review* 14, no. 2–3 (2000): 237–58, doi:10.1080/08913810008443559; Kay Lehman Schlozman, Sidney Verba, and Henry E. Brady, *The Unheavenly Chorus: Unequal Political Voice and the Broken Promise of American Democracy* (Princeton, NJ: Princeton University

Press, 2012), p. 351; David Lowery and Kathleen Marchetti, "You Don't Know Jack: Principals, Agents and Lobbying," *Interest Groups & Advocacy* 1, no. 2 (October 2012): 139–70, doi:10.1057/iga.2012.15.

2. Scott Ainsworth and Itai Sened, "The Role of Lobbyists: Entrepreneurs with Two Audiences," *American Journal of Political Science* 37, no. 3 (August 1993): 834, doi:10.2307/2111576.

3. Armen A. Alchian and Harold Demsetz, "Production, Information Costs, and Economic Organization," *American Economic Review* 62 (1972): 777–95; Oliver E. Williamson, "Transaction-Cost Economics: The Governance of Contractual Relations," *Journal of Law and Economics* 22, no. 2 (October 1, 1979): 233–61; Oliver E. Williamson, *The Economic Institutions of Capitalism: Firms, Markets, Relational Contracting* (New York; London: Free Press; Collier Macmillan, 1985); Oliver E. Williamson, "Comparative Economic Organization: The Analysis of Discrete Structural Alternatives," *Administrative Science Quarterly* 36 (1991): 269–96; Michael C. Jensen and William H. Meckling, "Theory of the Firm: Managerial Behavior, Agency Costs, and Capital Structure," *Journal of Financial Economics*, no. 3 (1976): 305–60; Eugene F. Fama, "Agency Problems and the Theory of the Firm," *Journal of Political Economy* 88, no. 2 (April 1980): 288–307; Steven N. S. Cheung, "The Contractual Nature of the Firm," *Journal of Law and Economics* 26, no. 1 (April 1983): 1–21; Eugene F. Fama and Michael C. Jensen, "Separation of Ownership and Control," *Journal of Law and Economics* 26, no. 2, Corporations and Private Property: A Conference Sponsored by the Hoover Institution (June 1983): 301–25; Oliver Hart, "An Economist's Perspective on the Theory of the Firm," *Columbia Law Review* 89, no. 7, Contractual Freedom in Corporate Law (November 1989): 1757–74; Bengt R. Holmstrom and Jean Tirole, "The Theory of the Firm," in *Handbook of Industrial Organizations*, vol. I (Amsterdam: Elsevier Science, 1989), 63–133; Bengt Holmstrom and Paul Milgrom, "The Firm as an Incentive System," *The American Economic Review* 84, no. 4 (September 1994): 972–91.

4. Bengt Holmstrom, "Moral Hazard and Observability," *The Bell Journal of Economics* 10, no. 1 (Spring 1979): 74–91; Steven Shavell, "Risk Sharing and Incentives in the Principal and Agent Relationship," *Bell Journal of Economics* 10, no. 1 (1979): 55–73; Gary J. Miller, "The Political Evolution of Principal-Agent Models," *Annual Review of Political Science* 8, no. 1 (2005): 203–25, doi:10.1146/annurev.polisci.8.082103.104840.

5. The other three, which have less relevance here, are "Initiative that lies with a unified principal"; "backward induction based on common knowledge"; and "ultimatum bargaining."

6. Bryan D. Jones and Frank R. Baumgartner, *The Politics of Attention: How Government Prioritizes Problems* (Chicago: University of Chicago Press, 2005).

7. Anthony Downs, *An Economic Theory of Democracy* (New York: Harper and Row Publishers, 1957).

8. Michael Watkins, Mickey Edwards, and Usha Thakrar, *Winning the Influence Game: What Every Business Leader Should Know about Government* (New York: Wiley and Sons, 2001), p. 65.

9. Watkins, Edwards, and Thakrar, *Winning the Influence Game*, p. 65.

10. Michael X. Delli Carpini and Scott Keeter, *What Americans Know about Politics and Why It Matters* (New Haven, CT: Yale University Press, 1997).

11. Watkins, Edwards, and Thakrar, *Winning the Influence Game*, p. 86

12. Kevin W. Hula, *Lobbying Together: Interest Group Coalitions in Legislative Politics* (Washington, DC: Georgetown University Press, 1999).

13. Alchian and Demsetz, "Production, Information Costs, and Economic Organization."

14. Kersh, "State Autonomy & Civil Society," p. 242.

15. Kersh, p. 242.

16. Kersh, p. 244.

17. Nicholas W. Allard, "Lobbying Is an Honorable Profession: The Right to Petition and the Competition to Be Right," *Stanford Law and Policy Review* 19, no. 1 (2008), 45.

18. See: "The Intimidation of Dr. John Buse and the Diabetes Drug Avandia," Committee Staff Report, U.S. Committee on Finance, November 2007.

19. Brian Kelleher Richter, Krislert Samphantharak, and Jeffrey F. Timmons, "Lobbying and Taxes," *American Journal of Political Science* 53, no. 4 (2009): 893–909, doi:10.1111/j.1540–5907.2009.00407.x.

20. Frank Yu and Xiaoyun Yu, "Corporate Lobbying and Fraud Detection," *Journal of Financial and Quantitative Analysis* 46, no. 06 (2012): 1865–91, doi:10.1017/S0022109011000457.
21. Eitan Goldman, Jörg Rocholl, and Jongil So, "Do Politically Connected Boards Affect Firm Value?" *Review of Financial Studies* 22, no. 6 (June 1, 2009): 2331–60, doi:10.1093/rfs/hhn088.
22. Jin-Hyuk Kim, "Corporate Lobbying Revisited," *Business and Politics* 10, no. 2 (September 28, 2008), http://www.degruyter.com/view/j/bap.2008.10.2/bap.2008.10.2.1193/bap.2008.10.2.1193.xml.
23. The Economist, "Money and Politics," *The Economist*, October 1, 2011, http://www.economist.com/node/21531014. There are, to be sure, causal inference difficulties in this analysis, because companies are not randomly assigned to lobby.
24. Mark S Mizruchi, *The Fracturing of the American Corporate Elite* (Cambridge, MA: Harvard University Press, 2013), http://search.ebscohost.com/login.aspx?direct=true&scope=site&db=nlebk&db=nlabk&AN=520,774; Benjamin C. Waterhouse, *Lobbying America: The Politics of Business from Nixon to NAFTA* (Princeton, NJ: Princeton University Press, 2013).
25. Timothy M. LaPira and Herschel F. Thomas, *Just How Many Newt Gingrich's Are There on K Street? Estimating the True Size and Shape of Washington's Revolving Door*, SSRN Scholarly Paper (Rochester, NY: Social Science Research Network, April 2, 2013), http://papers.ssrn.com/abstract=2,241,671.
26. Peter H. Stone, *Casino Jack and the United States of Money: Superlobbyist Jack Abramoff and the Buying of Washington* (New York, NY: Melville House, 2010).
27. http://www.vsadc.com/about/, accessed 4/21/2014
28. http://www.ogilvygr.com/About_Us.aspx, accessed 4/21/2014
29. http://www.qga.com/experts, accessed 4/21/2014
30. Kersh, "State Autonomy & Civil Society," p. 248.
31. T. W. Farnam, "Revolving Door of Employment between Congress, Lobbying Firms, Study Shows," *The Washington Post*, September 13, 2011, sec. Politics, http://www.washingtonpost.com/politics/study-shows-revolving-door-of-employment-between-congress-lobbying-firms/2011/09/12/gIQAxPYROK_story.html.
32. Jordi Blanes i Vidal, Mirko Draca, and Christian Fons-Rosen, "Revolving Door Lobbyists," *American Economic Review* 102, no. 7 (December 2012): 3731–48, doi:10.1257/aer.102.7.3731; Marianne Bertrand, Matilde Bombardini, and Francesco Trebbi, *Is It Whom You Know or What You Know? An Empirical Assessment of the Lobbying Process*, Working Paper (National Bureau of Economic Research, February 2011), http://www.nber.org/papers/w16765; Lee Drutman and Alexander Furnas, "K Street Pays Top Dollar for Revolving Door Talent," *Sunlight Foundation*, January 21, 2014, http://sunlightfoundation.com/blog/2014/01/21/revolving-door-lobbyists-government-experience/.
33. Conor Mcgrath, *Lobbying in Washington, London, And Brussels: The Persuasive Communication of Political Issues* (Lewiston, N.Y: Edwin Mellen Pr, 2005).

Chapter 8

1. James M. Buchanan and Gordon Tullock, *The Calculus of Consent: Logical Foundations of Constitutional Democracy* (Ann Arbor, MI: University of Michigan Press, 1967); John R. Lott, "A Simple Explanation for Why Campaign Expenditures Are Increasing: The Government Is Getting Bigger," *Journal of Law and Economics* 43, no. 2 (October 1, 2000): 359–94, doi:10.1086/467459.
2. Non-defense discretionary spending covers funding of most government agencies, and therefore seems like a reasonable proxy for the size of government. Defense spending is very responsive to wars, and it dwarfs all other government agencies.
3. David Bicknell Truman, *The Governmental Process; Political Interests and Public Opinion*, vol. 1 (New York: Knopf, 1951).
4. John Mark Hansen, *Gaining Access: Congress and the Farm Lobby, 1919–1981*, 1st ed. (Chicago: University Of Chicago Press, 1991).
5. Beth L. Leech et al., "Drawing Lobbyists to Washington: Government Activity and the Demand for Advocacy," *Political Research Quarterly* 58, no. 1 (March 2005): 29.

6. Baumgartner and colleagues extend this analysis further, adding more data in support of congressional attention, but find mixed results for presidential attention. See: Frank R. Baumgartner et al., "Congressional and Presidential Effects on the Demand for Lobbying," *Political Research Quarterly* 64, no. 1 (March 1, 2011): 3–16, doi:10.1177/1065912909343578.

7. David Lowery and Virginia Gray, "The Population Ecology of Gucci Gulch, or the Natural Regulation of Interest Group Numbers in the American States," *American Journal of Political Science* 39, no. 1 (February 1, 1995): 1–29, doi:10.2307/2111755; Virginia Gray and David Lowery, "Reconceptualizing PAC Formation: It's Not a Collective Action Problem, and it may Be an Arms Race," *American Politics Research* 25, no. 3 (July 1, 1997): 319–46, doi:10.1177/1532673X9702500304; Virginia Gray and David Lowery, "Interest Group Politics and Economic Growth in the U.S. States," *The American Political Science Review* 82, no. 1 (March 1, 1988): 109–31, doi:10.2307/1958061; Virginia Gray and David Lowery, *The Population Ecology of Interest Representation: Lobbying Communities in the American States* (Ann Arbor, MI: University of Michigan Press, 2000).

8. Lowery and Gray, "The Population Ecology of Gucci Gulch, or the Natural Regulation of Interest Group Numbers in the American States," 25.

9. Lowery and Gray, "The Population Ecology of Gucci Gulch, or the Natural Regulation of Interest Group Numbers in the American States," 10.

10. David Lowery et al., "Living in the Moment: Lags, Leads, and the Link Between Legislative Agendas and Interest Advocacy," *Social Science Quarterly* 85, no. 2 (June 1, 2004): 463–77, doi:10.1111/j.0038–4941.2004.08502014.x.

11. I rely on a cross-walk developed by Timothy M. LaPira and Beth Leech that links Center for Responsive Politics sector codes with Policy Agenda Projects topic codes.

12. Baumgartner et al., "Congressional and Presidential Effects on the Demand for Lobbying," 201.

13. Thanks to Timothy M. LaPira for this important point.

14. David C. Mowery, *Ivory Tower and Industrial Innovation: University-Industry Technology Transfer Before and After the Bayh-Dole Act in the United States* (Palo Alto, CA: Stanford University Press, 2004).

15. Juan Williams, "Reagan Signs Orphan Drug Bill Despite Reservations," *Washington Post*, January 5, 1983 .

16. Philip J. Hilts, "Senate Passes Bill to Charge Makers for Drug Approval," *New York Times*, October 8, 1992,.

17. Timothy M. LaPira, "The Allure of Reform: The Increasing Demand for Health Care Lobbying From Clinton's Task Force to Obama's Big [Expletive] Deal," in *Interest Group Politics*, 8th ed., ed. Allan Cigler and Burdett Loomis (Washington, DC: CQ Press, 2012).

18. Bill Frist, "Keeping Doctors Up to Date on Drugs," *Washington Post*, February 1, 1996,.

19. Mark Suzman, "Compromises Pave Way for FDA Reform," *Financial Times*, November 21, 1997.

20. Deborah McGregor, "Senate Vote Gives Bush Victory on Healthcare Medicare Legislation," *Financial Times*, November 26, 2003, sec. THE AMERICAS & MIDDLE EAST.

21. Richard Benedetto, "BioShield Bill Is Signed into Law," *USA TODAY*, July 22, 2004,

22. Michael Barbaro, "Bioshield Too Little For Drug Industry; Companies Want More Protection From Financial Loss," *Washington Post*, July 26, 2004, sec. Financial; E01, .

23. Sara Miles, *How to Hack a Party Line: The Democrats and Silicon Valley* (Berkeley, CA: University of California Press, 2002).

24. Kenneth Noble, "Piracy Ban Nears for Silicon Chips," *New York Times*, October 10, 1984,.

25. Thomas Friedman, "U.S. Seeking to Ease Restrictions On Export of High-Tech Products," *New York Times*, February 25, 1994,

26. John Schwartz, "The Net Impact of the New Copyright Bill," *Washington Post*, May 18, 1998,

27. Susan Crawford, *Captive Audience: The Telecom Industry and Monopoly Power in the New Gilded Age*, 1st ed. (New Haven, CT: Yale University Press, 2013); Patrick R. Parsons, *Blue Skies: A History of Cable Television* (Philadelphia: Temple University Press, 2008); Gary

Mucciaroni and Paul J. Quirk, *Deliberative Choices: Debating Public Policy in Congress*, annotated edition (Chicago: University Of Chicago Press, 2006), 122–55.

28. Mark Landler, "Stymied, SBC Seeks to Void Portion of Law," *New York Times*, July 3, 1997, sec. Business, http://www.nytimes.com/1997/07/03/business/stymied-sbc-seeks-to-void-portion-of-law.html.

29. Edmund Sanders, "Baby Bells Push to Ease Access to High-Speed Internet Market," *Los Angeles Times*, April 26, 2001, http://articles.latimes.com/2001/apr/26/business/fi-55806.

30. J.H. Snider, "FCC Lets the Telecom Giants Steal from You," *Sacramento Bee*, April 7, 2002.

31. William K. Black, *The Best Way to Rob a Bank Is to Own One: How Corporate Executives and Politicians Looted the S&L Industry*, updated edition (Austin, TX: University of Texas Press, 2014); Martin Mayer, *The Greatest-Ever Bank Robbery: The Collapse of the Savings and Loan Industry* (New York, NY: Scribner, 1990); Lawrence J. White, *The S&L Debacle: Public Policy Lessons for Bank and Thrift Regulation* (New York: Oxford University Press, 1991).

32. Keith Bradsher, "Interstate-Banking Bill Gets Final Approval in Congress," *New York Times*, September 14, 1994,

33. Stephen Labaton, "Congress Passes Wide-Ranging Bill Easing Bank Laws," *New York Times*, November 5, 1999,

34. Crawford, *Captive Audience*; Parsons, *Blue Skies*; Mucciaroni and Quirk, *Deliberative Choices*.

35. Financial Crisis Inquiry Commission, *The Financial Crisis Inquiry Report, Authorized Edition: Final Report of the National Commission on the Causes of the Financial and Economic Crisis in the United States* (PublicAffairs, 2011), 48.

36. Commission, *The Financial Crisis Inquiry Report, Authorized Edition*.

37. As I do elsewhere, I remove 1996 because of concerns about potential data discontinuity.

38. Henry E. Brady et al., "Corporate Lobbying Activity in American Politics," in Paper given at the American Political Science Association Annual Meeting (Chicago, IL, 2007).

39. Brady et al., "Corporate Lobbying Activity in American Politics."

40. If a company were to increase its sales by 10 percent year-to-year, marginal company lobbying would be expected to increase by 0.02. If a company were to increase its sales by 50 percent year-to-year, marginal company lobbying would be expected to increase by 0.07.

41. Even a doubling of company size predicts only a change of 0.016 in marginal lobbying presence.

Chapter 9

1. While it is more common to use a log transformation when variables are left-skewed, the square root transformation fits the reality of lobbying far better. The results do not depend on this transformation.

2. Charles E. Lindblom, "The Science of 'Muddling Through,'" *Public Administration Review* 19, no. 2 (April 1, 1959): 79–88, doi:10.2307/973677; Otto A. Davis, M. A. H. Dempster, and Aaron Wildavsky, "A Theory of the Budgetary Process," *The American Political Science Review* 60, no. 3 (September 1, 1966): 529–47, doi:10.2307/1952969; Frank R. Baumgartner and Bryan D. Jones, *Agendas and Instability in American Politics* (Chicago: University of Chicago Press, 1993); Bryan D. Jones and Frank R. Baumgartner, *The Politics of Attention: How Government Prioritizes Problems* (Chicago: University of Chicago Press, 2005).

3. Christopher H. Achen, "Why Lagged Dependent Variables Can Suppress the Explanatory Power of Other Independent Variables," working paper, November 2, 2001; Zvi Griliches, "A Note on Serial Correlation Bias in Estimates of Distributed Lags," *Econometrica* 29, no. 1 (January 1, 1961): 65–73, doi:10.2307/1907688; Douglas A. Hibbs, "Problems of Statistical Estimation and Causal Inference in Time-Series Regression Models," in *Sociological Methodology*, ed. Hebert L. Costner (San Francisco: Jossey-Bass, 1974), 252–308.

4. I estimated models with these variables separately and I did not find any consistently significant or substantial effects.

5. I experimented with other transformations, but I did not find any consistently significant or substantial effects.
6. Henry Brady et al., "Political Activity by American Corporations," in paper given at the Midwest Political Science Association Annual Meeting, 2007; Davis F. Taylor, "The Relationship between Firm Investments in Technological Innovation and Political Action," *Southern Economic Journal* 63, no. 4 (April 1, 1997): 888–903, doi:10.2307/1061229.
7. In order to calculate this variable, I collected data on government contracts for each company for 1981, 1991, and 2001. Then I arranged industries by how much they sold to the government. I considered the seven industries that sell the most to government as major sellers. These industries are: defense aerospace/electronics, computers/Internet, telecom services, misc. manufacturing, pharmaceuticals/health products, automotive, and chemical & related manufacturing.
8. Brady et al., "Political Activity by American Corporations."
9. I ran a series of Hausman tests in order to determine that fixed effects models are more appropriate than random effects models for this particular data.
10. Cheng Hsiao, *Analysis of Panel Data* (New York, NY: Cambridge University Press, 2003).
11. Nathaniel Beck and Jonathan N. Katz, "What To Do (and Not to Do) with Time-Series Cross-Section Data," *American Political Science Review* 89, no. 03 (1995): 645, doi:10.2307/2082979.
12. N. Beck and J. N. Katz, "Nuisance vs. Substance: Specifying and Estimating Time-Series-Cross-Section Models," *Political Analysis* 6, no. 1 (January 1, 1996): 1–36, doi:10.1093/pan/6.1.1; Nathaniel Beck, "TIME-SERIES–CROSS-SECTION DATA: What Have We Learned in the Past Few Years?" *Annual Review of Political Science* 4, no. 1 (2001): 271–93, doi:10.1146/annurev.polisci.4.1.271; Christian B. Hansen, "Asymptotic Properties of a Robust Variance Matrix Estimator for Panel Data When Is Large," *Journal of Econometrics* 141, no. 2 (December 2007): 597–620, doi:10.1016/j.jeconom.2006.10.009.
13. Admittedly, this removes cases where companies go in and out of lobbying, but these cases are relatively rare in the data.
14. What this means is that a 10 percent increase in sales is associated with an increase in marginal lobbying presence of 0.05 ($0.53 \times \log[1.1]$). (Taking the natural log of 1.1 allows us to estimate the impact of a 10 percent increase in the independent variable (sales)) An increase of 20 percent in sales is associated with a 0.1 increase in marginal lobbying presence, and an increase of 50 percent in the value of sales is associated with an increase of 0.21 ($0.53 \times \log[1.5]$). An increase of 0.21 is the equivalent of the increase of the square root of 5 (2.24) to the square root of 6 (2.45). It is also a little more than the equivalent of the increase in the square root of 25 (5) to the square root of 27 (5.20).
15. However, there are a few caveats to this conclusion. The most significant caveat arises from the limits of my measure of government attention, since it is based on an inherently imperfect crosswalk between industry categories and policy agenda categories. It is also only a measure of government attention in the primary industry of a company. However, one of the consequences of the growth of lobbying is that companies have generally expanded their interests beyond their primary industry. It also measures salient forms of government attention, like hearings and bills. This means that I am not capturing lobbying efforts on issues of lower salience, including small tweaks to larger bills, or agency rulemakings, even though there is good reason to think that they are an important part of lobbying. To draw the most conservative conclusion, then, we can say that increasing levels of highly salient government attention in a company's primary industry do not lead companies to expand their lobbying presence. This does not mean that government activity exerts no pull on companies, just that it doesn't do it in any predictable way.
16. Baumgartner and Jones, *Agendas and Instability in American Politics.*

Chapter 10

1. Lydia DePillis, "'Shame on Us': How Businesses Brought the Debt Limit Mess onto Themselves," *Washington Post*, 2013, http://www.washingtonpost.com/blogs/wonkblog/wp/2013/09/29/shame-on-us-how-businesses-brought-the-debt-limit-mess-onto-themselves/.

2. Stephen Ansolabehere, John M. de Figueiredo, and James M. Snyder Jr., "Why Is There so Little Money in U.S. Politics?," *The Journal of Economic Perspectives* 17, no. 1 (January 1, 2003): 105–30; Frank R. Baumgartner et al., *Lobbying and Policy Change: Who Wins, Who Loses, and Why* (Chicago: University of Chicago Press, 2009); Frank R. Baumgartner and Beth L. Leech, *Basic Interests: The Importance of Groups in Politics and in Political Science* (Princeton, NJ: Princeton University Press, 1998).

3. Baumgartner et al., *Lobbying and Policy Change*.

4. Baumgartner et al., *Lobbying and Policy Change*; Jacob S. Hacker and Paul Pierson, "Winner-Take-All Politics: Public Policy, Political Organization, and the Precipitous Rise of Top Incomes in the United States," *Politics & Society* 38, no. 2 (June 1, 2010): 152–204, doi:10.1177/0032329210365042.

5. Steven M. Teles, "Kludgeocracy in America," *National Affairs*, 2013.

6. Bill Frenzel, "The Tax Code Is A Hopeless Complex, Economy-Suffocating Mess," *Forbes*, April 4, 2013, http://www.forbes.com/sites/billfrenzel/2013/04/04/the-tax-code-is-a-hopeless-complex-economy-suffocating-mess/.

7. Mark S Mizruchi, *The Fracturing of the American Corporate Elite* (Cambridge, MA: Harvard University Press, 2013), p. 4.

8. DePillis, "'Shame on Us.'"

9. Arthur Meier Schlesinger, *The Cycles of American History* (Boston: Houghton Mifflin, 1986); Andrew S. McFarland, "Interest Groups and Political Time: Cycles in America," *British Journal of Political Science* 21, no. 3 (July 1, 1991): 257–84.

10. David Vogel, *Fluctuating Fortunes: The Political Power of Business in America* (New York: Basic Books, 1989).

11. Joseph E. Stiglitz, *The Roaring Nineties: A New History of the World's Most Prosperous Decade*, Reprint edition (New York: W. W. Norton & Company, 2004).

12. Thomas Edsall, "The Shadow Lobbyist," *New York Times*, 2013, http://opinionator.blogs.nytimes.com/2013/04/25/the-shadow-lobbyist/; Thomas B. Edsall, "The Unlobbyists," *New York Times*, December 31, 2013, http://www.nytimes.com/2014/01/01/opinion/edsall-the-unlobbyists.html.

13. David Vogel, "Why Businessmen Distrust Their State: The Political Consciousness of American Corporate Executives," *British Journal of Political Science* 8, no. 1 (January 1, 1978): 45–78.

14. Michael Watkins, Mickey Edwards, and Usha Thakrar, *Winning the Influence Game: What Every Business Leader Should Know about Government* (New York: Wiley and Sons, 2001), p. 101. One lobbyist quoted in this book said that: "CEOs … will talk about themselves as victims of government. They never think of themselves as partners."

15. David Espo, "Pelosi Says She Would Drain GOP 'Swamp'." Associated Press, October 6, 2006.

16. Bruce E. Cain and Lee Drutman, "Congressional Staff and the Revolving Door: The Impact of Regulatory Change," *Election Law Journal: Rules, Politics, and Policy* 13, no. 1 (March 1, 2014): 27–44, doi:10.1089/elj.2013.0213.

17. Peter H. Stone, *Casino Jack and the United States of Money: Superlobbyist Jack Abramoff and the Buying of Washington* (New York, NY: Melville House, 2010).

18. Sheryl Gay Stolberg, "On First Day, Obama Quickly Sets a New Tone," *New York Times*, January 21, 2009, sec. U.S./Politics, http://www.nytimes.com/2009/01/22/us/politics/22obama.html.

19. Julian E. Barnes, "Raytheon Lobbyist Picked for Deputy Defense Post," *Los Angeles Times*, January 23, 2009, http://articles.latimes.com/2009/jan/23/nation/na-deputy-defense-secretary23.

20. James A. Thurber, "The Contemporary Presidency: Changing the Way Washington Works? Assessing President Obama's Battle with Lobbyists," *Presidential Studies Quarterly* 41, no. 2 (2011): 358–74, doi:10.1111/j.1741-5705.2011.03858.x.

21. Timothy M. LaPira, "Erring on the Side of Shady: How Calling out 'Lobbyists' Drove Them Underground," *Sunlight Foundation*, April 1, 2014, http://sunlightfoundation.com/blog/2014/04/01/erring-on-the-side-of-shady-how-calling-out-lobbyists-drove-them-underground/.

22. Thurber, "The Contemporary Presidency."

23. Heather K. Gerken and Alex Tausanovitch, "A Public Finance Model for Lobbying: Lobbying, Campaign Finance, and the Privatization of Democracy," *Election Law Journal: Rules, Politics, and Policy* 13, no. 1 (March 1, 2014): 75–90, doi:10.1089/elj.2013.0212.
24. James Madison, *Federalist #10.*
25. Robert H. Salisbury, "Interest Representation: The Dominance of Institutions," *The American Political Science Review* 78, no. 1 (March 1, 1984): 64–76, doi:10.2307/1961249; David M. Hart, "'Business' Is Not an Interest Group: On the Study of Companies in American National Politics," *Annual Review of Political Science* 7, no. 1 (2004): 47–69, doi:10.1146/annurev.polisci.7.090803.161829.
26. Mancur Olson, *The Logic of Collective Action; Public Goods and the Theory of Groups,* vol. 124 (Cambridge, MA: Harvard University Press, 1965).
27. James Q. Wilson, *The Politics of Regulation* (New York: Basic Books, 1980); R. Douglas Arnold, *The Logic of Congressional Action* (New Haven, CT: Yale University Press, 1990); Theodore J. Lowi, *The End of Liberalism: The Second Republic of the United States,* vol. 2 (New York: Norton, 1979).
28. Zephyr Teachout, "Original Intent," *Democracy Journal,* 2009, http://www.democracyjournal.org/11/6666.php.
29. http://opengovfoundation.org/the-madison-project/
30. http://www.popvox.com/
31. Bengt Holmstrom, "Moral Hazard and Observability," *The Bell Journal of Economics* 10, no. 1 (Spring 1979): 74–91.
32. Lorelei Kelly, *Congress' Wicked Problem: Seeking Knowledge Inside the Information Tsunami* (Washington, DC: New America Foundation, 2012).
33. Dakota S. Rudesill, "Closing the Legislative Experience Gap: How a Legislative Law Clerk Program Will Benefit the Legal Profession and Congress," *Washington University Law Review* 87 (2010 2009): 699. See http://www.congressionalclerkship.com
34. Gerken and Tausanovitch, "A Public Finance Model for Lobbying," 88–9.
35. Gary Mucciaroni and Paul J Quirk, *Deliberative Choices: Debating Public Policy in Congress* (Chicago: University of Chicago Press, 2006).
36. Ryan Grim and Sabrina Siddiqui, "Call Time for Congress Shows How Fundraising Dominates Bleak Work Life," *Huffington Post,* January 8, 2013, http://www.huffingtonpost.com/2013/01/08/call-time-congressional-fundraising_n_2,427,291.html.
37. Lee Drutman, *The Political 1% of the 1% in 2012* (The Sunlight Foundation, June 24, 2013), http://sunlightfoundation.com/blog/2013/06/24/1pct_of_the_1pct/.
38. Paul Blumenthal, "Chris Murphy: 'Soul-Crushing' Fundraising Is Bad for Congress," *Huffington Post,* May 7, 2013, http://www.huffingtonpost.com/2013/05/07/chris-murphy-fundraising_n_3,232,143.html.
39. Charles Edward Lindblom, *Politics and Markets: The World's Political Economic Systems* (New York: Basic Books, 1977), p. 356.
40. Nicholas W. Allard, "Lobbying Is an Honorable Profession: The Right to Petition and the Competition to Be Right," *Stanford Law and Policy Review* 19, no. 1 (2008).
41. Martin Gilens and Benjamin I. Page, "Testing Theories of American Politics: Elites, Interest Groups, and Average Citizens," *Perspectives on Politics* 12, no. 3 (2014); Martin Gilens, *Affluence and Influence: Economic Inequality and Political Power in America* (Princeton University Press, 2012).

INDEX

Note: Figures and tables are indicated by page numbers in *italics*.